ECONOMIES OF VIRTUE

THE CIRCULATION OF 'ETHICS' IN AI

INC Theory on Demand #46
Economics of Virtue — The Circulation of 'Ethics" in AI

Edited by: Thao Phan, Jake Goldfein, Declan Kuch and Monique Mann
Copy Editor: Elena Gomez
Cover Design: Katja van Stiphout
Design and EPUB development: Jasmin Leech

Published by the Institute of Network Cultures, Amsterdam 2022

ISBN print: 9789492302960
ISBN EPUB: 9789492302977

Contact
Institute of Network Cultures
Amsterdam University of Applied Sciences (HVA)
Faculty of DMCI
Benno Premsela Huis
Rhijnspoorplein
Room 04A07
1019 GC Amsterdam
The Netherlands
Email: info@networkcultures.org
Web: www.networkcultures.org

Order a copy or download this publication for free at:
www.networkcultures.org/publications

Subscribe to the INC newsletter:
www.networkcultures.org/newsletter

institute of
network cultures

TABLE OF CONTENTS

SECTION III: ACTION

ECONOMIES OF VIRTUE

THAO PHAN, JAKE GOLDENFEIN, DECLAN KUCH, AND MONIQUE MANN

What does 'AI ethics' do? Who does it serve? What is its purpose? If we ask those invested in questions of technology and social, political, and environmental justice, or those engaged in on the ground inquiry with communities affected by automated decision-making, or working inside of regulatory institutions, the answer we might expect is 'nothing at all.' The fast-moving wave of critique that defined the "tech lash" is now being subsumed by an even larger wave of what Elettra Bietti calls "ethics bashing."[1] Where the tech lash centered on exposing the bad behavior of some of the world's largest tech corporations, this next wave addresses the rise of 'ethics' as a new industrial agenda, focusing on actions such as the establishment of AI ethics boards, hiring AI ethics teams, and funding AI ethics research. Critics have fairly interpreted these actions as efforts to instrumentalize ethics,[2] to reduce it to another form of industrial capital,[3] or to co-opt and capture researchers as part of efforts to control public narratives.[4]

Many critical accounts aim to bring transparency and accountability to fields that are themselves concerned with questions of transparency and accountability in AI systems. The turn within AI ethics conferences, most notably the Association of Computing Machinery's annual Fairness, Accountability, and Transparency conference (FAccT), to include whole streams that turn the gaze of inquiry back onto the organisation and its values, its processes of governance, and its sponsorship policies, signals a significant reflexive turn within these communities.[5] The intended audience for these discussions are people who, in many cases, work under the broad umbrella of AI ethics. Although an increasing number of scholars and activists now seek to disavow and indeed challenge both the terms 'AI' and 'ethics', for those who work outside the academy—the people who do not spend their days on Twitter, reading articles on Medium, Wired or the MIT Technology Review—'AI ethics' is broadly what the general public think we do. If we consider ethics as 'an internalised aspirational mode of enquiry that aims at a better world'

---

1   Elettra Bietti, 'From Ethics Washing to Ethics Bashing: A View on Tech Ethics from Within Moral Philosophy', *SSRN Electronic Journal*, 2021: 211 & 217.
2   Bietti, 'From Ethics Washing to Ethics Bashing: A View on Tech Ethics from Within Moral Philosophy'.
3   Thao Phan, Jake Goldenfein, Monique Mann, and Declan Kuch, 'Economies of Virtue: The Circulation of "Ethics" in Big Tech', *Science as Culture*, 4 November 2021, 1–15.
4   Meredith Whittaker, 'The Steep Cost of Capture', *Interactions* 28, no. (6) (2021): 50–5.
5   See, for example, Abeba Birhane, Elayne Ruane, Thomas Laurent, Matthew S. Brown, Johnathan Flowers, Anthony Ventresque, and Christopher L. Dancy, 'The Forgotten Margins of AI Ethics' in *2022 ACM Conference on Fairness, Accountability, and Transparency*, 948–58. FAccT '22. New York, NY, USA: Association for Computing Machinery, 2022; Ben Gansky, and Sean McDonald, 'CounterFAccTual: How FAccT Undermines Its Organizing Principles' in *2022 ACM Conference on Fairness, Accountability, and Transparency*, 1982–92. Seoul Republic of Korea: ACM, 2022; Young, Meg, Michael Katell, and P.M. Krafft. 'Confronting Power and Corporate Capture at the FAccT Conference' in *2022 ACM Conference on Fairness, Accountability, and Transparency*, 1375–86. Seoul Republic of Korea: ACM, 2022. For further discussion, see 'Drop Outs' in this volume.

and 'a more just society,'[6] then many would not object to this title. Rather the objection stems from what ethics has become. In short, what it is made to do, who it serves, and the purposes it *does*, rather than *should*, fulfil.

When posed with this question, 'what does AI ethics do?', the answer, in reality, is very rarely 'nothing at all.' As the growing corpus of critical literature shows, the 'ethics' of AI ethics is much more malleable, more pliable, and more amenable to strategic operationalization than anticipated. Ethics, it's said, can be washed[7] and bashed.[8] It can operate as a rubber stamp[9] or an empty gesture.[10] It can be a fig leaf,[11] a seductive diversion,[12] or, as Lily Hu writes in her searing analysis, it can be a performative theatre: 'Silicon Valley, with its long financial strings, plays the tech ethics marionette; "ethics" is a show, and they know it.'[13] Put simply, ethics as deployed by Big Tech does worse than nothing. It is divisive, contested, and more often than not enables the troubling practice of 'business as usual.' At its worst, AI ethics is not just useless but 'dangerous, hoarding expertise and funding that should be devoted to more effective work.'[14] For these reasons, celebrated tech journalists like Karen Hao[15] have scolded the AI ethics community:

[t]alk is just that—it's not enough. For all the lip service paid to these issues, many organizations' AI ethics guidelines remain vague and hard to implement. Few companies can show tangible changes to the way AI products and services get evaluated and approved. We're falling into a trap of ethics-washing, where genuine action gets replaced by superficial promises.

This collection takes its point of departure from here. In our initial call for contributions, we invited scholars and activists to respond to the growing trend of AI ethics bashing by focusing specifically on the financial structures that support AI ethics and its effects on the people who perform this work. We—the editors of this collection—asked: who

6   Bietti, 'From Ethics Washing to Ethics Bashing', 211 & 217.
7   Ben Wagner, 'Ethics as an Escape from Regulation. From "Ethics-Washing" to Ethics-Shopping?' in *Being Profiled*, Amsterdam: Amsterdam University Press, 2018, 84–9.
8   Bietti, 'From Ethics Washing to Ethics Bashing'.
9   Rashida Richardson in Bobbie Johnson and Gideon Lichfield, 'Hey Google, Sorry You Lost Your Ethics Council, So We Made One for You', *MIT Technology Review* blog, 8 April 2019, https://medium.com/mit-technology-review/hey-google-sorry-you-lost-your-ethics-council-so-we-made-one-for-you-28ee6c33576a.
10   Jake Metcalf in Johnson & Lichfield, 'Hey Google, Sorry You Lost Your Ethics Council, So We Made One for You'.
11   Adam Greenfield in Johnson & Lichfield, 'Hey Google, Sorry You Lost Your Ethics Council, So We Made One for You'.
12   Julia Powles and Helen Nissenbaum, 'The Seductive Diversion of 'Solving' Bias in Artificial Intelligence', *OneZero* blog, 7 December 2018, https://onezero.medium.com/the-seductive-diversion-of-solving-bias-in-artificial-intelligence-890df5e5ef53.
13   Lily Hu, 'Tech Ethics: Speaking Ethics to Power, or Power Speaking Ethics?' *Journal of Social Computing*, 2 (3, 2021): 240.
14   Luke Munn, 'The Uselessness of AI Ethics', *AI and Ethics*, 23 August 2022: n.p.
15   Karen Hao, 'In 2020, Let's Stop AI Ethics-Washing and Actually Do Something,' *MIT Technology Review*, https://www.technologyreview.com/2019/12/27/57/ai-ethics-washing-time-to-act/.

funds research into the ethics of AI technologies? How might these funding arrangements cement or exacerbate hierarchies of power? And how does an industry-sponsored agenda on ethics impact the production of knowledge about AI systems?

In our call, we suggested that in response to campaigners, industry insiders, and civil society actors raising concerns about 'bad AI,' there was now a wave of social science–led research around AI ethics. Joining the growing chorus, we expressed concern that, as the field of inquiry and practice grew, it too was at risk of an ethical crisis, one that brought into relief the complex positionality of researchers in this area. The social and political pressures that initially compelled companies to behave more ethically has since morphed into varying infiltrations of research culture in the form of conference sponsorship, formal research partnerships, joint industry-academic appointments, and more.[16]

This influx of industry funding is, of course, a symptom of a broader set of problems: the politicization of tertiary education, the cultivation of a hostile culture towards a perceived 'left intellectualism,' and the one–two neoliberal punch of funding withdrawal for public institutions the world over, coupled with growing incentives to acquire external industry funding. In Australia, for instance, a broken funding system has meant that 1) the few government grant sources that are available offer less than they did a decade ago and are mostly accessible to already wealthy institutions, 2) the grants are primarily structured to incentivise research deemed 'commercializable' or of value to industry, and 3) even if researchers make it through the highly competitive process,[17] project success can still be subject to political interference.[18] The slow withdrawal of public funding for public tertiary education has meant that universities must turn to other forms of income for survival. Again, to use the example of Australia, universities now approach education as a secondary enterprise to the real business of managing investment portfolios alongside other forms of profiteering, hiring former industry executives to manage universities as they would a large corporation. The result is that universities value teaching and research to the extent that they can be translated into metrics informing international rankings, which can then be cashed out in international student fees. At the same time, the trickle-

---

16   See Phan et al, 'Economies of Virtue: The Circulation of "Ethics" in Big Tech' and Whittakker, 'The Steep Cost of Capture'.

17   The Australian Research Council's DECRA (Discovery Early Career Researcher Award), the most prestigious grant available for Australian scholars in their early years, has an average 17 percent success rate. In 2022, there was a slight improvement, with 19.7 percent success rate (see Australian Research Council, 'Selection Report: Discovery Early Career Research Award 2022 | Australian Research Council,' Australian Government | Australian Research Council, 2022. https://www.arc.gov. au/funding-research/funding-outcome/selection-outcome-reports/selection-report-discovery-early-career-research-award-2022). For further discussion on the Australian Research Council and funding see Richardson's chapter in this volume.

18   Gregory Michael McCarthy and Kanishka Jayasuriya, 'A Review into How University Research Works in Australia Has Just Begun—It Must Confront These 3 Issues', *The Conversation*, 20 September 2022, https://theconversation.com/a-review-into-how-university-research-works-in-australia-has-just-begun-it-must-confront-these-3-issues-190551.

down effect of financial discipline pressures universities to extract as much from workers as possible, including systematic wage theft from staff.[19]

These factors place AI ethics in the awkward position of being financially dependent on the organisations they seek to hold to account. As Hu argues, '[i]t is an uncomfortable fact that however much external advisory boards and universities claim to be "third parties", ethical tech institutions are in fact parasitic on the continual moral failures and disappointments of a hegemonic tech industry.'[20] For Hu, these relationships are mutually reinforcing, with corporations using AI ethics as means to dissimulate political demands for change, and tech advocacy groups capitalising on the clout and resources that industry partnerships afford.[21] STS scholar Lee Vinsel has referred to this phenomena as 'criti-hype'—the kinds of self-serving criticism 'that both feeds and feeds on hype' concerning emerging technologies.[22]

Indeed, this volume itself began its life from a small research grant ($9,000 AUD) targeted at early career researchers in Australia. This 'workshop programme grant' was funded by the Academy of the Social Sciences in Australia, an organization supported primarily by Australian Commonwealth grants and Fellowship subscriptions.[23] As early and mid-career researchers ourselves, the institutional expectations to attract funding neatly collided with the realization that topics on AI, and especially the ethical dimensions of AI, were eminently fundable. While we were always motivated by our commitment to earnestly explore the topic of funding, labour, and AI ethics, the practical demands of requiring resources and institutional support were never far away.

As researchers based in the humanities and social sciences, we were lucky in that the questions we sought to answer did not require expensive hardware, compute power, access to large datasets, or server space—requirements that often force the hand of many of our colleagues in STEM faculties. Rather, our demands were more rudimentary: time. Both *our* time and the time of the various interlocutors we have engaged with throughout the lifespan of this project. In most circumstances, funding can do more than secure resources. It can also work to accumulate clout and authority, bestowing legitimation and accolades on those who receive it. With funding, we could pay for catering and copyediting, as well as administrative and research assistance to host workshops and develop publications. But in its most valuable form, the funding gave us the prestige necessary to ask for others to donate their time to our project and to give ourselves permission to take our own time back from the institution.

19   Julie Hare, 'Wage Theft Is "Systemic": 21 Universities under Investigation', *Australian Financial Review*, 20 October, 2021, https://www.afr.com/work-and-careers/education/wage-theft-is-systemic-21-universities-under-investigation-20211020-p591kw.
20   Hu, 'Tech Ethics: Speaking Ethics to Power, or Power Speaking Ethics?', 240.
21   Hu, 'Tech Ethics: Speaking Ethics to Power, or Power Speaking Ethics?', 243.
22   Lee Vinsel, 'You're Doing It Wrong: Notes on Criticism and Technology Hype.' *Medium* blog, 1 February, 2021, https://sts-news.medium.com/youre-doing-it-wrong-notes-on-criticism-and-technology-hype-18b08b4307e5.
23   socialsciences.org.au/publications/annual-report-2021/.

We mention this here in some detail because it is precisely these kinds of mundane, practical negotiations and institutional demands that dictate the conditions of labour for those engaged in the work of AI ethics. Rampant forms of precarity, insecurity, and normalized cultures of exhaustion and overwork have meant that these kinds of reflexive and critical conversations can rarely take place unless they can also be mobilized in service of strategic goals and personal metrics. These pressures are palpable in areas like the humanities and social sciences, who have been on the receiving end of faculty funding cuts and who have, for decades, struggled against a conservative-led culture war.[24] In this context, it's no surprise that many turn to profitable topics, like AI ethics, and to industry-funded grants as a means for survival.

It's under these disheartening conditions inside of universities that Big Tech succeeds, in the famous words of Fred Moten and Stefano Harney, in '[turning] insurgents into state agents.'[25] That 'AI ethicist' has now become a legitimate job title precisely illustrates Moten and Harney's argument. Former critics now make their wage through teaching specialized courses and degrees on the social, political, and ethical dimensions of AI, producing a new generation of professional technocrats that ostensibly do AI better than the generation previous. As Ben Tarnoff has incisively argued, one of the unexpected effects of the techlash has been 'a mass credentialing event for a new class of experts as "AI ethics," "responsible innovation," and similar pursuits attract significant funding and visibility.'[26] These forms of professionalization and credentialing only serve in the interests of corporate actors who were once the targets of critique. To riff on Moten and Harney, AI ethics is 'more than an ally' to Big Tech's corporate agenda, 'it is its attempted completion.'[27]

In the following sections, we turn more explicitly to the themes and concepts that underpin this anthology. We begin with a brief account of the rise of AI ethics before discussing what we see as the contemporary reification of ethics into a commodity form. We then introduce each of the chapters, outlining the ways in which they illustrate the vast and variegated network of circulations that define what we call an 'economy of virtue' before closing with a brief discussion on the trajectory for AI ethics from here.

The Rise of AI Ethics

The term 'tech-lash' entered the mainstream in 2013, with *The Economist*'s Adrian Wooldridge suggesting the public mood was shifting against Silicon Valley's tech elite.[28] Public perceptions

---

24   Joel Barnes. 'Defunding Arts Degrees Is the Latest Battle in a 40-Year Culture War', *The Conversation*, 3 July 2020, http://theconversation.com/defunding-arts-degrees-is-the-latest-battle-in-a-40-year-culture-war-141689.

25   Fred Moten and Stefano Harney, 'The University and the Undercommons', *Social Text* 22, (2, 2004): 101—15.

26   Ben Tarnoff, 'Postcript to J. Khadijah Abdurahman's "A Body of Work That Cannot Be Ignored"', *Logic* magazine, 2021, https://logicmag.io/beacons/a-body-of-work-that-cannot-be-ignored/.

27   Moten and Harney, 'The University and the Undercommons', 106.

28   Alan Wooldridge, 'The Coming tech-lash', *The Economist*, 18 November 2013, https://www.economist.com/news/2013/11/18/the-coming-tech-lash.

of 'Big Tech' were shaken by the industry's growing contributions to material inequality, failed (and decidedly untrendy) consumer products like Google Glass, repeated privacy failures, unjustified tax breaks, and problematic politics.[29] Google's effort to 'organize the world's information,'[30] for instance, was reinterpreted as harboring the capacity to produce profound social harm. Analysts were realizing that companies once seen as standard-bearers for liberatory rhetorics like the 'open internet' had now leveraged their control over online services and data flows into worrying forms of profiteering and domination. Far from facilitating a revolutionary break from the prevailing socio-economic situation, Silicon Valley's promises of liberation were exposed as just another expression of industrial capitalism. Within the academy, critical scholars had been describing the contradictions between Silicon Valley's counter-cultural self-presentation and its relentless pursuit of capital for some time.[31] But the legitimation of AI ethics as a field of inquiry, alongside and as part of the tech-lash, incentivised additional high-profile academics across social and technical disciplines to produce new critical analyses of tech industry services and structures.

One of Big Tech's primary products—machine learning (ML)—was at the forefront of this re-evaluation. There was growing recognition that it frequently generates biased outcomes, deeply affecting the lives of marginalised people. In 2013, mainstream news began reporting on how ML technologies, by virtue of being trained on historical (and historically biased) data, reproduced forms of gendered and racialised discrimination.[32] Awareness was growing around the mistakes, misrecognitions, and problematic profiling performed by algorithmic scoring systems in domains like employment, social services, and policing.[33]

With clear capacities for harm and massive commercial interest, machine-learning became the set of techniques around which AI ethics oriented itself as a field. Early technical work on fairness in machine-learning classification, for instance by Cynthia Dwork et. al. (including Moritz Hardt, an early organizer of the FATML conference),[34] explored ways to do 'fair' classification, drawing on notions of equality and fairness in the political theory of H. Peyton Young, John Roemer, and John Rawls. Once the political and social relevance of these technical issues was exposed, questions of fairness and bias were quickly targeted by the humanities and social sciences.

In March 2013, Latanya Sweeney, Founder and Director of the Harvard University Data Privacy Lab, published an influential paper on racial discrimination in online ad delivery,

---

29   A good example is Peter Thiel's libertarian interest in sea-steading, see generally F. Manjoo, 'Silicon Valley has an Arrogance Problem', *Wall Street Journal*, 3 November 2013.
30   Google's famous self-stated mission since it was founded in 1998. For further discussion on this slogan, see 'Open Secrets' in this volume.
31   Fred Turner, *From Counterculture to Cyberculture*, University of Chicago Press: Chicago, 2006; Morozov, *To Save Everything, Click Here*, Public Affairs: New York City, 2013b.
32   John Burn-Murdoch, 'The problem with algorithms: magnifying misbehaviour', *Guardian*, 14 August 2013.
33   Luke Dormehl, 'Algorithms Are Great and All, But They Can Also Ruin Lives', *Wired*, 19 November 2014, https://www.wired.com/2014/11/algorithms-great-can-also-ruin-lives/.
34   Cynthia Dwork, M. Hardt, T. Pitassi, O. Reingold, & R. Zemel, 'Fairness Through Awareness', 2011, https://arxiv.org/abs/1104.3913.

bringing critical attention to how commercial platforms reproduced patterns of racial discrimination via their ad delivery system.[35] Soon after, Kate Crawford, then a Principal Researcher at Microsoft Research, published 'The Hidden Biases in Big Data' in *The Harvard Business Review*.[36] Crawford framed fixing (big) data science as the next frontier in studying the relationship between technology and society, recommending technologists interface with social scientists and that computational sciences come to terms with qualitative methods. In *The Atlantic*, Nicholas Diakopoulas connected the problem of bias with that of opacity in machine learning.[37] Additionally, Safiya Noble helped bring many of these issues regarding data-driven systems, commercial interest, and racial bias together in her research highlighting the racial and gender bias in search engines.[38] In August 2014, Solon Barocas and Andrew Selbst made available their article 'Big Data's Disparate Impact,'[39] intricately outlining the ways big data technologies generated discriminatory treatment in legally meaningful ways.

Around 2014, civil society also turned its attention to social justice concerns associated with big data and AI. The Leadership Conference on Civil and Human Rights, for instance, published its 'Civil Rights Principles for the Era of Big Data' in February 2014,[40] outlining the need for accountability and fairness to tackle embedded discrimination. That agenda was given more specificity by organisations like Upturn,[41] who connected the potential harms of data driven decision-making with broader issues of social justice. Shortly after, Obama's White House (the Executive Office of the President) published its 2014 report on Big Data, identifying bias and discrimination in big data as risks of significant material and immaterial harms.

Concerns around algorithmic bias and fairness in machine learning were also connected with related scholarly interests in algorithmic accountability. New York University hosted a conference on Governing Algorithms in May 2013, asking how to turn the 'problem of algorithms into an object of productive inquiry?'[42] Data & Society also articulated a research

35   Latanya Sweeney, 'Discrimination in Online Ad Delivery: Google Ads, Black Names and White Names, Racial Discrimination, and Click Advertising', *Queue* 11 (3, 2013): 10–29.8.
36   Kate Crawford, 'The Hidden Biases in Big Data', *Harvard Business Review*, 1 April 2013, https://hbr.org/2013/04/the-hidden-biases-in-big-data.
37   Nicolas Diakopoulos, 'Race Against the Algorithms', *The Atlantic*, 4 October 2013, https://www.theatlantic.com/technology/archive/2013/10/rageagainst-the-algorithms/280255/.
38   Safiya Noble, 'Missed Connections: What Search Engines Say About Women', *Bitch* magazine, Spring 2012 (54), https://www.bitchmedia.org/issue/54; S. Noble, 'Google Search: Hyper-visibility as a Means of Rendering Black Women and Girls Invisible—InVisible Culture', *Invisible Culture*, 19., https://ivc.lib.rochester.edu/googlesearch- hyper-visibility-as-a-means-of-rendering-black-women-and-girls-invisible/; Safiya Noble, *Algorithms of Oppression: How Search Engines Reinforce Racism*, NYU Press: New York City, 2013.
39   Solon Barocas, and Aandre Selbst, 'Big Data's Disparate Impact', *California Law Review*, 104, (3), (June 2016): 671 - 732.
40   https://civilrights.org/2014/02/27/civil-rights-principles-era-big-data.
41   Upturn, *Civil Rights, Big Data and Our Algorithmic Future: A September 2014 Report on Social Justice and Technology*, 2014, https://bigdata.fairness.io/wp- content/uploads/2015/04/2015-04-20-Civil-Rights-Big-Data-and-Our-Algorithmic-Future-v1.2.pdf.
42   See https://governingalgorithms.org/.

agenda around algorithmic accountability in March 2014.[43] In February 2015, NYU hosted its Algorithms and Accountability Conference, building on the 2013 event, and expressly outlining its topic as the challenges of algorithmic power in terms of transparency, fairness, and equal treatment, hosting speakers primarily from the humanities and social sciences. A more expressly technical forum had also coalesced as the 2014 FATML workshop, interested in exploring 'how to characterise and address these issues with computationally rigorous methods,'[44] and offering a venue for broadly technical solutions within a complex and inter-disciplinary problem definition. This workshop ran until 2018 and was supplemented the same year with the larger and more interdisciplinary FAT* Conference (which in 2019 became affiliated with ACM, and changed its name to FAccT in 2020), bringing the social scientific and technical fields together. There are now a multitude of specialized AI Ethics workshops, professional organizations, and conferences, both standalone and as part of broader technical events, investigating issues such as algorithmic bias, the falsehood of technical objectivity, and solutions in the form of accountability, transparency, and fairness.

Despite AI Ethics emerging as a response to the failures of industry, Big Tech has long played a central role in supporting the field from its earliest days, and continues to participate in the scholarly environment with significant funding and support. Unquestionably, industry support of AI Ethics research has enabled a great deal of high quality, independent scholarship. But at the same time, it raises complex questions around the positionality of researchers and the institutional dynamics that define the 'value' of research.

Considering the commercial applications and tools that constitute the core subject of AI ethics analysis, it is no surprise that industry and academia have coalesced around these particular problems. However, it is precisely the development of networks of stakeholders with markedly different interests and values that has enabled the new forms of *circulation* described here as an 'economy of virtue.'[45] As Lily Hu points out with respect to the flagship AI ethics conference: 'FAccT researchers are, generally-speaking, not shouting into the void; quite the opposite, many are in fact meeting at post-conference corporate-sponsored cocktail parties to discuss collaborations across institutions and interests.'[46] Indeed, events like FAccT in essence operate as an interface between academia and industry, providing a platform that enables the consolidation of these groups and their competing interests. They create social and professional networks that can either lead to partnerships and collaborations or act as pipelines to direct employment in industry. The scale of these flagship events has also meant that they rely on the funding of Big Tech to subsidise the logistical costs of hosting. This creates particular obligations between professional societies and the organizations that they seek to hold to account; obligations that ensure doors always remain open to the flow of industrial interests.

---

43   Alex Rosenblat, Tamara. Kneese, and danah boyd, 'Algorithmic Accountability: A Workshop Primer Produced For: The Social, Cultural & Ethical Dimensions of "Big Data"', 17 March 2014, New York, NY, https://www.datasociety.net/pubs/2014-0317/AlgorithmicAccountabilityPrimer.pdf.

44   See, for example, https://www.fatml.org/.

45   For further discussion, see Phan et al, "Economies of Virtue: The Circulation of "Ethics" in Big Tech'.

46   Lily Hu, 'Tech Ethics: Speaking Ethics to Power, or Power Speaking Ethics?' *Journal of Social Computing* 2 (3, 2021): 243.

These social and intellectual exchanges have grounded the reification of research, researchers, and reputations into commodity forms capable of circulating between and through industrial and academic institutions. These circulations take a number of shapes, drawing in, producing, and exchanging both explicitly financial as well as reputational forms of value for all involved. For instance, scholarly ethics outputs might become levers for acquiring industry funding, industry supported scholarly platforms, or industry appointments. At the same time, universities endorse these developments, trading on the influx of external money, prestige, and 'impact' associated with industry engagement. All the while Big Tech benefits from the enhancement and legitimation of their ethical credentials and endeavours.

Such circulations harbour the contradiction that high-value ethics commodities only acquire and sustain value through having limited 'ethical effects.' That is, in order to circulate freely between the academy and industry, the ethical content (in terms of effects on the world—or at least the business to which they are directed) must be effaced or at least constrained. As the abhorrent treatment of prominent AI ethics researcher Timnit Gebru by her former employer Google demonstrates,[47] when the ethics commodity fundamentally challenges business models, the appointments and status offered in exchange disappear (and worse). It may be that the use-value of ethics commodities acquired by industry manifests elsewhere—not in the guiding of meaningful change in industrial and technical practice, but in the construction of reputational edifices capable of 1) shielding commerce from structural critique that could impact profit, and 2) incentivizing the AI ethics field's progression in congenial directions. The multitude of forms ethics might take, the channels of its circulation, and the work that it does or does not do, as well as the ways its imperatives intersect with the experience of researchers, are precisely the subjects explored in the contributions to this edition.

Contributions to this volume

This volume is a collective response to the reification of ethics into commodity forms. It explores how industry participation in ethical AI research has created a new economy of virtue—a massive network of actors variously situated across industry, civil society, and universities producing and circulating ethics as a service and as a product. The authors bring both critical perspectives and firsthand experiences of the challenges, dilemmas, and opportunities that life within this economy affords. Their experiences are diverse, hailing from a range of disciplinary backgrounds, including law, anthropology, criminology, media and communication studies, STS, political economy, and more. Where some of the authors are seasoned academics, professors with decades of experience in the field, others are at the beginning of their careers, entering industry at the peak of the AI ethics funding frenzy.

47   J. Khadijah Abdurahman, 'On the Moral Collapse of AI Ethics' *Medium* blog, 8 December 2020, https://upfromthecracks.medium.com/on-the-moral-collapse-of-ai- ethics-791cbc7df872. Karen Hao, 'A Leading AI Ethics Researcher Says She's Been Fired from Google', *MIT Technology Review*, 3 December 2020, https://www.technologyreview.com/ 2020/12/03/1013065/google-ai-ethics-lead-timnit-gebru-fired/.

They do, however, have a shared investment in issues of technology, power, and social justice, and while few (if any) would call themselves 'AI ethicists,' they are nevertheless all intimately intertwined with the controversies and debates that have followed the development of the field.

In the chapters that follow, these authors give voice and testimony to the tactics and strategies of commodification and resistance. Each chapter explores these dynamics as they unfold across different sites and terrains. When these stories are placed together, we begin to see common trajectories and flows between actors, institutions, and interests. It is a sad irony that the more ethics circulates as a commodity, the less ethical work it is able to do. Yet, as discussed above and as the chapters will illustrate, even in its commodity form, AI ethics can always be put to work to do something, to serve someone's interests.

This collection is arranged into three sections: subjects, sites, and actions. In the first section, the authors draw on their own subjectivities and subjective experiences to narrate the contradictions and dilemmas that these complex arrangements of funding place workers within.

In 'Your Thoughts for a Penny? Capital, Complicity and AI Ethics,' Corinne Cath and Os Keyes describe the industry sponsorship of PhD scholarships and collaborative projects as a cunning investment. They provide vignettes from their experiences as PhD students across the U.S. and the U.K., providing illuminating detail on how people on the ground navigate and negotiate the tensions and discomfort that can arise when one's wage is tied to one's enemy. 'Critique does not avoid complicity,' they write, and as their examples demonstrate, in many cases it operates as a mode of recuperation. They end with a call for feminist refusal, a position that helps situate researchers in relations of power by acknowledging that no engagement—however critical—is outside of it.

In 'Extractivist Ethics,' Sarah Pink describes ethics as 'the bait through which trust in technology is extracted from publics or users.' She argues that techno-solutionist approaches to design creates a disconnection between producers and everyday people, which in turn cultivates an instrumentalist approach to ethics. Human ethical values have purpose insofar as they can be used to make 'ethical machines' that can then be showcased to engender trust. She calls for a return to everyday ethics, which by their nature are slippery and unstable and therefore less amenable to the forms of capture and investment, at least as industry actors would imagine it.

In the final essay in this section, Rodrigo Ochigame describes the framing of ethics as a kind of 'amicable criticism' that can serve as a 'leverage for entering into business relationships.' Like Cath and Keyes, he describes his time as a graduate student researcher working in the AI ethics groups the MIT Media Lab. He provides candid commentary on the ethical scandals that shrouded the lab and its former director, Joichi Ito, offering an unflinching assessment of the role of the Media Lab in sustaining the agendas of Silicon Valley. Originally published on the investigative journalism website *The Intercept*, Ochigame's essay is a stunning example of speaking out against the sordid dynamics that most only hear through whispers. We are honoured to republish the essay with his permission here.

In the second section of this volume, 'sites,' we turn to situated case studies to understand how 'ethical' practice is leveraged by Big Tech within specific domains of AI application.

In 'Ecocide Isn't Ethical: Political Ecology and Capitalist AI Ethics,' Sy Taffel, Laura Bedford and Monique Mann describe AI ethics as a way for corporations to frame ethical practice away from anthropogenic forms of planetary harm. They discuss in detail the social and ecological impacts of AI and ML, moving between sites of resource extraction, data centres, and e-waste processing. This contribution provides a damning critique of how the fantasy of 'green AI' operates to sustain unjust, unethical, and decidedly ecocidal corporate practices.

For Angela Daly, the corporate agenda driving AI ethics has made it abstract, disconnected and apolitical. Like Sarah Pink, she also calls for an analytic return to sites in everyday life to understand the complex lived realities of people on the ground and to highlight the inadequacy of abstracted ethical principles. Turning to the specific example of facial recognition, Daly departs from the hifalutin world of ethical principles and instead brings attention to a world of ethical negotiation that is enacted through protest, dissensus, and organizing.

In their chapter on global standards and standard-setting, Tsvetelina Hristova and Liam Magee outline how ethics is used as a vehicle for the socialization of risk, allowing it to scale up and be turned into a form of value. Their work expands the sites and practices typically associated with economies of virtue, turning to the highly bureaucratized zones of ISO (International Standards Organisation) frameworks and subcommittees. Here, they examine how middle-power countries approach standards setting as an economic and political strategy, the effect of which is the transformation of ethics into a literal exportable commodity.

Finally, Michael Richardson closes this section with his chapter on the quintessential site for the study of paradoxes in ethics: defence and military AI. He describes how a focus on ethics insulates researchers working with departments of defence from the squeamish questions of lethal violence while at the same time justifying the use of autonomous weapons to intensify impact and injuries. He writes, 'Defence researchers and companies can not only *be* virtuous, but also can *make* war virtuous too.' He underscores how decreases in state funding push universities to diversify income streams through corporate and military partnerships. 'Universities,' he reminds us, 'are, after all, institutions of empire and colony even more than they are sites of learning, knowledge-making and dissent.'

The third and final section, 'action,' concludes the volume with two interviews with prominent scholars and activists, reflecting on moments of direct action against the politics of industry money and influence. Through these discussions we're given a glimpse at the alternatives, into what activism might achieve, and the kinds of reflexivity that scholars need to understand the complex forces and imperatives shaping their working lives and subjectivities. In 'Open Secrets' with Meredith Whittaker, Jathan Sadowski and Thao Phan, and 'Dropouts' with Lilly Irani, Alex Hanna, J. Khadijah Abdurahman, and Jake Goldenfein, scholars with rich experience from across different positions in the Economy of Virtue describe the different ways institutions hijack our sense of self as researchers, and how our efforts to (re)imagine and/or (re)define the university may be better spent on organising ourselves as university workers as in any other industrial enterprise.

With their rich and diverse experience across sectors, these scholars describe the complexities of funding in the context of community, collegiality, and supporting people to earn a wage, as well as how they're leveraged into tools of internalised discipline. With personal understanding of the internal mechanics of industry influence over the academy, and how alliances form around funding prerogatives, they describe the way these institutions encourage certain types of critical work, while simultaneously subverting radical efforts that might undermine industrial interests or funding relationships. The alternatives they offer is workplace organization as a tool to break scholars away from prerogatives of prestige that serve the interests of those with power over us, and in so doing to de-commodify the work performed by scholars in the economy of virtue.

Conclusion: From AI Ethics to the Economy of Virtue

This anthology is part of a growing body of literature within the AI ethics/AI and social responsibility literature that attempts to produce 'self-reflexive critiques of the conditions of knowledge creation.'[48] This style of critique builds on a long tradition in which researchers approach their own practices, communities, and institutions as objects for critical analysis and reflexivity. Exemplary forms of this style are found in areas such as critical race studies, Indigenous studies, Black Feminist theory, and other strands of feminist scholarship.[49] While the tenor of this work is often critical, the intention is to instigate positive change and to hold organizations and research communities accountable to the standards and values that they espouse. In recent years, many scholars have turned their attention to the growing interface between industry and the academy, and the impact on the topic of ethics—both as a domain of research (e.g. bioethics, AI ethics) and as a set of guiding principles that manage the creation of knowledge (e.g. diversity, equity, and inclusion programs).[50]

The contribution offered in this edition is an effort to highlight the complexities of researcher positionality in this field, and expose the dilemmas we all face when making choices about the research, methods, and partners we pursue. Many of the contributors have direct experience in industry, research-focused arms of industry, or university faculties and

---

48   Whittaker, 'The Steep Cost of Capture'.
49   See, for example, Sara Ahmed, *On Being Included: Racism and Diversity in Institutional Life*, Duke University Press, 2012; bell hooks, *Talking Back: Thinking Feminist, Thinking Black*. 2 edition. Routledge, 2014; Aileen Moreton-Robinson, *Talkin' Up to the White Woman: Aboriginal Women and Feminism*, Univ. of Queensland Press, 2000.
50   See Sara Ahmed, 'The Language of Diversity.' *Ethnic and Racial Studies* 30, no. (2) (March 2007): 235–56; Ruha Benjamin, *Race After Technology: Abolitionist Tools for the New Jim Code*. 1 edition. Cambridge, UK; Medford, MA: Polity, 2019; Carl Elliott, *White Coat, Black Hat: Adventures on the Dark Side of Medicine*. 1st edition. Beacon Press, 2010; Anna Lauren Hoffmann, 'Terms of Inclusion: Data, Discourse, Violence.' *New Media & Society*, September 16, 2020, doi. 146144482095872.

research institutes that receive funding and other kinds of support from industry.[51] Several of the contributions build from personal experience, provide insight into the institutional and organizational arrangements of Big Tech, and give testimony to the conditions of labour that shape research practice within these contexts. We have no interest in calling out colleagues for the choices they are compelled to make under capitalism. Our interest is understanding the ways industry both establishes and takes advantage of the incentive structures operating in this research environment. We hope this facilitates further reflexive analyses by university workers on the conditions of their own work in this domain.

Central to knowledge creation in scholarly contexts are mechanisms for the evaluation of research and researchers.[52] This has long been a contentious space, and indeed an area in which Big Tech has become increasingly central.[53] In the curation and production of this edition, we adopted a model of collective editorship where (lead) chapter authors were allocated other chapters to review. Our intention in doing so was to implement a constructive approach to 'peer-review' that was designed to discourage disciplinary gatekeeping, and accommodate the challenging topics and themes explored throughout the edited collection. Our aim was to encourage reviewers to be accountable for their feedback while constructively working closely together to improve the quality of the text and argument. We also hoped to participate in mechanisms that enhance the scholarly community's control over the conditions of its own work.

We—the editors—experienced this as a solidarity-building exercise far removed from the anonymous peer review processes through which commercial publishers extract academic labor in ways typically unrecognized by university incentives structures, and generally experienced as unappreciated and unenjoyable by workers. The same desire to (re)imagine and (re)define the university work experience influenced our choice of publisher—the Institute of Network Cultures (INC)—a press which has a history and reputation of multidisciplinary knowledge production and engagement that responds to urgent matters relating to digital networks through open access publishing and advocacy.

But these are, of course, marginal actions in the context of a research ecology defined by the dynamics outlined in the following chapters. How to find a path forward and navigate economies of virtue is an epic challenge. This collection of texts is part of the process of naming the dynamics of tech capture, co-optation, and compromise. The hope is for scholars, advocates, activists, and policy-makers to incorporate these reflexive critiques of the conditions of knowledge creation and dissemination, and the compromises and trade-offs faced by knowledge workers over whom interested institutions have power. This is certain to be uncomfortable given the politics of collegial proximity that inform academic prestige networks. But naming these dynamics is

51   See Powles and Nissenbaum, 'The Seductive Diversion of 'Solving' Bias in Artificial Intelligence'; Ochigame, 'The Invention of "Ethical AI"'; Gebru, 'For Truly Ethical AI, Its Research Must Be Independent from Big Tech'; Abdurahman, 'Fired for Speaking Out Against Anti-Blackness and Ethnic Cleansing: Open Letter to Cornell Tech' and 'On the Moral Collapse of AI Ethics'; Whittaker, 'The Steep Cost of Capture'; Young, et al, 'Confronting Power and Corporate Capture at the FAccT Conference'.
52   Pierre Bourdieu, *Science of Science and Reflexivity,* University of Chicago Press: Chicago, 2004.
53   Jake Goldenfein and Daniel Griffin, 'Google Scholar: Platforming the Scholarly Economy', *Internet Policy Review* 11(3, 2022) (online).

the only way to address them and to stage questions that allow us to envision and demand alternative futures.

Funding Disclosures

This work was supported by the Australian Research Council's Centre of Excellence for Automated Decision-Making & Society [Grant Number CE200100005]. In particular, we wish to acknowledge the Melbourne Law School node of the Centre for its financial support in bringing the book to fruition. Declan Kuch acknowledges support of the Vice Chancellor's Fellowship scheme at Western Sydney University for assistance with printing. This volume builds on the 'Economies of Virtue: The Circulation of 'Ethics' in AI and Digital Culture' workshop hosted at Deakin University 8–9 July 2021, funded by the Academy of the Social Sciences in Australia, Workshop Program Grant 2021.

References

Abdurahman, J. Khadijah. 'On the Moral Collapse of AI Ethics' *Medium* blog,8 December 2020, https://upfromthecracks.medium.com/on-the-moral-collapse-of-ai-ethics-791cbc7df872.

———. J. Khadijah. 'Fired for Speaking Out Against Anti-Blackness and Ethnic Cleansing: Open Letter to Cornell Tech', *Medium* blog, 3 June, 2021, https://upfromthecracks.medium.com/fired-for-speaking-out-against-anti-blackness-and-ethnic-cleansing-open-letter-to-cornell-tech-3b3f669cf69f.

———. 'On the Moral Collapse of AI Ethics', *Medium* blog, 7 December, 2020, https://upfromthecracks.medium.com/on-the-moral-collapse-of-ai-ethics-791cbc7df872.

Ahmed, Sara. *On Being Included: Racism and Diversity in Institutional Life*. Durham: Duke University Press, 2012.

———. 'The Language of Diversity', *Ethnic and Racial Studies* 30 (2, 2007): 235–56.

Australian Research Council. 'Selection Report: Discovery Early Career Research Award 2022 | Australian Research Council.' Australian Government | Australian Research Council, 2022. https://www.arc.gov.au/funding-research/funding-outcome/selection-outcome-reports/selection-report-discovery-early-career-research-award-2022.

Barnes, Joel. 'Defunding Arts Degrees Is the Latest Battle in a 40-Year Culture War', *The Conversation*, 3 July 2020, http://theconversation.com/defunding-arts-degrees-is-the-latest-battle-in-a-40-year-culture-war-141689.

Barocas, Solon, and Andrew D. Selbst. "Big Data's Disparate Impact." *California Law Review* 104 (3, 2016): 671–732.

Benjamin, Ruha. *Race After Technology: Abolitionist Tools for the New Jim Code*. 1 edition. Medford, MA: Polity, 2019, https://ebookcentral-proquest-com.ezproxy-b.deakin.edu.au/lib/deakin/detail.action?docID=5820427.

Bietti, Elettra. 'From Ethics Washing to Ethics Bashing: A View on Tech Ethics from Within Moral Philosophy', *SSRN Electronic Journal*, 2021.

Birhane, Abeba, Ruane, Elayne, Laurent, Thomas, Brown, Matthew S., Flowers, Johnathan, Ventresque, Anthony, and Dancy, Christopher L. 'The Forgotten Margins of AI Ethics' in *2022 ACM Conference on Fairness, Accountability, and Transparency*, 948–58. FAccT '22. New York, NY, USA: Association for Computing Machinery, 2022.

Bourdieu, Pierre. *Science of Science and Reflexivity*, trans. Richard Nice, Chicago: University of Chicago Press, 2004.

Burn-Murdoch, John. 'The Problem with Algorithms: Magnifying Misbehaviour', *Guardian*, 14 August 2013, https://www.theguardian.com/news/datablog/2013/aug/14/problem-with-algorithms-magnifying-misbehaviour.

Crawford, Kate. 'The Hidden Biases in Big Data', *Harvard Business Review*, 1 April 2013, https://hbr.org/2013/04/the-hidden-biases-in-big-data.

Diakopoulos, Nicholas. 'Rage Against the Algorithms', *The Atlantic*, 3 October 2013, https://www.theatlantic.com/technology/archive/2013/10/rage-against-the-algorithms/280255/.

Dormehl, Luke. 'Algorithms Are Great and All, But They Can Also Ruin Lives.' Accessed October 14, 2022. https://www.wired.com/2014/11/algorithms-great-can-also-ruin-lives/.

Dwork, Cynthia, Moritz Hardt, Toniann Pitassi, Omer Reingold, and Richard Zemel. 'Fairness through Awareness.' In *Proceedings of the 3rd Innovations in Theoretical Computer Science Conference on - ITCS '12*, 214–26. Cambridge, Massachusetts: ACM Press, 2012.

Elliott, Carl. *White Coat, Black Hat: Adventures on the Dark Side of Medicine*, Boston: Beacon Press, 2010.

———. 'Why Clinical Ethicists Are Not Activists', *Hastings Center Report* 51 (4, 2021): 36–7.

Gansky, Ben, and Sean McDonald. 'CounterFAccTual: How FAccT Undermines Its Organizing Principles' in *2022 ACM Conference on Fairness, Accountability, and Transparency*, 1982–92. Seoul Republic of Korea: ACM, 2022.

Gebru, Timnit. 'For Truly Ethical AI, Its Research Must Be Independent from Big Tech', *Guardian*, 6 December 2021, https://www.theguardian.com/commentisfree/2021/dec/06/google-silicon-valley-ai-timnit-gebru.

Goldenfein, Jake, and Daniel Griffin. 'Google Scholar – Platforming the Scholarly Economy', *Internet Policy Review* 11, no. 3, 29 September 2022, https://policyreview.info/articles/analysis/google-scholar-platforming-scholarly-economy.

Hao, Karen. 'A Leading AI Ethics Researcher Says She's Been Fired from Google', *MIT Technology Review*, 3 December 2020, https://www.technologyreview.com/2020/12/03/1013065/google-ai-ethics-lead-timnit-gebru-fired/.

———. 'In 2020, Let's Stop AI Ethics-Washing and Actually Do Something', *MIT Technology Review*, 27 December 2019, https://www.technologyreview.com/2019/12/27/57/ai-ethics-washing-time-to-act/.

Hare, Julie. 'Wage Theft Is "Systemic": 21 Universities under Investigation', *Australian Financial Review*, 20 October 2021, https://www.afr.com/work-and-careers/education/wage-theft-is-systemic-21-universities-under-investigation-20211020-p591kw.

Hoffmann, Anna Lauren. 'Terms of Inclusion: Data, Discourse, Violence', *New Media & Society*, 16 September 2020, 146144482095872.

hooks, bell. *Talking Back: Thinking Feminist, Thinking Black*, London: Routledge, 2014.

Hu, Lily. 'Tech Ethics: Speaking Ethics to Power, or Power Speaking Ethics?' *Journal of Social Computing* 2 (3, 2021): 238–48.

Johnson, Bobbie, and Gideon Lichfield. 'Hey Google, Sorry You Lost Your Ethics Council, So We Made One for You', *MIT Technology Review* (blog), 8 April 2019, https://medium.com/mit-technology-review/hey-google-sorry-you-lost-your-ethics-council-so-we-made-one-for-you-28ee6c33576a.

Manjoo, F. 'Silicon Valley Has an Arrogance Problem—WSJ', *Wall Street Journal*, 3 November 2013, https://www.wsj.com/articles/SB10001424052702303661404579175712015473766.

McCarthy, Gregory Michael, and Jayasuriya, Kanishka. 'A Review into How University Research Works in Australia Has Just Begun—It Must Confront These 3 Issues', *The Conversation*, 20 September 2022, http://theconversation.com/a-review-into-how-university-research-works-in-australia-has-just-begun-it-must-confront-these-3-issues-190551.

Moreton-Robinson, Aileen. *Talkin' Up to the White Woman: Aboriginal Women and Feminism*, Brisbane: University of Queensland Press, 2000.

Morozov, Evgeny. *To Save Everything, Click Here*, New York: PublicAffairs, 2014.

Moten, Fred, and Stefano Harney. 'The University and the Undercommons', *Social Text* 22 (2, 2004): 101–15.

Munn, Luke. 'The Uselessness of AI Ethics', *AI and Ethics*, 23 August 2022.

Noble, Safiya. *Algorithms of Oppression: How Search Engines Reinforce Racism*, New York: NYU Press, 2018.

———. 'Google Search: Hyper-Visibility as a Means of Rendering Black Women and Girls Invisible—InVisible Culture', *Invisible Culture*, no. 19 (October 2013), https://ivc.lib.rochester.edu/google-search-hyper-visibility-as-a-means-of-rendering-black-women-and-girls-invisible/.

———. 'Missed Connections: What Search Engines Say About Women.' *Bitch* magazine, Spring 2012, https://www.bitchmedia.org/issue/54.

Ochigame, Rodrigo. 'The Invention of 'Ethical AI': How Big Tech Manipulates Academia to Avoid Regulation', *The Intercept* (blog), 20 December 2019, https://theintercept.com/2019/12/20/mit-ethical-ai-artificial-intelligence/.

Phan, Thao, Jake Goldenfein, Monique Mann, and Declan Kuch. 'Economies of Virtue: The Circulation of "Ethics" in Big Tech', *Science as Culture*, 4 November 2021, 1–15.

Powles, Julia, and Helen Nissenbaum. 'The Seductive Diversion of 'Solving' Bias in Artificial Intelligence', *OneZero* (blog), 7 December 2018, https://onezero.medium.com/the-seductive-diversion-of-solving-bias-in-artificial-intelligence-890df5e5ef53.

Rosenblat, Alex, and Tamara Kneese. 'Algorithmic Accountability', n.d., 6.

Sweeney, Latanya. 'Discrimination in Online Ad Delivery: Google Ads, Black Names and White Names, Racial Discrimination, and Click Advertising', *Queue* 11 (3, 2013): 10–29.

Tarnoff, Ben. 'Postcript to J. Khadijah Abdurahman's "A Body of Work That Cannot Be Ignored"', *Logic* magazine, 25 December 2021, https://logicmag.io/beacons/a-body-of-work-that-cannot-be-ignored/.

Turner, Fred. *From Counterculture to Cyberculture: Stewart Brand, the Whole Earth Network, and the Rise of Digital Utopianism* (illustrated edition) Chicago: University of Chicago Press, 2008.

Upturn. 'Civil Rights, Big Data and Our Algorithmic Future: A September 2014 Report on Social Justice and Technology', 2014, https://bigdata.fairness.io/wp-content/uploads/2015/04/2015-04-20-Civil-Rights-Big-Data-and-Our-Algorithmic-Future-v1.2.pdf.

Vinsel, Lee. 'You're Doing It Wrong: Notes on Criticism and Technology Hype', *Medium* blog, 1 February 2021, https://sts-news.medium.com/youre-doing-it-wrong-notes-on-criticism-and-technology-hype-18b08b4307e5.

Wagner, Ben. 'Ethics As An Escape From Regulation. From "Ethics-Washing" to Ethics-Shopping?' in *Ethics As An Escape From Regulation. From 'Ethics-Washing' To Ethics-Shopping?*, 84–9. Amsterdam: Amsterdam University Press, 2018.

Whittaker, Meredith. 'The Steep Cost of Capture', *Interactions* 28 (6, 2021): 50–5.

Wooldridge, Adrian. 'The Coming Tech-Lash', *The Economist*, 18 November 2013, https://www.economist.com/news/2013/11/18/the-coming-tech-lash.

Young, Meg, Michael Katell, and P.M. Krafft. 'Confronting Power and Corporate Capture at the FAccT Conference' in *2022 ACM Conference on Fairness, Accountability, and Transparency*, 1375–86. Seoul Republic of Korea: ACM, 2022.

SECTION I:
SUBJECTS

YOUR THOUGHTS FOR A PENNY? CAPITAL, COMPLICITY AND AI ETHICS

CORINNE CATH AND OS KEYES

Introduction

The rise in concerns about the harms of algorithmic technologies and reformist efforts to address these harms is accompanied by a critical flank of research and researchers who advocate more radical interventions—and for good reason. Concerns about 'ethics-washing', 'ethics-shopping' and 'ethics theater'[1] are repeatedly validated by examples of companies seeking to water down research that brings scrutiny to inherent harms rooted in AI business models and corporate power consolidation.[2] These concerning dynamics occur against the backdrop of the growing lobbying power of the tech sector,[3] as well as increased neoliberalization that sees government and independent sources of funding for academic research reduced and supplanted by industry funding. The growing role of such corporate funding with a direct interest in business-friendly results is distinctly visible in academic research on AI ethics.[4]

This worrisome dynamic brings up a number of issues about what it means to do research into the ethics of AI technologies. It raises questions about who 'owns' AI ethics,[5] and by extension: who is responsible for maintaining ethical standards in academic research? Similarly, the role of private industry in research funding raises questions about the subtle and pernicious

---

1   See Mona Sloane, 'Inequality is the Name of the Game: Thoughts on the Emerging Field of Technology, Ethics and Social Justice', Weizenbaum Conference, Berlin, 16–17 May 2019; also Ben Wagner, 'Ethics As An Escape From Regulation. From "Ethics-Washing" To Ethics-Shopping?', in *Being Profiled*, Amsterdam: Amsterdam University Press, 2018; and Corinne Cath and Fieke Jansen, 'Dutch Comfort: The Limits of AI Governance Through Municipal Registers.' *arXiv e-prints* (2021): arXiv–2109.

2   Algorithm Watch, 'AlgorithmWatch Forced to Shut down Instagram Monitoring Project after Threats from Facebook'. *AlgorithmWatch*, 13 August 2021, https://algorithmwatch.org/en/instagram-research-shut-down-by-facebook/ and Issie Lapowsky, 'How Tech Giants Court and Crush the People Who Study Them', Protocol—The People, Power and Politics of Tech, 19 March 2021, https://www.protocol.com/nyu-facebook-researchers-scraping.

3   Pawel Popiel, 'The Tech Lobby: Tracing the Contours of New Media Elite Lobbying Power.' *Communication Culture & Critique* 11.4 (2018): 566–85 and Max Bank, Felix Duffy, Verena Leyendecker, and Margarida Silva, 'The Lobby Network; Big Tech's Web of Influence in the EU', Corporate Europe Observatory and Lobby Control e.V, 2021, https://corporateeurope.org/en/2021/08/lobby-network-big-techs-web-influence-eu.

4   Corinne Cath, 'Governing Artificial Intelligence: Ethical, Legal and Technical Opportunities and Challenges', *Philosophical Transactions of the Royal Society A: Mathematical, Physical and Engineering Sciences* 376 (2018) and Agathe Balayn and Seda Gürses, 'If AI Is the Problem, Is Debiasing the Solution?' Brussels, Belgium: EDRi, 2021, https://edri.org/our-work/if-ai-is-the-problem-is-debiasing-the-solution/.

5   Jacob Metcalf and Emanuel Moss, 'Owning Ethics: Corporate Logics, Silicon Valley, and the Institutionalization of Ethics', *Social Research: An International Quarterly* 86, (no. 2, 2019): 449–76.

ways in which corporations exert pressure over academic work, even when funding is formally described as 'no strings attached'. Last but not least, the changing landscape of academic funding leads to novel challenges regarding the impact of industry influence on the research agendas, as well as the career trajectories, of the next generation of academics, like the authors of this contribution.

The key question we ask is where and how one draws the line—a question that is both descriptive and normative. In this chapter, we examine both aspects by drawing from auto-ethnographic methods[6] and presenting our experiences in the form of stories in which the authors, each entangled in this reality of industry funding in different ways, reflect on our experiences. We examine how our work is shaped by industry funding, how we negotiate our own lines in the sand regarding when or how we are paid 'pennies for our thoughts', and how these negotiations and lines evolve over time. Engaging in both individual reflection and dialogic exchange, we ask ourselves (and each other):

What lessons can be learned from the ethnographic realities of working on AI in academic settings in which research is reliant on industry funding?

Answering this question, one that confronts many researchers, will help us provide new insights into how corporate power plays out in the context of academic research on AI ethics.

We argue that although boundaries can be (and often are) drawn between 'conventional' and 'critical' data ethics perspectives and actors, reality is often more complex. Engagement does not mean an absence of misgivings, as Su, Lazar & Irani adroitly document.[7] Likewise, critique does not avoid complicity.[8] Behind every perspective and position are *people*, navigating their own relation to, and alienation from, their values in a research environment of finite resources and corporate capture.[9]

Even absent such an environment, some degree of compromise is a consequence of having to work with and in relation to other people and organizations with different interests and perspectives. Indeed, as Nick Seaver puts it, one vital site of ethics is how 'people negotiate among apparently competing values'.[10] Our chapter elucidates what that negotiation can look like in practice and what lessons can be learned for others trying to navigate what it means to do, and relate to, ethics in academic settings and industry-funded AI research.

---

6   Carolyn Ellis, Tony E. Adams, and Arthur P. Bochner, 'Autoethnography: An Overview', *Forum Qualitative Sozialforschung / Forum: Qualitative Social Research* 12.1 (2001) and Deborah Reed-Danahay, *Auto/Ethnography: Rewriting the Self and the Social*, Oxford; New York: Routledge, 1997.

7   Norman Makato Su, Amanda Lazar, and Lilly Irani, 'Critical Affects: Tech Work Emotions Amidst the Techlash', *Proceedings of the ACM on Human-Computer Interaction* 5, CSCW1 (2021).

8   Fred Moten and Stefano Harney, 'The University and the Undercommons: Seven theses', *Social Text* 22.2 (2004).

9   Cath, 'Governing Artificial Intelligence' and Meredith Whittaker, 'The Steep Cost of Capture', *Interactions* 28.6 (2021): 50–5.

10   Nick Seaver 'CARE AND SCALE: Decorrelative Ethics in Algorithmic Recommendation', *Cultural Anthropology* 36 (no. 3, 2021): 509–37.

Two themes surface throughout this reflection. First, the power of corporations to indirectly shape research, not by setting the content but rather by drawing the contours of acceptable critique. Second is the relationships that are possible and impossible due to the role of industry funding. The emergence of these two distinct themes and the role of feminist refusal in our shared experience,[11] as PhD researchers who started their research three years and 4,488 miles apart, speaks to the expansive influence of corporate power, the implications this has for research, and the possibilities for the next generation of scholars working on AI ethics through industry funded means.

This chapter is organized as follows. First, we position our work and experiences in recent literature on navigating values in academia, by focusing on the capital, complicity, and articulation work of AI ethics. In doing so, we demonstrate a link between our individual experiences as junior scholars working on AI ethics and the broader dynamics of capture of, and resistance through, research documented in the literature. We show that the work of many scholars working at the intersection of AI and ethics is shaped by the funding realities of contemporary academia, and that efforts to simplistically escape these realities are themselves entangled in questions of power. Second, we introduce two short auto-ethnographic stories (in the sense used by Sotiropoulou and Cranston),[12] based on our research experiences.

Corinne considers the subtle power dynamics of industry funding on AI ethics research and its implications for the next generation of scholars. Os focuses on how funding shapes the network of relations that researchers build and those that, by extension, remain out of reach. We subsequently put our respective experience in conversations with each other, to draw broader conclusions about how AI ethics relates to questions of power, a key theme of this edited collection. We conclude by arguing that it is increasingly difficult for academia to be a bastion of critical thought on AI, given its enmeshment with industry interest and networks. If it ever was possible for the academe to play such a role,[13] these conclusions call for a radical rethinking of how research on AI ethics is funded and the creation of novel networks of counter-power and care, within and outside of the academe.

Positioning Us: Ongoing Debates About AI Ethics

Efforts to describe and/or demarcate AI ethics often rely on the idea of 'waves'—of successive, differing lines of scholarship and thought.[14] Although this is common, we worry that it risks rendering invisible and unintelligible scholarship that was 'out of time': too radical, too early, or

---

11   Bonnie Honig, *A Feminist Theory of Refusal*, Cambridge: Harvard University Press, 2021 and Audra
      Simpson, 'The Ruse of Consent and the Anatomy of "Refusal": Cases from Indigenous North America
      and Australia.' *Postcolonial Studies* 20.1 (2017): 18–33.
12   Panagiota Sotiropoulou and Sophie Cranston, 'Critical Friendship: An Alternative, 'Care-ful' Way to Play
      the Academic Game.' *Gender, Place & Culture* (2022).
13   Thao Phan, et al., 'Economies of Virtue: The Circulation of "Ethics" in Big Tech', *Science as Culture*
      (2021): 121–35.
14   Frank Pasquale, 'Machines Judging Humans: The Promise and Perils of Formalizing Evaluative Criteria',
      in *Proceedings of the AAAI/ACM Conference on AI, Ethics, and Society*, New York, 7–8 February 2020.

too conventional, too late.[15] Instead, we would subdivide AI ethics research based on its *form of critique*: into internal critique that seeks to alter scholarship from 'within the [scholarship] itself' and *immanent critique* (which, while involved with the practices being analyzed, relies on 'context-transcending claims').[16]

Internal critique operates within the norms of existing forms of governance. In the case of AI ethics, we can see this in proposals for voluntary or involuntary codes of ethics,[17] proposals to operationalize and orient AI researchers towards notions of 'algorithmic fairness', and attempts at developing binding regulations that implicitly further the inevitability thesis of AI—that many politicians, academics, and business leaders subscribe to.[18] It is often this type of critique that finds favor with corporate funders and, as such, has taken up much of the air in discussions about AI ethics.

Operating counter to this, immanent critique draws from broader normative understandings in the hope of achieving not only reformist, but transformative, effects. In the context of AI, this is often referred to as 'critical data studies', i.e., research that takes issue not only with the outcomes of algorithmic systems but also with the very premises on which such systems are designed, the political economies that make them possible, and the discursive cultures AI simultaneously depends on and enables.[19] For example, Green and Vijoen outline the limits of algorithmic thought and its technical formalism to argue that many of the harms of AI occur outside of these limits and need to be addressed in social rather than technical terms.[20] Similarly, in a recent report for European Digital Rights organization EDRi,[21] the authors argue that the root causes of power imbalances of AI must be addressed. Likewise, Powles and Nissenbaum argue that deference to AI by focusing on improving the technology from within limits not only critical conversation about the role of technology, but also the role of ethics, law, and the media in limiting AI harms.[22] Critical scholars like Powles, Nissenbaum, Balayn, and Gürses contend that focusing on 'technical debiasing of systems', while popular, is insufficient and oversimplifies the socio-technical impacts of AI as functions of its technical design. They make a strong statement that the seduction of such internal critiques and improvements

---

15   Clare Hemmings, *Why Stories Matter*, Durham: Duke University Press, 2011.
16   Rahel Jaeggi, *Critique of Forms of Life*, Cambridge: Harvard University Press, 2018.
17   See Anna Jobin, Marcello Ienca, and Effy Vayena, 'The Global Landscape of AI Ethics Guidelines',
      Nature Machine Intelligence 1.9 (2019).
18   Cath & Jansen, 'Dutch Comfort'.
19   Lina Dencik, 'The Datafied Welfare State: A Perspective from the UK' in Andreas Hepp, Juliane Jarke,
      and Leif Kramp (eds) *The Ambivalences of Data Power: New Perspectives in Critical Data Studies*,
      Palgrave Macmillan UK: 2021; Cami Rincón, Os Keyes, and Corinne Cath, 'Speaking from Experience:
      Trans/Non-Binary Requirements for Voice-Activated AI', *Proceedings of the ACM on Human-Computer
      Interaction* (2021), and Linnet Taylor, 'Public Actors Without Public Values: Legitimacy, Domination and
      the Regulation of the Technology Sector', *Philosophy & Technology*, 2021.
20   Ben Green and Salomé Viljoen, 'Algorithmic Realism: Expanding the Boundaries of Algorithmic Thought'
      in *Proceedings of the 2020 Conference on Fairness, Accountability, and Transparency* 2020, Barcelona
      Spain, 2020: ACM.
21   Balayn and Gürses, 'If AI Is the Problem, Is Debiasing the Solution?'.
22   Powles, Julia, and Helen Nissenbaum, 'The Seductive Diversion of "Solving" Bias in Artificial
      Intelligence', Medium, 2018, https://medium.com/s/story/the-seductive-diversion-of-solving-bias-in-
      artificial-intelligence-890df5e5ef53.

belies their simplicity, rather than its suitability for addressing the inevitable questions of power and governance invoked by AI.

Understandably, these researchers engaging with the socio-technical nature of AI have turned their eye to 'AI ethics itself'. Conventional AI ethics, they argue, is hobbled by and fundamentally tied to the economic, social, and political interests of AI industry leaders. This type of immanent critique is less likely to receive industry funding, given its focus on deconstructing the power relations that sustain the hype around AI systems.

Yet there is a growing need for such immanent critique that highlights what AI ethics 'does'. This type of critique can serve as a meta-analysis of the field of AI ethics and push back against narrow critique that elides structural change to the political and economic realities that sustain it. Researchers worry, for instance, that proposals for 'fairness' or ethical codes risk constituting forms of 'ethics washing',[23] providing the illusion of ethical behavior over harmful organizations and processes. Similarly, there are many concerns that conventional ideas of AI ethics—-and the practitioners engaging in them—-are complicit in enabling unjust futures, with the vast inequalities in political and economic power between technology companies and the communities they harm resulting in a field at risk of, if not already subject to, 'regulatory capture'.[24]

On both sides of this often tense divide are not only principles and practices but also *people*. These people, contrary to classical sociology, are not 'cultural dopes' ignorant of the wider processes they participate in and advance. Instead they are agentic creatures often aware of and (as Su et al, and Cath, respectively, demonstrate)[25] responsive to this back-and-forth. The question then becomes what these response could look like; how people already navigate these tensions, and how to do so in a 'better' way.

We, the authors, know this all too well, because we are both early-career scholars working in the field of AI ethics. Corinne Cath recently finalized her PhD in the UK and Os Keyes is currently a PhD Candidate in the United States. Before her PhD Corinne worked in politics and for various non-profit organizations; before theirs, Os was a data scientist at both for- and non-profit organizations. Our respective research topics—civil society participation in debates about technology governance and structures of domination—reflect our personal backgrounds, interests, and identities. In acknowledging positionality as queer, trans, white, and European scholars we recognize our backgrounds are irrevocably tied to our research and how we pursue the creation of knowledge about AI ethics. Throughout this piece, we draw from auto-ethnographic epistemologies and methods to outline how knowledge about AI ethics cannot be separated from the people undertaking that research, and how their expertise is (epistemically or materially) supported. The auto-ethnographic stories below are synthesized write-ups of our experiences and conversations that reflect in broad strokes

---

23   Wagner, 'Ethics as an Escape From Regulation'.
24   Whittaker, 'The steep cost of capture'.
25   Su et al., 'Critical Affects' and Cath, 'Governing Artificial Intelligence'.

the types of issues we encountered.[26] These broader compilations of our experiences demonstrate the pervasiveness of the influence of industry on AI ethics research across the different contexts and time spans we did our PhD research.

Corinne's Story: The Impossibility of 'No Strings Attached' Industry Research Funding

In 2016, I started a PhD at a famously old university in Europe. Over the course of my PhD program, I took and taught courses with various professors at this university who included me in ongoing research projects. It was exciting and validating to be involved in their research. Given the proximity of my university to the London-based tech scene and my background as an anthropologist of computing cultures, some of the work I became involved in naturally included research for large, well-known social media companies. Often, this work would be around particular thorny topics, like the ethics of using AI in content moderation at scale. Sometimes this research would be peer-reviewed and public facing, in other cases it would be for internal company purposes. Sometimes the senior researchers I worked with received funding from these tech companies to undertake research.

I had a personal interest in being involved in such industry-driven efforts; it allowed me to peek inside the machine and get a sense of what priorities and politics drive internal decision-making in Big Tech companies. The focused nature of the research, and the trust relationship between the senior researchers I worked with and the companies, meant that the information shared was more elaborate and the people we spoke to less reserved. These experiences provided important insights for an anthropologist of computing communities and cultures, like myself. Even if I would not be able to explicitly write about what I heard or saw, doing this kind of work, I reasoned, would sharpen my overall understanding of the tech sector, and thus my critique. I still believe this to be the case but looking back now, I see how such research can expand the toolbox of these companies in pushing back critics as much as it sharpens researchers' analysis of harms caused.

Notably absent in my industry projects was explicit engagement with some of the most well-known eroding and harmful effects of the tech sector: its surveillance-based data collection and business model. This absence is surprising, given existing academic critique of this business model,[27] and the extent to which it is at the root of many of the ethical concerns that follow. When I made suggestions that would touch on these business models, it was often the senior researchers that would be the first line of defense against including such critiques in our research. The response I received would inevitably read along the lines of:

26   Carolyn Ellis, Tony E. Adams, and Arthur P. Bochner, 'Autoethnography: An Overview' *Forum Qualitative Sozialforschung / Forum: Qualitative Social Research* 12.1 (2011) and Ingo Winkler, 'Doing Autoethnography: Facing Challenges, Taking Choices, Accepting Responsibilities', *Qualitative Inquiry* 24.4 (2018).

27   Frank Pasquale, *The Black Box Society: The Secret Algorithms That Control Money and Information*, Cambridge: Harvard University Press, 2016, and O'Neil, Cathy, *Weapons of Math Destruction: How Big Data Increases Inequality and Threatens Democracy*, New York: Crown, 2016.

'We can't tell this company to change their business model, even though we all know it is part of the problem, because they will not give up their golden goose.'

On multiple occasions, I inquired whether there was something in the terms of reference of our research grants with the companies that prevented us from highlighting these structural concerns. I would receive many answers that eventually were a version of the following: 'No, we can say what we want. There are no strings attached to this funding. But we will not tell them to change the business model.'

The idiom 'no strings attached' meant that the funding presumably came without any requirements for the content of the research. This statement was true in only the narrowest reading of the sentence. The signed agreements between academics and industry funders might not have spelled out any limitations on the nature of the critique, or its direction towards the structural forces underpinning industry success. Yet, the unspoken agreements around scope, including the practice of doing the research without veering into immanent critique, did pose real limits. In many of the steps preceding the start of the research, industry funders took decisions that meant that they were likely to invite academics that were willing to improve industry status quo, rather than 'disrupt' it.

There is a clear place in academia for people who want to provide internal, rather than immanent, critique by working with companies. I do not critique that choice. The problem, however, is the silent power exerted through funding, in that companies do not mete out funding to academics equally. Rather, various companies, as I learned through being involved in such efforts, seek out academics whose research agendas align with their corporate incentives. Or in other words, they select research that stays within the bounds of internal critique. There are of course exceptions to this rule, and I do not mean to say that all academics who receive industry funding are stopped from making hard-hitting structural critiques. That being said, I saw firsthand how tech companies employ strategic amplification and elevation strategies. A dynamic that Whittaker describes as: 'Industry elevates their weakest critic.'[28]

Industry can and does shape research by creating and strengthening a network of researchers that presents soft, stable, and predictable critique that does not focus too heavily on disrupting the status quo. It is the relations that industry builds with certain academics where much of their power over research agendas resides. This dynamic has direct implications for junior scholars. Industry funding shapes research; not by directly commanding certain outcomes but by amplifying questions that industry is comfortable answering. It thereby shapes the contours of reasonable critique and which harms industry should answer to or not. Simultaneously, funding such internal criticism allows these companies to appear earnestly engaged with academic research while enabling them to sideline those academics deemed too radical, too critical, or too daring.

There are a number of recent examples of this dynamic playing out beyond my direct experiences that bolster my analysis. Recent examples include Google funding a university

---

28   Whittaker, 'The Steep Cost of Capture'.

think tank that champions critique of applying anti-trust regulation to Big Tech on the one hand[29], and firing internal and external academic critics on the other[30]. We each need to make a decision about our level of comfort with this reality—and root our decisions to accept industry funding in a strong set of explicit politics that allows us to carefully weigh the impact of complicity or refusal, not just for ourselves but for the kind of relations it encourages us to build, with whom and for whom. In their section, Os will pick up on precisely this question of relationship building and how it features in the ability of industry funding to shape research agendas.

Os's Story: 'All Our Relations', or, How Networking Distorts Networks

In early 2019 I was awarded a Microsoft Ada Lovelace Fellowship. This was very prestigious: of 100 finalists (approximately—I was too busy trying not to throw up from nerves to count), there were five winners, across nearly every STEM field. But it was a big deal regardless of the prestige. It offered three years of tuition, salary, and consequently, three years of focusing on research.

Unlike Corinne's experience, the fellowship didn't come with any ongoing involvement by the sponsor. The expectations were simply that I'd do research that interested me (and stay enrolled). But that lack of interference didn't mean that enabling me was the only consequence. Two others are worth highlighting: the impact the fellowship had on Microsoft, and the impact it had on my personal–professional relationships within research.

The impact on Microsoft made itself known pretty quickly. One of my areas of research expertise is facial recognition (FRT), a technology I firmly believe should be staked through the heart and left at a crossroads. At this point, hating FRT is a family tradition: one grand-advisor was worried about it ten years ago.[31] Another was worried about it *two decades* ago.[32] So it came as an unpleasant surprise—although not, in my most cynical moments, an unexpected one—when I found myself at the Washington state legislature to testify as an expert witness on the need to regulate FRT, where we were opposed by … Microsoft. Their argument was multifaceted, but one vital part of it was that regulation was unneeded because they could be trusted to address FRT's various biases themselves. Specifically, what FRT needed was the involvement of diverse, expert stakeholders from a range of marginalized communities. In other words: people like me.

29   Daisuke Wakabayashi, 'Big Tech Funds a Think Tank Pushing for Fewer Rules. For Big Tech', *The New York Times*, 24 July 2020.
30   Cade Metz and Daisuke Wakabayashi, 'Google Researcher Says She Was Fired Over Paper Highlighting Bias in A.I.', *The New York Times*, 3 December 2020.
31   Susan Leigh Star, 'This Is Not a Boundary Object: Reflections On the Origin of a Concept', *Science, Technology, & Human Values* 35.5 (2010): 601–17.
32   Phil Agre, 'Your Face is Not a Bar Code: Arguments Against Automatic Face Recognition in Public Places', *Whole Earth* 106.2001 (2001): 74–7.

Now: no company is a monolith. I am perfectly willing to accept that a large segment of Microsoft Research (who funded the fellowship) are opposed to FRT, even as the company as a whole advocates and sells it. And, obviously, the lawyer did not specifically mean me; they had no idea who I am. But the fact of the matter is that the *reason* Microsoft can spend its money paying someone who wants to set fire to one of their products is because they feel it does something for them. It lets them pretend the solution is 'in-house'; it lets them recuperate critique. It positions fellows as in the same role that Fred Moten skewers critical academia for playing; as tasked with *perfecting* technoscience, in being not an alternative to conventional ways of doing but 'its attempted completion'.[33] This is not to say critical, funded work cannot be effective. It is to say that critique is only *one* of its effects.

Even if the fellowship had not (in a tiny way) changed a Microsoft PR strategy, it certainly changed me. One way in which this happened was via a common secondary clause in the fellowship: that as well as a stipend and tuition, fellows also got priority access to Microsoft Research internships. On the surface, this seems like a win–win; Microsoft gets to try to persuade PhD students of the joys of joining them full time post-graduation, while those students get to eat something other than ramen.

But there's another consequence, too, of doing the work, of being in that place, with those people. To be in an internship is to be in relation to people, to have a drastically lowered cost of access to some (very smart and kind) researchers. I have met some of my favorite people, including Corinne, through such opportunities. But thanks to the limited time we have on this earth and our constrained capabilities within it, we can only relate to so many people. And so, by creating the possibilities of close relations with some, these opportunities limit the possibility of relations with others. The fellowship afforded me access to new collaborators, and expanded the time available for interactions within professional research circles. But in doing so, it took away from (and weakened) my ties to the people who had got me this fellowship in the first place; to the people and communities that motivate my work.

Discussion

Conventionally, a discussion section acts to wrap an analysis together, exploring the underlying themes and then compressing them into fixed lessons, lenses, or implications for practice. In attempting to write this, we struggled to point unambiguously in any one direction, for the simple reason that there are, here, no easy answers. Jones states that 'the choice…[is] between research that is 'engaged' or 'complicit'',[34] but it is hard to find a spot free of complicity (if such a spot even exists).

---

33   Moten and Harney, 'The University and the Undercommons'.
34   Richard G. Jones, 'Putting Privilege Into Practice Through "Intersectional Reflexivity": Ruminations, Interventions, and Possibilities', in *Reflections: Narratives of Professional Helping* (2010), quoting Dwight Conquergood, 'Between Rigor and Relevance: Rethinking Applied Communication,' *Applied Communication In the 21st Century*, London: Routledge, 1995.

Rather than write a discussion-section-as-usual, then, we drew inspiration from the conversational approach of Bellanova et al.,[35] and the conversational approach of our writing process. Like Sotiropoulou and Cranston,[36] we see our conversational approach, and the friendship that belies it, as building the radical practice of care ethics in academia. This practice is needed to critically reflect on, and where necessary resist, the influence of industry funding on independent research. We decided to present a series of lenses that are *not* fixed; that are ambiguous, uncertain, sometimes in tension, just like the dynamics we are discussing.

From these lenses, we identified two answers to the question *'What lessons can be learned from the ethnographic realities of working on AI in academic settings in which research is reliant on industry funding?'* The first theme is the importance of the networks and relationships created and never pursued due to the steering force of industry funding. The second theme is the soft and pernicious power of industry funding and its eroding impact on critical research at both the individual and systemic level.

I: Answering: Just Say No

The most instinctive response to the quandaries of complicity is to demand a 'no'; to demand the purity of refusing to be complicit at all; to demand that a researcher refuse to stand there. Such a view has the advantage of moral clarity, but quickly becomes messier, precisely as researchers such as Shotwell and scholars of explicitly feminist notions of refusal have made clear.[37]

But who, quite literally, can afford to do this? Research into AI ethics is increasingly precarious outside of the large for-profits we are concerned with, and there is differential access to those resources that *do* exist. Anecdotally, but unsurprisingly, we have also seen differential consequences for saying 'yes'. The senior academics in Corinne's example can survive the reputational cost of engaging with such funders—-the stock of their power makes it easier for people to excuse their complicity, and harder to experience the consequences, than more junior scholars.

Second: where do we stand otherwise? Universities have their own moral ambiguity, as has already been noted by Phan et al.[38] Shifting to community-based groups and networks is the ideal, but those groups often lack the funding to sustain researchers, and have many more immediately critical things to spend it on. Here, non-industry and government funders could play a critical role to ensure that there are many hubs of organizations and individuals doing critical work. A good recent example is the Distributed Artificial

---

35 Bellanova, Rocco, Kristina Irion, Katja Lindskov Jacobsen, Francesco Ragazzi, Rune Saugmann, and Lucy Suchman. 'Toward a Critique of Algorithmic Violence.' International Political Sociology (2021.)15 (1): 121–50. https://doi.org/10.1093/ips/olab003.
36 Sotiropoulou and Cranston, 'Critical Friendship'.
37 Alexis Shotwell, *Against Purity: Living Ethically in Compromised Times*, Minneapolis: University of Minnesota Press, 2016.
38 Phan et al., 'Economies of Virtue'.

Intelligence Research Institute (DAIR) set up by Dr. Timnit Gebru, funded by a number of not-for-profit foundations. More such places of counter-power are needed—as is structuring them in a way that recognizes the risks of associating 'non-profit' with 'beneficial to a community.'[39]

II: Answering: Take the Money and Run

'The only ethical relationship with the university,' Fred Moten says, 'is a criminal one,'[40] by which he means that researchers should maximize what they take from an institution that demands a ruthless work ethic (and operates from an unjust premise) but offers little resources in return. If that motto is true of universities, it goes double for many companies in the tech sector. The tension of participation—that these organizations do have resources we want—is resolved (or at least, altered), by taking the money and running.

The concern with that approach is that it is a tactic and not a strategy. It might be possible to get an industry-backed grant once or twice and run. Yet eventually, industry funders will catch on. Furthermore, when it comes to supporting research, even fierce industry competitors exchange notes. This should come as no surprise to those monitoring the same five professors being asked to sit on the ethics board, council, or oversight mechanism *du jour*. A take-the-money-and-run reputation will eventually precede you, closing down possible relationships—criminal or otherwise. Additionally, taking your penny and running will eventually lead to a situation where you are functionally saying 'no', by being excluded from the pool of fundable academics, and, because of the collective nature of reputations, you may be seen as speaking for your students as well.

III: Pivoting the Question: Feminist Refusal

Part of the reason these two answers are so dissatisfying is that there is no such thing as a transcendentally satisfying answer. Another, however, is that they ask the *wrong question*. In both cases, the question is, 'What do I, a singular person, singularly do?' To approach things this way is to miss two vital facets of feminist and/or virtuous practices; that they are often relational, involving assemblages of people, and that (partly as a result of this) they are *practices*. Answers are contingent on circumstance, and the pursuit of them alters those circumstances and in turn demands a reevaluation of our ongoing actions.

The point where we settle, then, is neither on accepting the costs of involvement nor refusing involvement as standalone answers, but instead on what Bonnie Honig frames as *feminist refusal*.[41] To engage in feminist refusal is not to 'say no' and be done with it. Rather, it begins with recognising that we are *never* outside relations of power. As such, we have responsibilities of care to those nestled more deeply within these power structures, to treat refusal as a tactic. To refuse purposefully, potentially-temporarily, with an eye to the future.

---

39   Incite! Women of Color Against Violence (eds), *The revolution will not be funded: Beyond the non-profit industrial complex*, Boston: South End Press, 2007.
40   Moten and Harney, 'The University and the Undercommons'.
41   Honig, 'A Feminist Theory of Refusal'.

Or: to remain enmeshed on a contingent basis, for a tactical purpose, in relation with the choices of others.

What does this look like in the case of researcher complicity in AI ethics? One hypothetical way it might manifest is by collaborating on a piece of industry-funded research, but with an explicit understanding of what the limits are of the change the company is willing to instigate and making analysis of those boundaries part and parcel of the research. Another would be to engage in conversation when invited by industry, to learn firsthand how they define the problem and the solution—-and use that knowledge to sharpen collective attempts at addressing harms. Yet, another would be to push the boundaries of which voices tech companies listen to by including directly impacted communities in the research design. Or to engage as an educator and use a collaboration to outline alternatives to the status quo, with an aim to generate change through internal research.

There are many parts of the research design, from theory, to data to methods, to the accessibility of the findings that should be part of our negotiation process by which we draw research contours and accept industry funding. Feminist refusal, then, is neither inherently incompatible with refusing funding nor embracing it—it simply demands that both be treated as tactics, undertaken with an awareness of, and in relation to, the choices of others. Further, linking to Audra Simpson's parallel thread of indigenous refusal,[42] we would argue that it requires us not only to make choices, but also to examine them on an ongoing basis. To look, in a relational fashion,[43] at the benefits and harms that come from our tentative answers having time to unfold in practice. This reflection needs to happen in and through trusted relationships, or 'critical academic friendship',[44] with peers, students, and mentors. To not simply answer this question but *re-answer* this question, from the perspective of the collective to define what is needed for the collective rather than 'what can I singularly do'.

Conclusion: What Do Our Experiences Tell us About the State of Research and its Future?

The picture we sketch is complex, it contains multitudes. Yet there are clear lessons to be learned from our experiences as early-career scholars doing research into the ethics of AI technologies. As qualitative researchers, we outline how feminist refusal, friendship, and a reorientation from the individual to the collective provides at least a partial answer to the question of effective resistance. We would also like to offer up reflexivity upon how academic knowledge is created, as key. Part of the problem is that many of the dynamics we described happen in the dark. It is difficult to be open and transparent about industry relations, which in turn makes it difficult to understand exactly how they influence research. We hope that these insights into the nuanced ways in which industry influence permeates academia leads to further develop existing descriptions of industry's impact as well as corporate denial of complicity in dulling tech critique.

---

42   Simpson, 'The Ruse of Consent and the Anatomy of "Refusal"'.
43   Abeba Birhane, 'Algorithmic Injustice: A Relational Ethics Approach', *Patterns* 2.2 (2021).
44   Sotiropoulou and Cranston, 'Critical Friendship'.

Our experiences from the ground up strengthen existing work critiquing the dangers of corporate capture by concretizing how it may influence independent thought in academia. It also provides a clear concern for the future of critical academic research, as few young scholars will be able to escape or avoid the structural pressure put on their institutions to play by the rules, and the machinery, of industry. The deep and resounding consequences of this 'new normal' of research raises the question what resistance can and should look like.

We have some thoughts on the question of effective resistance. We call on other early-career scholars to seek out like minded communities and friendships that can support continued critical reflection and dialogue about the impact of individual decisions on the collective body of the academe. Likewise, we ask for tenured faculty to further model and engage in such reflexivity, as they are both closest to the action and least likely to be burned by providing openness. We would like to emphasize the call made by others regarding the need to organize tech workers and academics into collectives that can resist corporate pressure.[45]

As for funders genuinely interested in transformative, rather than reformist, change, we would say: look outside the network. Look at projects and organizations that do not fit the quintessential mold of academic institutions, formal charities and companies. Look at projects that do not promise large-scale payoffs. Look at community groups; look at big changes in small spaces. Accept that your involvement may, in turn, be subject to its own necessary scrutiny. Furthermore, this piece is also a call to action to governments interested in holding tech accountable to seriously consider funding critical academic research. Finding good research will require looking at which scholars and what questions are currently out of bounds for industry funding, and identifying those scholars that are asking research questions from the perspective of the social impact of technology and its collective good, rather than those focused on narrow—penny wise but pound foolish—questions around how to make the AI industry more ethical.

Funding Disclosures

Corinne's contribution to this research was not funded; Os is funded by a Microsoft Ada Lovelace Fellowship.

References

Agre, Phil. 'Your Face is not a Bar Code: Arguments Against Automatic Face Recognition in Public Places', *Whole Earth* 106.2001 (2001): 74–77.

Algorithm Watch. 'AlgorithmWatch Forced to Shut down Instagram Monitoring Project after Threats from Facebook', *AlgorithmWatch* blog, 13 August 2021, https://algorithmwatch.org/en/instagram-research-shut-down-by-facebook/.

Balayn, Agathe, and Gürses, Seda. 'If AI Is the Problem, Is Debiasing the Solution?', Brussels Belgium: EDRi, 2021, https://edri.org/our-work/if-ai-is-the-problem-is-debiasing-the-solution/.

---

45   See INCITE!, 'The Revolution will Not be Funded', Whittaker, 'The Steep Cost of Capture', and Ben Tarnoff, *The Making of the Tech Worker Movement*, New York, NY, USA: *Logic* magazine, 2019, https://logicmag.io/the-making-of-the-tech-worker-movement/.

Bank, Max, Duffy, Felix, Leyendecker, Verena, and Silva, Margarida. 'The Lobby Network: Big Tech's Web of Influence In the EU', Corporate Europe Observatory and LobbyControl e.V, 2021, https://corporateeurope.org/en/2021/08/lobby-network-big-techs-web-influence-eu.

Bellanova, Rocco, Kristina Irion, Katja Lindskov Jacobsen, Francesco Ragazzi, Rune Saugmann, and Lucy Suchman. 'Toward a Critique of Algorithmic Violence.' International Political Sociology (2021.)15 (1): 121–50. https://doi.org/10.1093/ips/olab003.

Birhane, Abeba. 'Algorithmic Injustice: A Relational Ethics Approach.' *Patterns* 2.2 (2021).

Cath, Corinne. 'Governing Artificial Intelligence: Ethical, Legal and Technical Opportunities and Challenges', *Philosophical Transactions of the Royal Society A: Mathematical, Physical and Engineering Sciences* 376 (2018).

Cath, Corinne, and Jansen, Fieke. 'Dutch Comfort: The Limits of AI Governance Through Municipal Registers', *arXiv e-prints* (2021): arXiv–2109.

Conquergood, Dwight. 'Between Rigor and Relevance: Rethinking Applied Communication', *Applied communication in the 21st century* (1995): 79–96.

Dencik, Lina. 'The Datafied Welfare State: A Perspective from the UK', in Hepp, Andreas, Jarke, Juliane, and Kramp, Leif (eds), *The Ambivalences of Data Power: New Perspectives in Critical Data Studies*, UK: Palgrave Macmillan, (2022):145–66.

Ellis, Carolyn, Adams, Tony E., and Bochner, Arthur P. 'Autoethnography: An Overview', *Forum Qualitative Sozialforschung / Forum: Qualitative Social Research* 12.1 (2010).

Green, Ben, and Viljoen, Salomé. 'Algorithmic Realism: Expanding the Boundaries of Algorithmic Thought' in *Proceedings of the 2020 Conference on Fairness, Accountability, and Transparency*, Barcelona, Spain: ACM, 2020: 19–31.

Hemmings, Clare. *Why Stories Matter*, Durham: Duke University Press, 2011.

Honig, Bonnie. *A Feminist Theory of Refusal*, Cambridge: Harvard University Press, 2021.

Incite! Women of Color Against Violence (eds). *The Revolution Will Not Be Funded: Beyond the Non-profit Industrial Complex*, Boston: South End Press, 2007.

Jaeggi, Rahel. *Critique of Forms of Life*, Cambridge: Harvard University Press, 2018.

Jobin, Anna, Ienca, Marcello, and Vayena, Effy. 'The Global Landscape of AI Ethics Guidelines', *Nature Machine Intelligence* 1.9 (2019): 389–99.

Jones, Richard G. 'Putting Privilege Into Practice Through "Intersectional Reflexivity": Ruminations, Interventions, and Possibilities', in *Reflections: Narratives of Professional Helping*, 2010.

Lapowsky, Issie. 'How Tech Giants Court and Crush the People Who Study Them', *Protocol—The People, Power and Politics of Tech* blog, 19 March 2021. https://www.protocol.com/nyu-facebook-researchers-scraping.

Metcalf, Jacob, and Moss, Emanuel. 'Owning Ethics: Corporate Logics, Silicon Valley, and the Institutionalization of Ethics', *Social Research: An International Quarterly* 86.2 (2019): 449–76.

Metz, Cade and Wakabayashi, Daisuke. 'Google Researcher Says She Was Fired Over Paper Highlighting Bias in A.I.', *The New York Times,* 3 December 2020.

Moten, Fred, and Harney, Stefan. 'The University and the Undercommons: Seven Theses', *Social Text* 22.2 (2004): 101–15.

O'Neil, Cathy. *Weapons of Math Destruction: How Big Data Increases Inequality and Threatens Democracy*, New York: Crown, 2016.

Pasquale, Frank. *The Black Box Society: The Secret Algorithms That Control Money and Information*, Cambridge: Harvard University Press, 2016.

———. 'Machines Judging Humans: The Promise and Perils of Formalizing Evaluative Criteria.', in *Proceedings of the AAAI/ACM Conference on AI, Ethics, and Society*, 2020.

Phan, Thao, et al. 'Economies of Virtue: The Circulation of 'Ethics' in Big Tech', *Science as Culture* 31.1 (2021): 1–15.

Popiel, Pawel. 'The Tech Lobby: Tracing the Contours of New Media Elite Lobbying Power', *Communication Culture & Critique* 11.4 (2018): 566–85.

Reed-Danahay, Deborah. *Auto/Ethnography: Rewriting the Self and the Social*, Oxford; New York: Routledge, 1997.

Rincón, Cami, Keyes, Os, and Cath, Corinne. 'Speaking from Experience: Trans/Non-Binary Requirements for Voice-Activated AI', in *Proceedings of the ACM on Human-Computer Interaction* 5.CSCW1 (2021): 132:1–132:27.

Seaver, Nick. 'CARE AND SCALE: Decorrelative Ethics in Algorithmic Recommendation', *Cultural Anthropology*. 36.3 (2021): 509–37.

Shotwell, Alexis. *Against Purity: Living Ethically in Compromised Times*, Minneapolis: University of Minnesota Press, 2016.

Simpson, Audra. 'The Ruse of Consent and the Anatomy of "Refusal": Cases from Indigenous North America and Australia', *Postcolonial Studies,* 20.1 (2017): 18–33.

Sloane, Mona. 'Inequality Is the Name of the Game: Thoughts on the Emerging Field of Technology, Ethics and Social Justice', Weizenbaum Conference, Berlin, Germany, 16–17 May 2019.

Sotiropoulou, Panagiota, and Cranston, Sophie. 'Critical Friendship: An Alternative, "Care-full" Way to Play the Academic Game', *Gender, Place & Culture* (2022): 1–22.

Star, Susan Leigh. 'This is Not a Boundary Object: Reflections on the Origin of a Concept', *Science, Technology, & Human Values,* 35.5 (2010): 601–17.

Su, Norman Makoto, Lazar, Amanda, and Irani, Lilly. 'Critical Affects: Tech Work Emotions Amidst the Techlash' in *Proceedings of the ACM on Human-Computer Interaction* 5.CSCW1 (2021): 1–27.

Tarnoff, Ben. *The Making of the Tech Worker Movement*. New York: *Logic* magazine, 2019, https://logicmag.io/the-making-of-the-tech-worker-movement/.

Taylor, Linnet. 'Public Actors Without Public Values: Legitimacy, Domination and the Regulation of the Technology Sector', *Philosophy & Technology*, (2021):1–26.

Wagner, Ben. 'Ethics As An Escape From Regulation. From "Ethics-Washing" To Ethics-Shopping?' in *Being Profiled*, Amsterdam University Press, 2018, 84–9.

Wakabayashi, Daisuke. 'Big Tech Funds a Think Tank Pushing for Fewer Rules. For Big Tech', *The New York Times*, 24 July 2020.

Whittaker, Meredith. 'The Steep Cost of Capture', *Interactions*, 28.6 (2021): 50–5.

EXTRACTIVIST ETHICS

SARAH PINK

Introduction

Let me take you to the moment I started to write this chapter about AI, ethics, and people, following links through reports and papers on ethics I found the AI4People's ethical framework. The intentions of such projects have societal wellbeing at heart, and contribute actively to the important argument that AI needs to be regulated and needs to do good. This made me feel uncomfortable as I began to read; knowing I was about to turn my anthropologist's eye to critique the logics of an agenda that seeks to make AI ethical, when surely I should be on the same page (*Spoiler alert: hold onto the page metaphor and don't click on the links until I ask you to*). To be clear, my critique is not of the AI4People's ethical framework in particular. Rather, the framework exemplifies how the metaphors, narratives, and structures that commonly frame good intentions towards ethical AI and People in dominant discourses betray a logic that is misaligned with everyday realities. My agenda, and my work as a whole, focuses on creating collaborative partnerships to work toward ethical futures, rather than simply writing endpoint outlines of what is wrong. But to make the connections/relations required for collaboration we need to make visible the cracks between approaches, disciplines, and logics.

The 'AI4People's Ethical Framework for a Good AI Society: Opportunities, Risks, Principles and Recommendations' report is 'committed to the development of AI technology in a way that secures people's trust, serves the public interest, and strengthens shared social responsibility' and it presents a set of recommendations towards ensuring this.[1] It is authored by a range of scholars and industry contributors who specialize in ethics from fields including philosophy, law, and computer science, but excluding the social sciences such as anthropology and qualitative sociology. While the report presents perfectly reasonable principles from the perspective of the societal structures in which we presently operate, the terminologies and concepts it uses to communicate its ideas are difficult to reconcile with those of an anthropological approach to people, ethics, and emerging technologies. First, the idea that people's trust can be 'secured' by particular developments in AI technology requires trust to be a fixed quality that can be extracted from people and captured. Second, the notion of 'the public interest' invokes a one-dimensional framing of people, rather than actual people in the messy contingency of their lives where real interests and everyday ethics play out. Third, by referring to 'social responsibility,' it focuses on a sociological unit or level of analysis, rather than on the experiential domain of life. That is, the AI4People agenda is inhabited by a striking absence of the experience and activity of actual people.

---

1   L. Floridi, J. Cowls, M. Beltrametti, et al. 'AI4People—An Ethical Framework for a Good AI Society: Opportunities, Risks, Principles, and Recommendations', *Minds & Machines* 28, (2018): 22, https://www.eismd.eu/wp-content/uploads/2019/11/AI4People%E2%80%99s-Ethical-Framework-for-a-Good-AI-Society_compressed.pdf.

In this chapter I argue for a people-focused approach which must be surfaced through engagement with theory and research in everyday worlds. Elsewhere I have defined 'techno-solutionist approaches to ethics as extractivist, where they seek to identify and capture human ethics values and invest them in machines with the intention that such ethical machines will engender trust.'[2] Here, I extend this argument, along with the premise that to be ethical, AI should not simply be for people, but be designed with people, attentive to diversity, specificity and locality. It should not seek to secure, gain or win people's trust or anything else after the event of its design, but should be created already within relations of trust, attentive to 'everyday ethics'.[3] By everyday ethics I mean ethics as they are lived out in and contingent on the circumstances of everyday life; where ethics are not necessarily fixed in such a way that they can be applied consistently across all situations, and are nuanced by the relationships between people, things and environment. My definition builds on ethics as understood in phenomenological anthropology, which 'reveals ethical life as a condition marked by ontological indeterminacy and ethical overload;'[4] in anthropology (as I practice it) ethics are indeterminate, 'contingent, emergent from the everyday worlds and circumstances of life.'[5] Such an understanding of ethics permeates anthropological research ethics as well as how we understand other people's ethics, and thus concerns equally the actions of the reflexive ethnographer.[6]

The AI4People's agenda is of course not alone in its approach, and it seeks to offer a solution to the question of how to make AI ethical, which aligns with the ways AI is being developed. In one sense, this is a step in an ethical direction. But it is also emblematic of a consistent and glaring gap in the dominant discourses advanced in the technology industry, government, and the engineering and computer sciences about how to make AI ethical. I believe that there is a common concern about people and AI across these disciplines and stakeholders, which we can better address by bringing people (encountered through collaborative ethnographic research practices, engagements, and interventions) into the debate. This means we need to ensure that everyday ways of knowing and diversity are at the forefront of the ways we consider ethics. But a glance at the AI4People report's web page[7] banner (*go to the link now*) assures me that the page is visibly gendered. Although the report itself was authored by men and women, this appears to be erased in the visual representation of the banner. The substantially outed[8] and critiqued 'manel' (all male panel)[9] lives on, and highlights that

---

2   S. Pink, 'Trust, Ethics and Automation: Anticipatory Imaginaries in Everyday Life' in S. Pink, D. Lupton, M. Berg & M. Ruckenstein (eds) *Everyday Automation*, London: Routledge, 2022.
3   Pink, 'Trust, Ethics and Automation'.
4   C. Mattingly and J. Throop, 'The Anthropology of Ethics and Morality', *Annual Review of Anthropology* 47.1 (2018): 483.
5   Pink, 'Trust, Ethics and Automation'.
6   M. Strathern (ed) *Audit Cultures: Anthropological Studies in Accountability*, London: Routledge, 2000; P. Pels, 'The Trickster's Dilemma: Ethics and the Technologies of the Anthropological Self' in M. Strathern (ed) *Audit Cultures*.
7   https://www.eismd.eu/featured/ai4peoples-ethical-framework-for-a-good-ai-society/.
8   @allmalepanels, https://twitter.com/allmalepanels?lang=en.
9   J.K. Rodriguez and E.A. Guenther, 'What's Wrong With "Manels" and what Can We Do About Them?' *The Conversation*, 15 October 2020, https://theconversation.com/whats-wrong-with-manels-and-what-can-we-do-about-them-148068.

the topic of extractivist ethics I am about to address also surfaces the gendered politics of technology, data, ethics, and academia.

Extractivist Ethics (Mining for Ethics)

The metaphors we use to refer to data, as well as automated, connected, and intelligent emerging technologies and systems are themselves sites of contestation, and with that they also constitute possible sites of investigation and intervention. Sally Wyatt suggests that as critical social scientists we need to contest the extractive metaphors used by industry and policy makers which frame data as a resource that can be mined.[10] In this chapter I outline a related mode of contestation, which instead of switching the metaphors involves applying them to ethics in order to interrogate how ethics are situated within approaches to data and emerging technologies such as AI, which scholars have already labelled as being extractivist.[11] I discuss how similar logics of extraction, which have been critiqued by critical data scholars, are applied to ethics in AI, and what this suggests regarding industry, policy, and research. I call this *extractivist ethics*.

So how are extractivist ethics constituted? On one level, as exemplified above, ethics become the bait through which trust in technology is extracted from publics or users. On another, as I have proposed elsewhere, in relation to the relationship between trust and ethics, techno-solutionist approaches to ethics can be defined as extractivist where 'they seek to identify and capture human ethics values and invest them in machines with the intention that such ethical machines will engender trust.'[12] This kind of causality typifies renderings of ethics in the engineering sciences. A good example is the well-known MIT moral machine experiment,[13] which I (and others) have discussed elsewhere,[14] but here take up in a new direction.

The moral machine is a game which serves as survey seeking to extract the moral judgments of thousands of people across the world in relation to a set of future self-driving car scenarios based on the 'Trolley Problem' (a philosophical conundrum where the person playing the game needs to decide whom from a choice of possible victims the train car should kill in an accident) by judging a series of scenarios presented online. There is perhaps nothing surprising that a game should be used to extract ethics from its players. Writing more generally of social media, Sheila Jasanoff notes how such technologies 'profit from people' by 'mining their thoughts, words, habits, bodies and emotions as resources to create new

---

10   S. Wyatt, 'Metaphors in Critical Internet and Digital Media Studies', *New Media & Society*, 23.2 (2021): 406–16.
11   S. Jasanoff, *The Ethics of Invention*. New York: W. W. Norton & Company, 2016; Wyatt, 'Metaphors'.
12   Pink, 'Trust, Ethics and Automation'.
13   E. Awad, S. Dsouza, R. Kim et al., 'The Moral Machine Experiment', *Nature*, 563 (2018): 59–64. See also: https://www.moralmachine.net/.
14   S. Pink, K. Raats, T. Lindgren, K. Osz, and V. Fors, 'An Interventional Design Anthropology of Emerging Technologies' in Maja Hojer Bruun, Ayo Wahlberg, Dorthe Brogaard Kristensen, Rachel Douglas-Jones, Cathrine Hasse, Klaus Høyer, and Brit Ross Winthereik (eds) *The Handbook for the Anthropology of Technology*, London: Palgrave, 2021; Pink, 'Trust, Ethics and Automation'.

marketable goods.'[15] Edmond Awad and colleagues (all men), have good intentions, as the AI4People authors discussed above. They are attentive to cultural difference and suggest that 'we can embrace the challenges of machine ethics as a unique opportunity to decide, as a community, what we believe to be right or wrong; and to make sure that machines, unlike humans, unerringly follow these moral preferences.'[16] Again, my quarrel is not so much with the sentiment but with an understanding of ethics which is disconnected from all the anthropological evidence of how ethics actually play out in the contingent circumstances of the everyday. As the philosopher Onora O'Neill has highlighted, the use of surveys or polls to quantify human sentiment, affective states, and contingent decisions is limited. For instance, polls on public trust 'offer no evidence about the judgements that people make when they decide to trust or refuse trust to particular individuals or institutions for particular matters, in which they often differentiate cases with some care.'[17] Equally questionable is the status of knowledge about ethics derived from responses to improbable ethical dilemmas which are subsequently suspended from their sources, rather than situated within realistic situations in which they actually unfold.

The implication of understanding ethics as contingent (as argued earlier) is that everyday ethics are slippery, they are incredibly difficult to capture, to invest in either organizations or machines, or to regulate. Thus, it follows that the assumptions it is possible to solve ethical problems that emerge after AI has become embedded in everyday life are limited. Typical solutions involving either designing ethical machines, or introducing regulation and governance, construct risk mitigation processes, based on logics which follow causal chains created externally to everyday life and its ethics. When instead we turn the focus to what it actually means to be human in the everyday—that is, the experience of being, feeling, and doing, ethics cannot be abstracted, fixed, or predetermined externally to the everyday. Instead, through giving 'primacy to first- and second- person positions', phenomenology draws our attention to the intersubjectivity and intercorporeality of ethics.[18] As Mattingly and Throop put it, 'Far from being a site of culturally well-articulated obligations or the imposition of normative moral orders that create docile subjects, scholars have empirically documented ways that the ethical can pose excessive demands that render lived experience uncanny.'[19] This means that while there are ongoing attempts to abstract ethics into regulations, such ethics are unlikely to ever be aligned with the ethical requirements of everyday life.

As such, in this section I have offered two very different answers to questions of the kind invoked by legal and STS scholar Sheila Jasinoff when she asks: 'Whose duty is it in today's complex societies to foresee or forestall the negative impacts of technology, and do we possess the necessary tools and instruments for forecasting and preventing harm?'[20] The MIT moral machine experiment tries to answer this question head on by both taking responsibility for forestalling the negative and creating tools through which to create ethical self-driving

---

15   Jasanoff, 259.
16   Awad et al., 63.
17   O. O'Neill, 'Accountable Institutions, Trustworthy Cultures', *Hague J Rule Law* 9 (2017): 405.
18   Mattingly and Throop, 483.
19   Mattingly and Throop, 485-6.
20   Jasanoff, 7.

cars that people will subsequently trust and adopt, and in doing so reduce traffic deaths and carbon emissions. But Mattingly and Throop ask a different question, which complicates both this response and the mode of responsibility it assumes: 'What is at stake in emphasizing the underdetermined nature of ethical life [...]? What does it mean to portray the human as characterized by potentiality or possibility rather than actuality? What does it mean to claim that there is an excessiveness to the ethical demand such that it cannot be reduced to following prescriptive norms or rules?'[21] In this context the answer is that because the ethics that will characterize the relations between people and self-driving cars (and by extension AI in general) are indeterminate, they can neither be extrapolated to machines nor be engaged to forecast and prevent harm.

Extractivist Ethics and Anticipatory Audits (Attracting Investment)

In this section I investigate how extractivist ethics could participate in the anticipatory visions of capitalism. These visions are key to capitalism occupying the future to maintain its structural hold on everyday life. As a resource that can be extracted, or as a bait to capture trust, ethics can be invested in trustworthy intelligent and automated machines, thus serving as the catalyst in causal chains of human trust, acceptance, and adoption of AI. Here, extracted ethics could participate in creating an anticipatory infrastructure through which ethical AI and ethical machines are seen as a technological solution to situations where public acceptance of automated technologies is perceived as a challenge,[22] and thus to attract investment in the technologies that are envisioned as solutions to societal problems.

To make investment and markets for AI plausible and realistic, extractivist ethics are also aligned with what I call the *anticipatory audit*. Anticipatory audits are part of what anthropologists have long since referred to as 'audit cultures.'[23] Many elements of audit culture are anticipatory by nature. Take, for example, university ethics committees.[24] This is an example I have discussed often but it is worth repeating here because it both connects with the academic research and funding context mentioned below, and is likely part of the experience of academic readers. Usually regulated by an institutional (or in some case national) body which sets the rules which define ethical research conduct, ethical approval involves ensuring that any risks of what is defined as unethical happening in our research are identified and mitigated *in advance*. However, when ethics are the subject of an anticipatory audit, the only way that ethics can be accounted for is by fixing them still, capturing them for measurement against ethical regulations. The result is to reassure our institutions that our research will in fact be ethical (and that they have minimized the possibility of conduct that

---

21   Mattingly and Throop, 'The Anthropology of Ethics and Morality', 486.
22   J. Stilgoe, T. Cohen, 'Rejecting Acceptance: Learning from Public Dialogue on Self-Driving Vehicles', *Science and Public Policy*, 48.6 (2021): 849–59.
23   For example, Strathern, *Audit Cultures*.
24   S. Pink, 'Ethics in a Changing World: Embracing Uncertainty, Understanding Futures, and Making Responsible Interventions' in (eds) S. Pink, V. Fors, T. O'Dell *Working in the Between: Theoretical Scholarship and Applied Practice*, Oxford: Berghahn, 2017. To be clear, I support ethical review processes because when they are done well, they provoke reflection as well as ethical conduct.

would be interpreted as unethical). The case of ethical AI is similar in that the ethical conditions that AI should manifest are prescribed in advance through ethics frameworks, and can therefore, like the ethics of researchers, the ethics of AI can also be audited before they are let loose into the world—that is, into everyday life environments.

As one of many examples, the website of the top consultancy firm PricewaterhouseCoopers (PwC) takes up the question of 'Responsible AI (RAI)', which it states 'is the only way to mitigate AI risks.'[25] Their 'Responsible AI Toolkit' includes a focus on ethics. Yet while the possibility that getting the ethics right will mitigate the risks is tempting to believe, what that actually means still appears to be in the balance; a 2019 review of international ethics frameworks found 'a global convergence emerging around five ethical principles [for AI] (transparency, justice and fairness, non-maleficence, responsibility and privacy), with substantive divergence in relation to how these principles are interpreted, why they are deemed important, what issue, domain or actors they pertain to, and how they should be implemented.'[26] Moreover, in 2021 the Pew Research Institute issued the findings of their survey of technology experts, to suggest that most did not believe that ethical AI design would be broadly adopted by 2030.[27]

However, of the most significant comments cited by the Pew were those by danah boyd, who pointed out that when AI systems are aligned with contemporary capitalism, 'which fetishizes efficiency, scale and automation,' they are antithetical to the ethical values of 'augmentation, localized context and inclusion.' boyd's insight connects with the everyday ethics outlined above, which emphasizes precisely how ethics are contingent and specific. As these points show, it is not just a question of what the ethics of AI are, but also a question of where it gets its ethics from and whose values they align with. As I have shown through the example of the moral machine experiment, there have been attempts to extract the ethics from the everyday by aggregating individual responses, but these inevitably fail to generate ethics that align with ethics in the everyday because they are extractive. We cannot mine ethics. Rather we have to get in there with them. It is the opposite of extraction; it requires blending and collaboration both in place and with the ongoing emergence of life.

Indeed, the similarities between the anticipatory ethics audits we experience as university academics and those AI systems are subject to don't stop at their common impulse to mitigate the risks related to what certain agents will do 'in the wild.' Both modes of anticipatory audit are also meant to account for, regulate, control, and mitigate any risks involved in the ethical behaviour of an active agent in the form of the AI or the researcher, over a passive agent in the form of a member of the public, a user or consumer, or a research participant. There are, however, several mismatches between anticipatory audits

25   PwC, https://www.pwc.com/gx/en/issues/data-and-analytics/artificial-intelligence/what-is-responsible-ai.html.
26   A. Jobin, M. Ienca, and E. Vayena, 'The Global Landscape of AI Ethics Guidelines', *Nat Mach Intell* 1 (2019): 389.
27   https://www.pewresearch.org/internet/2021/06/16/experts-doubt-ethical-ai-design-will-be-broadly-adopted-as-the-norm-within-the-next-decade/.

of ethics and the everyday ethics in which the academic researchers or the AI systems and technologies (who or which have been audited) will be let loose. The everyday worlds where their anticipated one-way ethical effects will be activated are in fact inhabited by very different ethics—the experiential ethics noted by Mattingly and Throop, which are contingent, contextual, embodied, intersubjective, and indeterminate.[28]

Funding Extractivist Ethics (The Gender of Funding)

Above I have outlined the inherent flaw in visions of human ethics as a determinate thing which can be extracted from society or garnered from experts as representing societal values, captured, and transferred into a machine.[29] Yet such approaches to ethics offer a (deceptively) simple response to a complex problem, with a causal chain of guarantees which mitigate the risks of AI doing future harm, *as well as* mitigating a set of risks around the research needed to create the knowledge and technologies that will apply the solution.

Research that proposes to embed predetermined ethical values into AI is relatively not risky because it shows a clear route to impact. It might, of course, entail other risks relating to the difficulties or uncertainties related to the technological discoveries that the researchers wish to make, which is a different thing. However, if you already believe that ethical AI—AI infused with societally endorsed ethical values—will make people trust, accept, and adopt technology that will benefit society and the environment, it's not a big leap to consequently assume that it's a good idea to fund research that will aim to produce AI that will only act according to desirable human ethics, and that will be governed by an ethics framework approved by experts. Thus an extractivist ethics agenda would ultimately be appealing to well-intentioned organizations and researchers involved in narratives and practices of dominant innovation agendas. It would subsequently support the academic careers of those whose work is funded through them, and oil the wheels of the machines of research funding, outputs, and impact that govern success in academia. One of the factors that appears to govern success in academia, at least in funding outputs, is gender. In 2019 an EU H2020 funded project titled 'Grant Allocation Disparities from a Gender Perspective' reported a set of 'indisputable facts:' there are fewer women than men in STEM disciplines and in senior academic positions, and women get fewer research grants, less funding, and lower evaluations.[30]

Extractivist Ethics and Everyday Ethics at the Impasse

In this chapter, I have proposed the concept of *extractivist ethics*, which I suggest creates a category through which to reveal and contest the dominant narratives concerning the

28   Mattingly and Throop, 'The Anthropology of Ethics and Morality'.
29   In this chapter I raise this issue specifically in relation to the question of the challenge of making ethical machines. This issue raises wider questions relating to how such a stance might be reconciled with the status of ethics, regulation, and governance in society, which is not within the scope of this chapter to address.
30   L. Cruz Castro and L. Sans Menéndez, *Literature Review Synthesis Report.* CSIS Institute of Public Goods and Policies, Madrid, 2019.

generation of trust and acceptance of and the constitution of markets for emerging technologies in society. I have explored the alignment of *extractivist ethics* to another concept—the *anticipatory audit.* I have suggested the risk mitigation paradigm that structures both extractivist ethics and the anticipatory audit, also aligns them to both corporate and research agendas, because they both promise paths to impact.

Approaches to ethical AI that call for ethics frameworks and regulation have good intentions. Luciano Floridi is right to advocate that 'Ethics-first is the right approach to set global standards for AI.'[31] However, for ethics to really come first, more work is needed. At the moment the logics of ethics from above through regulation are not compatible with ethics as they occur in the everyday contexts that they ultimately seek to (ethically) impact on. Everyday ethics cannot entertain the certainties that extractivist ethics, as articulated in relation to ethical machines, desire. In part this concurs with another point boyd makes in the Pew Survey, that '[w]e misunderstand ethics when we think of it as a binary, when we think that things can be ethical or unethical;' such binaries indeed coincide with the idea that machines can be made ethical. Seeing ethics participating in predictable causal sequences is similarly incorrect. Ethics cannot participate in predictable chains of reactions, simply because they are not static. These anthropological interpretations of ethics complicate the STEM models of ethical machines and their promise of beneficial impact on society. They are moreover difficult to work with, and teach, because they are slippery, tricky, and don't stay still. But besides this they proffer another challenge to the societal structures that make STEM valued in research because as boyd puts it: 'We cannot meaningfully talk about ethical AI until we can call into question the logics of late-stage capitalism.'

There is a politics to everyday ethics, which, as I hinted at the beginning of this chapter, which also requires us to attend to questions of gender. Gender is intersectional, not binary, meaning that both my own references to all male panels, research teams and the possibility of bias in research funding outcomes towards men, all need to be nuanced with other modes of difference, inequality, and inequity. However, the evidence suggests that AI is emerging within a gendered enterprise of research and development, which frequently favours men, and to move forward we need to empower other voices. A starting point could be to borrow Point 6 of the Feminist Data Manifest-no,[32] to 'refuse the expansion of forms of [data science] *ethics frameworks* that normalize[s] a condition of [data] *ethics* extractivism and is defined primarily by the drive to monetize and hyper-individualize the human experience.' When ethics (as facets of human experience) are extracted from the everyday, or are used as bait to capture other everyday feelings like trust, in order to constitute anticipated markets, they are effectively being commodified. Like feminist data scholars we should instead: 'commit to centering creative and collective

---

31   L. Floridi, 'Establishing the Rules for Building Trustworthy AI', *Nat Mach Intell* 1 (2019): 262.
32   Feminist Data Manifest-No, https://www.manifestno.com/home; Point 6 of the Feminist Data
      Manifesto reads: 'We refuse the expansion of forms of data science that normalizes a condition of
      data extractivism and is defined primarily by the drive to monetize and hyper-individualize the human
      experience. We commit to centering creative and collective forms of life, living, and worldmaking that
      exceed the neoliberal logics and resist the market-driven forces to commodify human experience.'

forms of life, living, and worldmaking that exceed the neoliberal logics and resist the market-driven forces to commodify human experience'.

Acknowledgments

This chapter has benefited from its original conceptualisation as part of the excellent Economies of Virtue workshop. I thank Thao Phan, Monique Mann, Jake Goldenfein, and Declan Kuch for their work and inspiration and I am especially grateful to Ellen Broad, Lorenn Ruster, Jake Goldenfein, and Declan Kuch for their wonderfully inspiring comments and review of the first version of this chapter.

Funding Disclosure

My work on this chapter is undertaken in my role as a Chief Investigator in the Australian Research Council–funded Centre of Excellence for Automated Decision-Making and Society (CE200100005) (2020–2027).

References

Awad, E., Dsouza, S., Kim, R. et al. 'The Moral Machine Experiment', *Nature* 563 (2018): 59–64.

Cruz Castro, L. and Sans Menéndez, L. *Literature Review Synthesis Report.* CSIS Institute of Public Goods and Policies, Madrid, 2019.

Floridi, L. 'Establishing the Rules for Building Trustworthy AI', *Nat Mach Intell* 1 (2019): 261–262.

Floridi, L., Cowls, J., Beltrametti, M. et al. AI4People—An Ethical Framework for a Good AI Society: Opportunities, Risks, Principles, and Recommendations. *Minds & Machines* 28, (2018): 689–707.

Jasanoff, S. *The Ethics of Invention*, New York: W. W. Norton & Company, 2016.

Jobin, A., Ienca, M. & Vayena, E. 'The Global Landscape of AI Ethics Guidelines', *Nat Mach Intell* 1 (2019): 389–99.

Mattingly, C. and J. Throop. 'The Anthropology of Ethics and Morality', *Annual Review of Anthropology* 47:1 (2018): 475–92.

O'Nell, O. 'Accountable Institutions, Trustworthy Cultures', *Hague J Rule Law* 9 (2017): 401–12.

Pels, P. 'The Trickster's Dilemma: Ethics and the Technologies of the Anthropological Self' in M. Strathern (ed) *Audit Cultures: Anthropological Studies in Accountability*, London: Routledge, 2000, pp. 147–84.

Pink, S. 'Ethics in a Changing World: Embracing Uncertainty, Understanding Futures, and Making Responsible Interventions' in xS. Pink, V. Fors, T. O'Dell (eds) *Working in the Between: Theoretical Scholarship and Applied Practice.* Oxford: Berghahn, 2017, pp. 29–51.

——. 'Trust, Ethics and Automation: Anticipatory Imaginaries in Everyday Life' in Pink, S., Lupton, D., Berg, M. and Ruckenstein, M. (eds) *Everyday Automation*, London: Routledge, 2022, 44–58.

Pink, S., Raats, K., Lindgren T., Osz, K. and Fors, V. 'An Interventional Design Anthropology of Emerging Technologies' in Hojer Bruun, M., Wahlberg, A., Brogaard Kristensen, D., Douglas-Jones, R., Hasse, C., Høyer, K., and Ross Winthereik, B. (eds) *The Handbook for the Anthropology of Technology*, London: Palgrave, 2021, pp. 183–200.

Stilgoe, J., T. Cohen, 'Rejecting Acceptance: Learning from Public Dialogue on Self-Driving Vehicles', *Science and Public Policy*, 48.6 (2021): 849–59.

Strathern, M. (ed). *Audit Cultures: Anthropological Studies in Accountability*, London: Routledge, 2000.

Wyatt, S. 'Metaphors in Critical Internet and Digital Media Studies', *New Media & Society*, 23.2 (2021): 406–16.

THE INVENTION OF 'ETHICAL AI': HOW BIG TECH MANIPULATES ACADEMIA TO AVOID REGULATION

RODRIGO OCHIGAME

This essay was originally published in The Intercept on 20 December 2019. It has been reprinted here with permission from the author.

The irony of the ethical scandal enveloping Joichi Ito, the former director of the MIT Media Lab, is that he used to lead academic initiatives on ethics. After the revelation of his financial ties to Jeffrey Epstein, the financier charged with sex trafficking underage girls as young as 14, Ito resigned from multiple roles at MIT, a visiting professorship at Harvard Law School, and the boards of the John D. and Catherine T. MacArthur Foundation, the John S. and James L. Knight Foundation, and the New York Times Company.

Many spectators are puzzled by Ito's influential role as an ethicist of artificial intelligence. Indeed, his initiatives were crucial in establishing the discourse of 'ethical AI' that is now ubiquitous in academia and in the mainstream press. In 2016, then-President Barack Obama described him as an 'expert' on AI and ethics. Since 2017, Ito financed many projects through the $27 million Ethics and Governance of Artificial Intelligence Fund, an initiative anchored by the MIT Media Lab and the Berkman Klein Center for Internet & Society at Harvard University. What was all the talk of 'ethics' really about?

For 14 months, I worked as a graduate student researcher in Ito's group on AI ethics at the Media Lab. I stopped on 15 August,2019, immediately after Ito published his initial 'apology' regarding his ties to Epstein, in which he acknowledged accepting money from the financier both for the Media Lab and for Ito's outside venture funds. Ito did not disclose that Epstein had, at the time this money changed hands, already pleaded guilty to a child prostitution charge in Florida, or that Ito took numerous steps to hide Epstein's name from official records, as *The New Yorker* later revealed.

Inspired by whistleblower Signe Swenson and others who have spoken out, I have decided to report what I came to learn regarding Ito's role in shaping the field of AI ethics, since this is a matter of public concern. The emergence of this field is a recent phenomenon, as past AI researchers had been largely uninterested in the study of ethics. A former Media Lab colleague recalls that Marvin Minsky, the deceased AI pioneer at MIT, used to say that 'an ethicist is someone who has a problem with whatever you have in your mind.'[1] Why, then, did AI researchers suddenly start talking about ethics?

At the Media Lab, I learned that the discourse of 'ethical AI,' championed substantially by Ito, was aligned strategically with a Silicon Valley effort seeking to avoid legally enforceable

---

1   In recently unsealed court filings, victim Virginia Roberts Giuffre testified that Epstein directed her to have sex with Minsky.

restrictions of controversial technologies. A key group behind this effort, with the lab as a member, made policy recommendations in California that contradicted the conclusions of research I conducted with several lab colleagues, research that led us to oppose the use of computer algorithms in deciding whether to jail people pending trial. Ito himself would eventually complain, in private meetings with financial and tech executives, that the group's recommendations amounted to 'whitewashing' a thorny ethical issue. 'They water down stuff we try to say to prevent the use of algorithms that don't seem to work well' in detention decisions, he confided to one billionaire.

I also watched MIT help the U.S. military brush aside the moral complexities of drone warfare, hosting a superficial talk on AI and ethics by Henry Kissinger, the former secretary of state and notorious war criminal, and giving input on the U.S. Department of Defense's 'AI Ethics Principles' for warfare, which embraced 'permissibly biased' algorithms and which avoided using the word 'fairness' because the Pentagon believes 'that fights should not be fair.'

Ito did not respond to requests for comment.

MIT lent credibility to the idea that Big Tech could police its own use of artificial intelligence at a time when the industry faced increasing criticism and calls for legal regulation. Just in 2018, there were several controversies: Facebook's breach of private data on more than 50 million users to a political marketing firm hired by Donald Trump's presidential campaign, revealed in March 2018; Google's contract with the Pentagon for computer vision software to be used in combat zones, revealed that same month; Amazon's sale of facial recognition technology to police departments, revealed in May; Microsoft's contract with the U.S. Immigration and Customs Enforcement revealed in June; and IBM's secret collaboration with the New York Police Department for facial recognition and racial classification in video surveillance footage, revealed in September. Under the slogan #TechWontBuildIt, thousands of workers at these firms have organized protests and circulated petitions against such contracts. From #NoTechForICE to #Data4BlackLives, several grassroots campaigns have demanded legal restrictions of some uses of computational technologies (e.g., forbidding the use of facial recognition by police).

Meanwhile, corporations have tried to shift the discussion to focus on voluntary 'ethical principles,' 'responsible practices,' and technical adjustments or 'safeguards' framed in terms of 'bias' and 'fairness' (e.g., requiring or encouraging police to adopt 'unbiased' or 'fair' facial recognition). In January 2018, Microsoft published its 'ethical principles' for AI, starting with 'fairness.' In May, Facebook announced its 'commitment to the ethical development and deployment of AI' and a tool to 'search for bias' called 'Fairness Flow.' In June, Google published its 'responsible practices' for AI research and development. In September, IBM announced a tool called 'AI Fairness 360,' designed to 'check for unwanted bias in datasets and machine learning models.' In January 2019, Facebook granted $7.5 million for the creation of an AI ethics center in Munich, Germany. In March, Amazon co-sponsored a $20 million program on 'fairness in AI' with the U.S. National Science Foundation. In April, Google cancelled its AI ethics council after backlash over the selection of Kay Coles James, the vocally anti-trans president of the right-wing Heritage Foundation. These corporate initiatives frequently cited academic research that Ito had supported, at least partially, through the MIT–Harvard fund.

To characterize the corporate agenda, it is helpful to distinguish between three kinds of regulatory possibilities for a given technology: (1) no legal regulation at all, leaving 'ethical principles' and 'responsible practices' as merely voluntary; (2) moderate legal regulation encouraging or requiring technical adjustments that do not conflict significantly with profits; or (3) restrictive legal regulation curbing or banning deployment of the technology. Unsurprisingly, the tech industry tends to support the first two and oppose the last. The corporate-sponsored discourse of 'ethical AI' enables precisely this position. Consider the case of facial recognition. This year, the municipal legislatures of San Francisco, Oakland, and Berkeley—all in California—plus Somerville, Massachusetts, have passed strict bans on facial recognition technology. Meanwhile, Microsoft has lobbied in favor of less restrictive legislation, requiring technical adjustments such as tests for 'bias,' most notably in Washington state. Some big firms may even prefer this kind of mild legal regulation over a complete lack thereof, since larger firms can more easily invest in specialized teams to develop systems that comply with regulatory requirements.

Thus, Silicon Valley's vigorous promotion of 'ethical AI' has constituted a strategic lobbying effort, one that has enrolled academia to legitimize it. Ito played a key role in this corporate-academic fraternizing, meeting regularly with tech executives. The MIT–Harvard fund's initial director was the former 'global public policy lead' for AI at Google. Through the fund, Ito and his associates sponsored many projects, including the creation of a prominent conference on 'Fairness, Accountability, and Transparency' in computer science; other sponsors of the conference included Google, Facebook, and Microsoft.

Although the Silicon Valley lobbying effort has consolidated academic interest in 'ethical AI' and 'fair algorithms' since 2016, a handful of papers on these topics had appeared in earlier years, even if framed differently. For example, Microsoft computer scientists published the paper that arguably inaugurated the field of 'algorithmic fairness' in 2012. In 2016, the paper's lead author, Cynthia Dwork, became a professor of computer science at Harvard, with simultaneous positions at its law school and at Microsoft. When I took her Harvard course on the mathematical foundations of cryptography and statistics in 2017, I interviewed her and asked how she became interested in researching algorithmic definitions of fairness. In her account, she had long been personally concerned with the issue of discriminatory advertising, but Microsoft managers encouraged her to pursue this line of work because the firm was developing a new system of online advertising, and it would be economically advantageous to provide a service 'free of regulatory problems.' (To be fair, I believe that Dwork's personal intentions were honest despite the corporate capture of her ideas. Microsoft declined to comment for this article.)

After the initial steps by MIT and Harvard, many other universities and new institutes received money from the tech industry to work on AI ethics. Most such organizations are also headed by current or former executives of tech firms. For example, the Data & Society Research Institute is directed by a Microsoft researcher and initially funded by a Microsoft grant; New York University's AI Now Institute was co-founded by another Microsoft researcher and partially funded by Microsoft, Google, and DeepMind; the Stanford Institute for Human-Centered AI is co-directed by a former vice president of Google; University of California, Berkeley's Division of Data Sciences is headed by a Microsoft veteran; and the MIT Schwarzman College of Computing is headed by a board member of Amazon. During my time at the Media Lab, Ito maintained frequent contact with the executives and planners of all these organizations.

Big Tech money and direction proved incompatible with an honest exploration of ethics, at least judging from my experience with the 'Partnership on AI to Benefit People and Society,' a group founded by Microsoft, Google/DeepMind, Facebook, IBM, and Amazon in 2016. PAI, of which the Media Lab is a member, defines itself as a 'multistakeholder body' and claims it is 'not a lobbying organization.' In an April 2018 hearing at the U.S. House Committee on Oversight and Government Reform, the partnership's executive director claimed that the organization is merely 'a resource to policymakers—for instance, in conducting research that informs AI best practices and exploring the societal consequences of certain AI systems, as well as policies around the development and use of AI systems.'

But even if the partnership's activities may not meet the legal threshold requiring registration as lobbyists—for example, by seeking to directly affect the votes of individual elected officials—the partnership has certainly sought to influence legislation. For example, in November 2018, the partnership staff asked academic members to contribute to a collective statement to the Judicial Council of California regarding a Senate bill on penal reform (S.B. 10). The bill, in the course of eliminating cash bail, expanded the use of algorithmic risk assessment in pretrial decision-making, and required the Judicial Council to 'address the identification and mitigation of any implicit bias in assessment instruments.' The partnership staff wrote, 'We believe there is room to impact this legislation (and CJS [criminal justice system] applications more broadly).'

In December 2018, three Media Lab colleagues and I raised serious objections to the partnership's efforts to influence legislation. We observed that the partnership's policy recommendations aligned consistently with their corporate agenda. In the penal case, our research led us to strongly oppose the adoption of risk assessment tools, and to reject the proposed technical adjustments that would supposedly render them 'unbiased' or 'fair.' But the partnership's draft statement seemed, as a colleague put it in an internal email to Ito and others, to 'validate the use of RA [risk assessment] by emphasizing the issue as a technical one that can therefore be solved with better data sets, etc.' A second colleague agreed that the 'PAI statement is weak and risks doing exactly what we've been warning against re: the risk of legitimation via these industry-led regulatory efforts.' A third colleague wrote, 'So far as the criminal justice work is concerned, what PAI is doing in this realm is quite alarming and also in my opinion seriously misguided. I agree with Rodrigo that PAI's association with ACLU, MIT and other academic / non-profit institutions practically ends up serving a legitimating function. Neither ACLU nor MIT nor any non-profit has any power in PAI.'

Worse, there seemed to be a mismatch between the partnership's recommendations and the efforts of a grassroots coalition of organizations fighting jail expansion, including the movement Black Lives Matter, the prison abolitionist group Critical Resistance (where I have volunteered), and the undocumented and queer/trans youth-led Immigrant Youth Coalition. The grassroots coalition argued, 'The notion that any risk assessment instrument can account for bias ignores the racial disparities in current and past policing practices.' There are abundant theoretical and empirical reasons to support this claim, since risk assessments are typically based on data of arrests, convictions, or incarcerations, all of which are poor proxies for individual behaviors or predispositions. The coalition continued, 'Ultimately, risk-assessment tools create a feedback-loop of racial profiling, pre-trial detention and conviction. A person's freedom should not be reduced to an algorithm.' By contrast, the partnership's statement focused on 'minimum requirements for responsible deployment,' spanning such topics as 'validity and data sampling bias, bias in statistical predictions; choice of the appropriate targets for prediction; human–computer interaction questions; user training; policy and governance; transparency and review; reproducibility, process, and recordkeeping; and post-deployment evaluation.'

To be sure, the partnership staff did respond to criticism of the draft by noting in the final version of the statement that 'within PAI's membership and the wider AI community, many experts further suggest that individuals can never justly be detained on the basis of their risk assessment score alone, without an individualized hearing.' This meek concession—admitting that it might not be time to start imprisoning people based strictly on software, without input from a judge or any other 'individualized' judicial process—was easier to make because none of the major firms in the partnership sell risk assessment tools for pretrial decision-making; not only is the technology too controversial but also the market is too small.[2]

In December 2018, my colleagues and I urged Ito to quit the partnership. I argued, 'If academic and nonprofit organizations want to make a difference, the only viable strategy is to quit PAI, make a public statement, and form a counter alliance.' Then a colleague proposed, 'There are many other organizations which are doing much more substantial and transformative work in this area of predictive analytics in criminal justice—what would it look like to take the money we currently allocate in supporting PAI in order to support their work?' We believed Ito had enough autonomy to do so because the MIT-Harvard fund was supported largely by the Knight Foundation, even though most of the money came from tech investors Pierre Omidyar, founder of eBay, via the Omidyar Network, and Reid Hoffman, co-founder of LinkedIn and Microsoft board member. I wrote, 'If tens of millions of dollars from nonprofit foundations and individual donors are not enough to allow us to take a bold position and join the right side, I don't know what would be.'[3]

Ito did acknowledge the problem. He had just received a message from David M. Siegel, co-chair of the hedge fund Two Sigma and member of the MIT Corporation. Siegel proposed a

---

2 Facial recognition technology, on the other hand, has a much larger market in which Microsoft, Google, Facebook, IBM, and Amazon all operate.

3 Omidyar funds *The Intercept*.

self-regulatory structure for 'search and social media' firms in Silicon Valley, modeled after the Financial Industry Regulatory Authority, or FINRA, a private corporation that serves as a self-regulatory organization for securities firms on Wall Street. Ito responded to Siegel's proposal, 'I don't feel civil society is well represented in the industry groups. We've been participating in Partnership in AI and they water down stuff we try to say to prevent the use of algorithms that don't seem to work well like risk scores for pre-trial bail. I think that with personal data and social media, I have concerns with self-regulation. For example, a full-blown genocide [of the Rohingya, a mostly Muslim minority group in Myanmar] happened using What's App and Facebook knew it was happening.'[4]

But the corporate-academic alliances were too robust and convenient. The Media Lab remained in the partnership, and Ito continued to fraternize with Silicon Valley and Wall Street executives and investors. Ito described Siegel, a billionaire, as a 'potential funder.' With such people, I saw Ito routinely express moral concerns about their businesses—but in a friendly manner, as he was simultaneously asking them for money, whether for MIT or his own venture capital funds. For corporate-academic 'ethicists,' amicable criticism can serve as leverage for entering into business relationships. Siegel replied to Ito, 'I would be pleased to speak more on this topic with you. Finra is not an industry group. It's just paid for by industry. I will explain more when we meet. I agree with your concerns.'

In private meetings, Ito and tech executives discussed the corporate lobby quite frankly. In January, my colleagues and I joined a meeting with Mustafa Suleyman, founding co-chair of the partnership and co-founder of DeepMind, an AI startup acquired by Google for about $500 million in 2014. In the meeting, Ito and Suleyman discussed how the promotion of 'AI ethics' had become a 'whitewashing' effort, although they claimed their initial intentions had been nobler. In a message to plan the meeting, Ito wrote to my colleagues and me, 'I do know, however, from speaking to Mustafa when he was setting up PAI that he was meaning for the group to be much more substantive and not just "white washing." I think it's just taking the trajectory that these things take.' Suleyman did not respond to requests for comment.

Regardless of individual actors' intentions, the corporate lobby's effort to shape academic research was extremely successful. There is now an enormous amount of work under the rubric of 'AI ethics.' To be fair, some of the research is useful and nuanced, especially in the humanities and social sciences. But the majority of well-funded work on 'ethical AI' is aligned with the tech lobby's agenda: to voluntarily or moderately adjust, rather than legally restrict, the deployment of controversial technologies. How did five corporations, using only a small fraction of their budgets, manage to influence and frame so much academic activity, in so many disciplines, so quickly? It is strange that Ito, with no formal training, became positioned as an 'expert' on AI ethics, a field that barely existed before 2017. But it is even stranger

---

4   Facebook has admitted that its platform was used to incite violence in Myanmar; news reports have documented how content on the Facebook platform facilitated a genocide in the country despite repeated warnings to Facebook executives from human rights activists and researchers. Facebook texting service WhatsApp made it harder for its users to forward messages after WhatsApp was reportedly used to spread misinformation during elections in India.

that two years later, respected scholars in established disciplines have to demonstrate their relevance to a field conjured by a corporate lobby.

The field has also become relevant to the U.S. military, not only in official responses to moral concerns about technologies of targeted killing but also in disputes among Silicon Valley firms over lucrative military contracts. On 1 November, 2019, the Department of Defense's innovation board published its recommendations for 'AI Ethics Principles.' The board is chaired by Eric Schmidt, who was the executive chair of Alphabet, Google's parent company, when Obama's defense secretary Ashton B. Carter established the board and appointed him in 2016. According to ProPublica, 'Schmidt's influence, already strong under Carter, only grew when [James] Mattis arrived as [Trump's] defense secretary.' The board includes multiple executives from Google, Microsoft, and Facebook, raising controversies regarding conflicts of interest. A Pentagon employee responsible for policing conflicts of interest was removed from the innovation board after she challenged 'the Pentagon's cozy relationship not only with [Amazon CEO Jeff] Bezos, but with Google's Eric Schmidt.' This relationship is potentially lucrative for Big Tech firms: The AI ethics recommendations appeared less than a week after the Pentagon awarded a $10 billion cloud-computing contract to Microsoft, which is being legally challenged by Amazon.

The recommendations seek to compel the Pentagon to increase military investments in AI and to adopt 'ethical AI' systems such as those developed and sold by Silicon Valley firms. The innovation board calls the Pentagon a 'deeply ethical organization' and offers to extend its 'existing ethics framework' to AI. To this end, the board cites the AI ethics research groups at Google, Microsoft, and IBM, as well as academics sponsored by the MIT-Harvard fund. However, there are caveats. For example, the board notes that although 'the term "fairness" is often cited in the AI community,' the recommendations avoid this term because of 'the DoD mantra that fights should not be fair, as DoD aims to create the conditions to maintain an unfair advantage over any potential adversaries.' Thus, 'some applications will be permissibly and justifiably biased,' specifically 'to target certain adversarial combatants more successfully.' The Pentagon's conception of AI ethics forecloses many important possibilities for moral deliberation, such as the prohibition of drones for targeted killing.

The corporate, academic, and military proponents of 'ethical AI' have collaborated closely for mutual benefit. For example, Ito told me that he informally advised Schmidt on which academic AI ethicists Schmidt's private foundation should fund. Once, Ito even asked me for second-order advice on whether Schmidt should fund a certain professor who, like Ito, later served as an 'expert consultant' to the Pentagon's innovation board. In February 2019, Ito joined Carter at a panel titled 'Computing for the People: Ethics and AI,' which also included current and former executives of Microsoft and Google. The panel was part of the inaugural celebration of MIT's $1 billion college dedicated to AI. Other speakers at the celebration included Schmidt on 'Computing for the Marketplace,' Siegel on 'How I Learned to Stop Worrying and Love Algorithms,' and Henry Kissinger on 'How the Enlightenment Ends.' As Kissinger declared the possibility of 'a world relying on machines powered by data and algorithms and ungoverned by ethical or philosophical norms,' a protest outside the MIT auditorium called attention to Kissinger's war crimes in Vietnam, Cambodia, and Laos, as well as his support of war crimes elsewhere. In the age of automated targeting, what atrocities will the U.S. military justify as governed by 'ethical' norms or as executed by machines beyond the scope of human agency and culpability?

No defensible claim to 'ethics' can sidestep the urgency of legally enforceable restrictions to the deployment of technologies of mass surveillance and systemic violence. Until such restrictions exist, moral and political deliberation about computing will remain subsidiary to the profit-making imperative expressed by the Media Lab's motto, 'Deploy or Die.' While some deploy, even if ostensibly 'ethically,' others die.

Funding Disclosure

The author worked as a graduate student researcher at the MIT Media Lab between July 2018 and August 2019. The report was written while the author was supported by a doctoral fellowship from the MIT Program in History, Anthropology, and Science, Technology, and Society, and a research fellowship (for different work in social science) from the Jain Family Institute. The author declined compensation from *The Intercept*.

SECTION II:
SITES

ECOCIDE ISN'T ETHICAL: POLITICAL ECOLOGY AND CAPITALIST AI ETHICS

SY TAFFEL, LAURA BEDFORD, AND MONIQUE MANN

Introduction

Emerging discourses surrounding new forms of extractivism associated with data and digital technologies are framed as 'the new oil';[1] as the key raw material that drives the information economy;[2] as a new form of circulatory capital;[3] or as a new type of colonialism.[4] While the framing varies, these conceptualizations of digital technoculture illuminate numerous harms that amplify existing social inequalities,[5] discriminate against certain groups of people[6] and enact predictive logics of control.[7] However, these 'new' forms of data-driven extractivism are not distinct from 'old' forms of extractivism associated with procuring the materials and energy required for digital technologies and infrastructures, or the social and environmental impacts associated with the enormous increases in production, consumption and waste which results from data processing, storage, and transmission in the 21st century.

Responses to harms associated with computational systems are often framed within the field of 'AI ethics,'[8] where a focus on enhancing privacy, or making AI more 'fair,' 'accountable,' and 'transparent', elides larger ethical questions relating to the significant harms to both present and future ecosystems associated with the energy, labour, and materials required for the production, maintenance, use, and waste disposal associated with AI. The planetary assemblages of code, carbon, cobalt, copper, and numerous other materials that compose

1   'The World's Most Valuable Resource Is No Longer Oil, but Data', *The Economist*, 6 May 2017, https://
     www.economist.com/leaders/2017/05/06/the-worlds-most-valuable-resource-is-no-longer-oil-but-data.
2   Nick Srnicek, *Platform Capitalism*, Cambridge: Polity, 2016.
3   Jathan Sadowski, 'When Data Is Capital: Datafication, Accumulation, and Extraction', *Big Data &
     Society* 6.1 (2019): 2053951718820549.
4   Nick Couldry and Ulises A Mejias, *The Costs of Connection: How Data Is Colonizing Human Life and
     Appropriating It for Capitalism*, Stanford: Stanford University Press, 2019; Monique Mann and Angela
     Daly, '(Big) Data and the North-in-South: Australia's Informational Imperialism and Digital Colonialism',
     Television & New Media 20.4 (2019): 379–95.
5   Virginia Eubanks, *Automating Inequality: How High-Tech Tools Profile, Police, and Punish the Poor*. New
     York: St. Martin's Press, 2018; Bridle, James, *New Dark Age: Technology and the End of the Future*,
     London: Verso Books, 2018.
6   Safiya Umoja Noble, *Algorithms of Oppression: How Search Engines Reinforce Racism*, New York: NYU
     Press, 2018; Thao Phan and Scott Wark, 'What Personalisation Can Do For You! Or: How to Do Racial
     Discrimination Without "Race"', *Culture Machine* 20 (2021): 1–29.
7   Bernard Stiegler, *Automatic Society: The Future of Work*, Cambridge: Polity, 2017; Mark Andrejevic,
     Automated Media, New York: Routledge, 2020.
8   Angela Daly, Thilo Hagendorff, Li Hui, Monique Mann, Vidushi Marda, Ben Wagner, Wayne Wei
     Wang, 'AI, Governance and Ethics: Global Perspectives' in Oreste Pollicino and Giovanni de Gregorio
     (eds) *Constitutional Challenges in the Algorithmic Society*, Cambridge: Cambridge University Press,
     2021.

contemporary AI plays a significant role in climate change and associated ecological crises of the Capitalocene.[9] Given the Paris Agreement targets to limit global heating to under 2 degrees Celsius above pre-industrial levels, and preferably to no more than 1.5 degrees,[10] any meaningful discussion of AI ethics must address a much broader set of concerns than it presently does. This includes acknowedging AI's contribution to the impacts of climate change including drought, biodiversity loss, flooding, extinctions, coastal submergence, and issues of food and water security, among many other material consequences. Omitting to address these harms when considering AI, we argue, is *unethical*. In this chapter we draw from the field of political ecology to explore what kinds of systemic and structural changes are needed for AI to be considered 'ethical'?

We argue that the ecocidal tendencies of current global economic arrangements, where digital technologies and AI are positioned as key drivers of economic growth (*and* the solution to the climate crisis itself,[11] requires a reframing of the ethics of AI. Technology cannot be understood as being neutral in taking us to this point of global ecological crisis and, further, its role will not be neutral as we address the crisis. It is critical, therefore, that we centre the *role of technology* in our prefiguration of future global arrangements. While political ecology focuses on making explicit the political, social, and economic dimensions of environmental crises that are often aberrantly perceived as being 'natural' and 'apolitical,' we draw on a growing body of literature which has centred this conceptual lens towards technology,[12] data,[13] the digital economy,[14] and e-waste.[15]

These recent works apply the framework of political ecology to demonstrate how the ecological and political-economic dimensions of digital technologies that are typically misidentified

9   Andreas Malm and Alf Hornborg, 'The Geology of Mankind? A Critique of the Anthropocene Narrative', *The Anthropocene Review* 1.1 (2014): 62–9; Jason W. Moore, *Anthropocene or Capitalocene?: Nature, History, and the Crisis of Capitalism*, Oakland: Pm Press, 2016; Christophe Bonneuil and Fressoz, Jean-Baptiste, *The Shock of the Anthropocene: The Earth, History and us,* London: Verso Books, 2016.

10   United Nations, 'Paris agreement' in *Report of the Conference of the Parties to the United Nations Framework Convention on Climate Change*, 21st Session, Paris: 2015, *https://unfccc.int/files/meetings/paris_nov_2015/application/pdf/paris_agreement_english_.pdf*.

11   Eric Nost and Emma Colven, 'Earth for AI: A Political Ecology of Data-Driven Climate Initiatives', *Geoforum* 130 (2022): 23–34.

12   Alf Hornborg, 'The Political Ecology of the Technocene' in Clive Hamilton, François Gemenne, and Christophe Bonneuil (eds) *The Anthropocene and the Global Environmental Crisis: Rethinking Modernity in a New Epoch*, London, Routeledge, 2015, pp. 177–83; Laura Bedford, Monique Mann, Reece Walters, and Marcus Foth, 'A Post-capitalocentric Critique of Digital Technology and Environmental Harm: New Directions at the Intersection of Digital and Green Criminology', *Beyond Cybercrime: New Perspectives on Crime, Harm and Digital Technologies, International Journal for Crime, Justice and Social Democracy (Special Issue)*, 11.1 (2022): 167–81.

13   Sy Taffel, 'Data and Oil: Metaphor, Materiality and Metabolic Rifts', *New Media & Society* (2021); Eric Nost and Jenny Elaine Goldstein, 'A Political Ecology of Data', *Environment and Planning E: Nature and Space* (2021).

14   Vasilis Kostakis, Andreas Roos, and Michel Bauwens, 'Towards a Political Ecology of the Digital Economy: Socio-Environmental Implications of Two Competing Value Models', *Environmental Innovation and Societal Transitions* 18 (2016): 82–100.

15   Graham Pickren, 'Geographies of E-Waste: Towards a Political Ecology Approach to E-Waste and Digital Technologies', *Geography Compass* 8.2 (2014): 111–24.

as being 'dematerialized' or 'artificial.' Both these terms effectively conceal the material dimensions of these artefacts, contributing to their frequent portrayal as apolitical, neutral, mathematical objects. Although ecology and technology are situated very differently with regards to an imagined nature/culture dualism, they share a tendency to be positioned as politically neutral issues that should be addressed by differing branches of the sciences rather than being understood as entangled with systems of power. This focus on power, inequalities, politics, and collective action is underpinned by political ecology's view of ethics as normatively being concerned with social action that redistributes power towards subaltern groups,[16] aligning the approach of political ecology with emerging arguments that discourse surrounding AI should 'transcend the language of "ethics" and engage with power and political economy.'[17] A key point here is that 'AI ethics' frequently becomes a way for powerful corporations to avoid regulation by adopting voluntary practices focused on technical fixes that fail to meaningfully address harms associated with AI.

While there has been some scholarly work to broaden AI ethics to include AI's ecological impacts,[18] these contributions have tended to be limited to narrow technical considerations. As such, we begin by contrasting a political ecology approach that centers ecological harms and inequitable power relations, with the discourse of 'green AI'[19] that focuses concern on the carbon costs of training ML models. While the ecology of AI includes the data centers where ML training and inference occurs, we argue that the impacts go far beyond data centers, situating those facilities within flows of energy, labour, knowledge, and the myriad materials necessary for AI systems to operate. Nonetheless, we begin our examination of the ecopolitical impacts of AI with data centres, as this has been both the central focus of the sustainable AI literature and a key site within critical studies of digital infrastructures.[20]

Subsequently, we critique two prominent, interconnected discourses that suggest digital technologies enable the maintenance of the socioeconomic status quo in the face of ecological crises. The first discourse argues that AI facilitates a hyper-efficient mode of production that decouples the production of wealth from material constraints, allowing the continuation of

---

16   Raymond L. Bryant and Lucy Jarosz, 'Ethics in Political Ecology: A Special Issue of Political Geography: Introduction: Thinking About Ethics in Political Ecology', *Political Geography* 23. 7 (2004): 807–12; Peter A. Walker 'Political ecology: where is the politics?.' *Progress in Human Geography* 31.3 (2007): 363--9.

17   Angela Daly, S. Kate Devitt, Monique Mann, 'AI Ethics Needs Good Data' In. Pieter Verdegem (ed), *AI for Everyone? Critical Perspectives*, London: University of Westminster Press, 2021.

18   Emma Strubell, Ananya Ganesh, and Andrew McCallum, 'Energy and Policy Considerations for Deep Learning in Nlp', arXiv preprint arXiv:1906.02243, 2019; David Patterson, Joseph Gonzalez, Quoc Le, Chen Liang, Lluis-Miquel Munguia, Daniel Rothchild, David So, Maud Texier, and Jeff Dean; 'Carbon Emissions and Large Neural Network Training', arXiv preprint arXiv:2104.10350, 2021.

19   Roy Schwartz, Jesse Dodge, Noah A. Smith, and Oren Etzioni, 'Green AI', *Communications of the ACM* 63.12 (2020): 54–63; Aimee van Wynsberghe, 'Sustainable AI: AI for Sustainability and the Sustainability of AI', *AI and Ethics* (2021): 1–6.

20   Mél Hogan and Asta Vonderau, 'The Nature of Data Centers', *Culture Machine* 18 (2019): 1–4 Brett Neilson and Ned Rossiter, 'Automating Labour and the Spatial Politics of Data Centre Technologies' in Mascha Will-Zocholl and Caroline Roth-Ebner (eds) *Topologies of Digital Work*, London: Palgrave Macmillan Cham, 2021, pp. 77–101.

economic business as usual. We demonstrate how this line of reasoning does not hold up to scrutiny when viewed through the lens of political ecology. The second discourse we critique is premised on the erroneous contention that technological innovation will straightforwardly solve contemporary ecological crises. We challenge techno-solutionist responses which recast a crisis of capitalism as a business opportunity for innovative tech corporations. Instead, we argue that the hegemonic discourse related to AI ethics legitimates ecocide while actively inhibiting the systemic and structural social, political, and cultural transformations that are required. This includes, for example recognizing ecocide in national international criminal law.[21]

We conclude by briefly outlining alternatives to hyper-efficient green growth and technological solutionism. We acknowledge that substantial debates exist within political ecology scholarship relating to the possible world we should strive for and how to get there. These debates extend to the role envisaged to be played by technology in both the transition and in the society being prefigured. These positions include degrowth, ecosocialism, conviviality, commoning, and public service models of digital infrastructure. It is beyond the scope of this short chapter to engage with all these perspectives in any depth. Nevertheless, highlighting these alternatives outlines postcapitalist pathways towards more ethical forms of AI. Emphasizing the structural causes of ecological harms associated with existing economic practices foregrounds how debates surrounding AI ethics function to legitimize and normalize AI's contributions to systemic ecocide rather than meaningfully challenge them. Consequently, employing the lens of political ecology, we add our voices to accounts which critique AI ethics as ethics-washing and/or greenwashing, instead contending that the focus needs to shift towards structural issues of power.[22]

(Not-so) Green AI

AI is resource-intensive in ways that are often overlooked. Recent debates surrounding AI, ethics and sustainability have largely focused on the carbon cost of training ML models.[23] This partly results from a prominent paper which estimated that a single training run of a specific ML model emits 284,019 kg of CO2e.[24] Although this estimate is staggeringly high,

---

21   Polly Higgins, *Eradicating Ecocide: Exposing the Corporate and Political Practices Destroying the Planet and Proposing the Laws to Eradicate Ecocide*, London: Shepard–Walwyn, 2016.

22   Ben Wagner, 'Ethics as an Escape from Regulation. From "Ethics-Washing" to Ethics-Shopping?' in Emre Bayamlioglu, Irina Baraliuc, Liisa Albertha Wilhelmina Janssens, and Mireille Hildebrandt (eds) *Being Profiled*, Amsterdam: Amsterdam University Press, 2018, 84–9; Yochai Benkler, 'Don't Let Industry Write the Rules for AI', *Nature*, 569.7754 (2019): 161–2.

23   Alexandre Lacoste, Alexandra Luccioni, Victor Schmidt, and Thomas Dandres, 'Quantifying the Carbon Emissions of Machine Learning' (preprint) arXiv:1910.09700, 2019; Roy Schwartz, Jesse Dodge, Noah A. Smith, and Oren Etzioni, 'Green AI'; E.M. Bender, Timnit Gebru, Angelina McMillan-Major, and Shmargaret Shmitchell, 'On the Dangers of Stochastic Parrots: Can Language Models Be Too Big??' *Proceedings of the 2021 ACM Conference on Fairness, Accountability, and Transparency*, 1 March 2021: 610–23.

24   Emma Strubell, Ananya Ganesh, and Andrew McCallum, 'Energy and Policy Considerations for Deep Learning in Nlp'.

equivalent to the lifetime emissions of 3,422 iPhone 13s,[25] it received little prominence in the original paper, which acknowledged that alternative hardware could reduce training time by a factor of 8.5, signaling the estimate had a substantial margin of error.[26] Indeed, subsequent research argues that erroneous assumptions, such as using the 'big' 213 million parameter Transformer model for the experiment rather than the 65 million parameter base model, entailed that the training run would have resulted in 15,200 kg CO2e in an average US data centre, or 3,200 kg CO2e using the hardware in Google's Georgia data centre where the real-world model ran.[27]

In fact, however, more pertinent to the ecological impacts of ML systems was Strubell et al.'s finding that another model, whose development they followed from inception to deployment as a case study, required *4789 training runs*, equivalent to '60 GPU's [graphics processing units] running constantly throughout the six-month duration of the project,'[28] highlighting the fallacy of focusing on the CO2 emissions of single training runs. Furthermore, far more energy is used running ML systems (what is known as inference) than training models. Nvidia estimate 80 to 90 percent of the cost of machine learning systems is inference rather than the initial training,[29] while Amazon Web Services state that inference accounts for up to 90 percent of the cost of machine learning.[30]

The data centers where high-performance computers are used in parallel to conduct training and inference for ML systems (alongside activities including data storage, web hosting, and video transcoding) are, of course, one area of intense energy and resource use. Estimates for global energy use within data centers vary widely, from 205 terawatt-hours (TWh)[31] to 400-500 TWh.[32] This equates to between one and two percent of all global electricity use. Forecast increases in data storage and processing, ML dataset size,

---

25 Apple, *iPhone 13 Product Environmental Report*, 14 September 2021, https://www.apple.com/environment/pdf/products/iphone/iPhone_13_PER_Sept2021.pdf.

26 Using Tensor processing units (TPU) specifically designed for machine-learning rather than graphics processing units (GPU) reduced training time from 274,120 hours down to 32,623 hours. CO2e figures were, however, only provided for training conducted on GPUs due to a lack of public information on energy draw for TPUs.

27 David Patterson, Joseph Gonzalez, Quoc Le, Chen Liang, Lluis-Miquel Munguia, Daniel Rothchild, David So, Maud Texier, and Jeff Dean, 'Carbon Emissions and Large Neural Network Training'.

28 Emma Strubell, Ananya Ganesh, and Andrew McCallum, 'Energy and Policy Considerations for Deep Learning in Nlp'.

29 George Leopold, 'AWS to Offer Nvidia's T4 Gpus for AI Inferencing', *HPC Wire*, 19 March 2019, https://www.hpcwire.com/2019/03/19/aws-upgrades-its-gpu-backed-ai-inference-platform/.

30 Jeff Barr, *Amazon EC2 Update—Inf1 Instances with AWS Inferentia Chips for High Performance Cost-Effective Inferencing*, 3 December 2019, https://aws.amazon.com/blogs/aws/amazon-ec2-update-inf1-instances-with-aws-inferentia-chips-for-high-performance-cost-effective-inferencing/.

31 Eric Masanet, Arman Shehabi, Nuoa Lei, Sarah Smith, and Jonathan Koomey, 'Recalibrating Global Data Center Energy-Use Estimates', *Science* 367.6481 (2020): 984–6.

32 S.E., Andrae Anders, 'Hypotheses for Primary Energy Use, Electricity Use and CO2 Emissions of Global Computing and its Shares of the Total Between 2020 and 2030', *WSEAS Transactions on Power Systems*, 15 (2020): 50–9; Rabih Bashroush and Andy Lawrence, *Beyond Pue: Tackling Its Wasted Terawatts*, Uptime Institute, January 2020, https://uptimeinstitute.com/beyond-pue-tackling-it%E2%80%99s-wasted-terawatts.

training, inference, and other computationally intensive tasks such as transcoding and streaming 8K video, mean that data centre energy use is estimated to rise to approximately 780 TWh by 2030.[33]

The past decade has seen a significant centralisation of data accompanied towards large cloud and hyperscale data centres. By 2021 there were 659 hyperscale data centres[34] (Synergy Research Group, 2021), a figure which has more than doubled since 2015.[35] Half of these are owned and operated by just three companies, Amazon, Microsoft, and Google.[36] Whereas historically, many businesses ran small, in-house centers, hyperscale data centres exemplify the logic of platform capitalism,[37] insofar as they leverage economies of scale and network effects that centralise facilities, with a few oligopolistic technology companies leasing space and compute to smaller businesses. One purported benefit of hyperscale data centres is an increase in energy efficiency,[38] a point we return to in the following section where we discuss efficiency and decoupling.

While carbon costs are important, the narrow focus of these studies masks the urgent necessity of meaningfully considering the ecological impacts of AI/ML that go far beyond the energy use associated with powering particular training models or inference within data centres. Instead, it requires analyzing the material and energy flows associated with the *entire* supply chain and assemblage of software, hardware and infrastructure required for ML systems to function. Political ecology here provides a useful alternative to existing 'green' and 'ethical' AI, both because of its focus on mapping the material and energy footprints of sociotechnical systems from cradle to grave, and its emphasis on ecological systems being thoroughly entangled with and affected by power, inequality and violence. Data centers also require enormous amounts of water.[39] Within data centers, vast amounts of heat are generated, requiring active cooling.[40] Water is central to the cooling process, with chilled water employed as a heat transfer mechanism to reduce air temperatures.[41] In 2014, U.S.-based data centers used approximately 626 billion litres of water.[42] While data center water consumption (1.7 billion litres/day) is a small fraction

33   Anders, 'Hypotheses for Primary Energy Use, Electricity Use and CO2 Emissions of Global Computing
     and its Shares of the Total Between 2020 and 2030'.
34   Synergy Research Group, *Hyperscale Data Center Count Grows to 659—ByteDance Joins the Leading
     Group*', 13 September 2021, https://www.srgresearch.com/articles/hyperscale-data-center-count-
     grows-to-659-bytedance-joins-the-leading-group.
35   Dan Swinhoe, 'Microsoft, Amazon, and Google Operate Half the World's 600 Hyperscale Data Centers',
     2021, https://www.datacenterdynamics.com/en/news/microsoft-amazon-and-google-operate-half-the-
     worlds-600-hyperscale-data-centers/.
36   Swinhoe, 'Microsoft, Amazon, and Google Operate Half the World's 600 Hyperscale Data Centers'.
37   Nick Srnicek, *Platform Capitalism*, Cambridge: Polity, 2016.
38   Arman Shehabi, Sarah J. Smith, Eric Masanet, and Jonathan Koomey, 'Data Center Growth in the
     United States: Decoupling the Demand for Services from Electricity Use', *Environmental Research
     Letters* 13.12 (2018): 124030.
39   Mél Hogan, 'Data Flows and Water Woes: The Utah Data Center', *Big Data & Society* 2.2: (2015): 1 -12.
40   Nicole Starosielski, 'Thermocultures of Geological Media', *Cultural Politics* 12.3 (2016): 293–309.
41   David Mytton, 'Data Centre Water Consumption', *Npj Clean Water* 4.1 (2021): 11.
42   Arman Shehabi et al., *United States Data Center Energy Usage Report*. U.S. Department of Energy
     Office of Scientific and Technical Information, 2016, https://www.osti.gov/biblio/1372902/.

of total water consumption (1218 billion liters/day)[43] acute and significant impacts of data centers on water availability are dependent on geographical location. For example, data centers in the western and south-western U.S. depend upon already scarce and stressed watersheds,[44] placing technology corporations in conflict with local communities and ecosystems. When ecological disasters occur, technology corporations are often prioritised over local people.[45]

While 'green AI' approaches[46] focus on reducing the electricity needed to train and run models within data centers, they rarely engage with the human and environmental costs associated with producing or disposing of hardware or the infrastructure that houses and cools that technology. These social and environmental harms include those associated with industries that extract conflict minerals like tantalum, tungsten, and gold from the Democratic Republic of Congo (DRC),[47] or where extraction is dependent on child labour such as cobalt from the DRC.[48] Unbridled extraction of other materials such as lanthanides (commonly known as rare earth minerals) leave a toxic legacy of localised environmental and human health impacts such as producing 'cancer villages' in China.[49]

Further to this, none of these materials come out of the ground ready for use in high-performance computing. Another set of energy-intensive extraction processes separates and purifies raw materials, resulting in significant levels of additional pollution. Processes of beneficiation remove most of the raw material that was extracted from the earth. In the case of copper, for example, as high-grade ores are increasingly depleted, the concentration within commercially viable ores has fallen from 2 percent to 0.8 percent,[50] meaning that over 99 percent of the mass of extracted material is waste/tailings.[51] The processes employed for purification require significant energy inputs and often require the use of toxic materials. For example, the silicon used in CPUs, GPUs and TPUs requires several stages of chemical processing to reach 99.999999999 percent purity,[52] before it undergoes processes of thermal oxidation, photolithography, plasma etching and doping,

---

43   Cheryl A. Dieter, Molly A. Maupin, Rodney R. Caldwell, Melissa A. Harris, Tamara I. Ivahnenko, John K. Lovelace, Nancy L. Barber, and Kristin S. Linsey, *Estimated Use of Water in the United States in 2015*, Reston, VA: U.S. Geological Survey, 2018.

44   Md Abu Bakar Siddik, Arman Shehabi, and Landon Marston, 'The Environmental Footprint of Data Centers in the United States', *Environmental Research Letters* 16.6 (2021): 064017.

45   Mél Hogan, 'Big Data Ecologies', *Ephemera* 18.3 (2018): 631–57.

46   Roy Schwartz, Jesse Dodge, Noah A. Smith, and Oren Etzioni, 'Green AI'; Bender, Gebru, McMillan-Major and Shmitchell, 'On the Dangers of Stochastic Parrots: Can Language Models Be Too Big??'.

47   Sy Taffel, *Digital Media Ecologies*, New York and London: Bloomsbury, 2019, 162–9.

48   Nicholas Niarchos, 'The Dark Side of Congo's Cobalt Rush', *The New Yorker*, 2021, https://www. newyorker.com/magazine/2021/05/31/the-dark-side-of-congos-cobalt-rush.

49   Julie Michelle Klinger, *Rare Earth Frontiers*, Ithaca, London: Cornell University Press, 2017.

50   Rembrandt H. E. M. Koppelaar and Hendrik Koppelaar, 'The Ore Grade and Depth Influence on Copper Energy Inputs', *BioPhysical Economics and Resource Quality* 1.2 (2016): 11.

51   We should note that cobalt is largely extracted as a by-product of mines that primarily extract copper and nickel.

52   Beiser Vince, *The World in a Grain: The Story of Sand and How It Transformed Civilization*, New York: Riverhead Books, 2018.

all of which are chemically and energetically intensive, requiring precise controls over substances and temperatures, some of which reach 1100°C.[53]

The matter and energy required for AI largely flow from the global economic periphery towards the burgeoning technomass in the economic core.[54] Contemporaneously, theories of data colonialism outline the flow of financial value and data from the economic periphery towards the core.[55] This ecologically unequal exchange (EUE),[56] is not incidental to, but comprises instead a constitutive element of global capitalism which has persisted throughout past and present forms of colonialism and imperialism.[57] Under conditions of EUE, raw materials and energy flow from periphery to core, while the periphery also functions as a 'dump' for much of the 50 million tons of toxic e-waste generated annually.[58] Recent research in ecological economics indicates that high income countries' usage of raw material exceeds domestic extraction by over 10 billion tons, while all regions except high-income countries are net providers of raw materials.[59]As we have demonstrated, this includes the raw materials required for AI.

While hardware located inside data centres is necessary for ML systems, a holistic and ethical appraisal should also include all the network and platform infrastructure that connects data centres to end-client devices. This includes undersea and terrestrial fibre-optic cables, internet exchange points and cable landing stations and many of the desktop, laptop, tablet, smartphone and IoT devices that engage with ML systems. Furthermore, ML systems require training data, for example, the ImageNet dataset that has been commonly used for image recognition were drawn from Flickr,[60] so the assemblage required for ML systems employing these datasets includes Flickr's platform infrastructure and the array of digital cameras, smartphones and computers that created the dataset. The images were

53   John Zhang and Kazunori Hoshino, *Molecular Sensors and Nanodevices* 2nd edition, Cambridge: Academic Press, 2019.
54   Alf Hornborg, *The Power of the Machine: Global inequalities of Economy, Technology, and Environment*, Lanham: Altamira Press, 2001.
55   Nick Couldry and Ulises A Mejias, *The Costs of Connection: How Data Is Colonizing Human Life and Appropriating It for Capitalism*, Stanford: Stanford University Press, 2019.
56   Alf Hornborg, 'Towards an Ecological Theory of Unequal Exchange: Articulating World System Theory and Ecological Economics', *Ecological Economics* 25.1 (1998): 127–36; Alf Hornborg and Joan Martinez-Alier, 'Ecologically Unequal Exchange and Ecological Debt', *Journal of Political Ecology* 23.1(2016): 328–33.
57   Raj Patel and Jason W. Moore, *A History of the World in Seven Cheap Things: A Guide to Capitalism, Nature, and the Future of the Planet*, New York: Verso, 2017; Andreas Malm and Alf Hornborg, 'The Geology of Mankind? A Critique of the Anthropocene Narrative', *The Anthropocene Review* 1.1 (2014): 62–9.
58   Vanessa Forti, Cornelis P. Balde, Ruediger Kuehr, and Garam Bel, *The Global E-Waste Monitor 2020: Quantities, Flows and the Circular Economy Potential*, Bonn, Geneva and Rotterdam: United Nations University/United Nations Institute for Training and Research, International Telecommunication Union, and International Solid Waste Association, 2020.
59   Christian, Dorninger, Alf Hornborg, David J. Abson, Henrik Von Wehrden, Anke Schaffartzik, Stefan Giljum, John-Oliver Engler, et al., 'Global Patterns of Ecologically Unequal Exchange: Implications for Sustainability in the 21st Century', *Ecological Economics* 179 (2021): 106824.
60   Katarina Sluis and Fei-Fei Li, *Where Did ImageNet Come From?*, November 2019, https://unthinking. photography/articles/where-did-imagenet-come-from.

labelled by humans sourced through Amazon Mechanical Turk—which pays workers well below minimum wage while failing to offer the protections associated with employment.[61] The exploitative and precarious human labour associated with such systems should also be recognised as a component of the ecology of an ML system.

Mapping the scale of the system required for contemporary ML goes far beyond a server in a data center and the energy it requires and the emissions it produces. It includes a vast array of devices, operations, facilities, and people located across the planet. Each device is itself an assemblage of materials whose extraction, processing and disposal are associated with a range of environmental, social, and labour justice issues, which remain neglected in most contemporary conceptions of 'ethical AI.' Acknowledging the scale of this assemblage and the range and severity of harms it inflicts on people and ecosystems unmasks any notion that AI under current extractivist capitalism arrangements of EUE is ethical, or that it could be regarded as ethical if only privacy concerns were addressed, biases were removed from training datasets so they are 'fairer,' or the models themselves were more 'transparent' and 'accountable.' Indeed, the current, extremely narrow framing of AI ethics largely serves to benefit technology corporations who enact minor technical modifications to ecologically calamitous technologies whilst boldly pronouncing that this proves they are acting ethically.

Efficiency, Technology, and Capitalism

The myopic focus on the energy costs of training models results in 'solutions' based on improving efficiency, reducing carbon costs by limiting the computational intensity or training dataset size of machine learning models.[62] These 'solutions' miss broader points around ML systems, supply chains and infrastructure; solely focusing on energy use within data centers fails to consider the upstream and downstream costs and externalities, or recognize the historical and ongoing relationships between technology, efficiency, and capitalism.

'Green AI'[63] advocates that increasing energy efficiency enables a decoupling of economic growth and environmental impacts, therefore reducing ecological harms from ML. Assessing this claim requires some context surrounding decoupling, technology and 'green growth.' Since the industrial revolution there have been strong positive correlations

---

61   Birgitta Bergvall-Kåreborn and Debra Howcroft, 'Amazon Mechanical Turk and the commodification of labour', *New Technology, Work and Employment*, 29.3 (2014): 213–23; Jathan Sadowski, 'The Internet of Landlords: Digital Platforms and New Mechanisms of Rentier Capitalism', *Antipode*, 52 (2020): 562–80.

62   Strubell, Ganesh, and McCallum, 'Energy and Policy Considerations for Deep Learning in NLP'; Schwartz, Dodge, Smith, and Etzioni, 'Green AI'; Patterson, Gonzalez, Le, Liang, Munguia, Rothchild, So, Texier, and Dean, 'Carbon Emissions and Large Neural Network Training'; Aimee van Wynsberghe, 'Sustainable AI: AI for Sustainability and the Sustainability of AI', *AI and Ethics* (2021): 1–6; Bender, Gebru, McMillan-Major, and Shmitchell 'On the Dangers of Stochastic Parrots: Can Language Models Be Too Big??'.

63   Schwartz, JDodge, Smith, and Etzioni, 'Green AI; van Wynsberghe, 'Sustainable AI: AI for Sustainability and the Sustainability of AI'.

between economic growth (measured in GDP) and both greenhouse gas (GHG) emissions and material footprints (i.e., the overall mass of materials used by a society).[64] The goal of decoupling is to allow economic growth to continue unabated while decreasing presently associated ecological harms. Here several key distinctions surrounding the form, scale, and rate of decoupling are required. The first distinction is between relative decoupling— which means that while rates of growth and GHG/material footprints diverge, there remain overall increases of resource use/harms—and absolute decoupling, where economic growth increases while GHG/material footprints decrease. A second important distinction involves the geographical scale of analysis. While there are numerous exemplars of OECD nations achieving absolute decoupling at a national level,[65] that decoupling has been achieved through offshoring industry and importing goods and materials, i.e., a form of regional decoupling predicated upon EUE. To avert ecological catastrophe, absolute decoupling must take place on a global rather than national or regional scale. Finally, for green growth to be ethical *and* sustainable, the absolute decoupling of economic growth from GHG emissions must be sufficiently rapid to meet (or indeed exceed) global environmental commitments such as the Paris Agreement.

Assuming continued economic growth of around 2 percent a year, this decoupling would require OECD nations to reduce emissions at a rate of 15 percent per annum until they reach zero.[66] While moving from fossil fuels to renewable energy does decouple GHG emissions from energy use, there is no empirical evidence to support this rate of absolute decoupling of GHG emissions from economic growth. Additionally, since 1990 global growth in material use has *outpaced* growth in GDP.[67] There is no contemporary evidence for any trend towards decoupling of economic growth and resource use; in fact for every unit of economic growth over this time, *more* resources have been required. While the current global material footprint is approaching 100 billion tons per annum—having more than doubled since 1990—a sustainable level is estimated to be 25–50 billion tons per annum.[68] Further, the vast majority of material footprint growth since 1990—81 percent at a per capita level—is attributable to high income nations, further demonstrating that the responsibility for current ecological crises is deeply inequitable.[69]

64   Thomas O. Wiedmann, Heinz Schandl, Manfred Lenzen, Daniel Moran, Sangwon Suh, James West, and Keiichiro Kanemoto, 'The Material Footprint of Nations', proceedings of the National Academy of Sciences 112.20 (2015): 6271–6276; Jason Hickel and Giorgos Kallis, 'Is Green Growth Possible?', *New Political Economy* (2019): 1–18.

65   See for example: Esther Sanyé-Mengual, Michaela Secchi, Sara Corrado, Antoine Beylot, and Serenella Sala, 'Assessing the Decoupling of Economic Growth from Environmental Impacts in the European Union: A Consumption-based Approach', *Journal of Cleaner Production,* 236 (2019): 117535.

66   Jason Hickel and Giorgos Kallis, 'Is Green Growth Possible?' *New Political Economy* (2019): 1–18.

67   Jason Hickel, *Less Is More: How Degrowth Will Save the World*, New York: Penguin Random House, 2020; Wiedmann, Schandl, Lenzen, Moran, Suh, West, and Kanemoto 'The Material Footprint of Nations'.

68   Stefan Bringezu, 'Possible Target Corridor for Sustainable Use of Global Material Resources', *Resources* 4.1 (2015): 25–54. These global figures are very coarse-grained, as differing materials have different impacts, as do the technologies and processes used for material extraction. Still, despite this homogenisation these figures are useful indicators of the rapid growth in material footprint since 1950.

69   Hickel *Less Is More 110* .

Moving from global aggregate figures to focus on efficiency and AI, digital technology has long involved a relative decoupling between metrics of performance and energy use.[70] Exemplifying these changes, data centres have become more energy efficient over time, particularly with the move towards hyperscale and cloud data centres.[71] The metric for measuring data center energy efficiency is power use effectiveness (PUE), a ratio demarcating the proportion of a data centers' energy use required for operating the IT equipment in comparison with the total energy required by the facility (which includes energy for cooling, lighting, etc.). An ideal PUE would be 1, signaling that total energy usage equals that used by the IT equipment. As of 2020, the US average PUE was 1.59, while certain data centers have achieved a ratio of 1.11.[72] However, PUE only measures efficiency, not the overall energy use of the facility,[73] or the total number of facilities. Accordingly, while facilities become more efficient, total data center energy use has grown.[74]

Efficiency gains are essential in shoring up capitalist economic growth and have been present throughout the history of computational development.[75] The problem is that efficiency gains are typically negated by rebound effects such as Jevons's paradox:[76] more efficiently using resources leads to overall increases in resource use. Nonetheless, it is in the economic interests of data centre owners to increase efficiency, which reduces costs, therefore enhancing profits. This is not to suggest that efficiency is 'bad', but within a growth-based capitalist economy, efficiency savings do not typically lead to absolute reductions of emissions or materials usage—they increase material input overall. As Foster and colleagues argue, 'An economic system devoted to profits, accumulation, and economic expansion without end will tend to use any efficiency gains or cost reductions to expand the overall scale of production.'[77] What is required, then, is a shift away from the conflation of exchange value (i.e., GDP) with social progress and abandoning the fairy-tale of endless economic growth. Our conclusion outlines strategies for achieving this, but we first turn to a second model for resolving ecological crises under 'green capitalism' via technological solutionism.[78]

---

70   Koppelaar and Koppelaar, 'The Ore Grade and Depth Influence on Copper Energy Inputs', 11; Taffel, 'Data and Oil'.
71   Anders, 'Hypotheses for primary energy use, electricity use and CO2 emissions of global computing and its shares of the total between 2020 and 2030'.
72   Patterson, Gonzalez, Le, Liang, Munguia, Rothchild, So, Texier, and Dean, 'Carbon Emissions and Large Neural Network Training'.
73   Gemma A. Brady, Nikil Kapur, Jonathan L. Summers, and Harvey M. Thompson, 'A Case Study and Critical Assessment in Calculating Power Usage Effectiveness for a Data Center', *Energy Conversion and Management* 76 (2013): 155–61.
74   Anders, 'Hypotheses for Primary Energy Use, Electricity Use and CO2 Emissions of Global Computing and its Shares of the Total Between 2020 and 2030', 53.
75   Stephan G. Bunker, 'Raw Materials and the Global Economy', *Society and Natural Resources* 9.4 (1996): 419–29.
76   William Stanley Jevons (1865) *The Coal Question*, 3rd edition, New York: Augustus M. Kelley, 1965.
77   John Bellamy Foster, Brett Clark, and Richard York, 'Capitalism and the Curse of Energy Efficiency', *Monthly Review* 62.6 (2010): 183.
78   Evgeny Morozov, *To Save Everything, Click Here: The Folly of Technological Solutionism*, London: Penguin, 2014. Our use of technological solutionism is related to the term's popularisation by Morozov, insofar as it demarcates a logic unique to 21st-century digital capitalism which seeks to resolve problems through optimization, efficiency and market-based computational technologies.

8

## The Fallacy of Technological Solutionism

New and emerging technologies are positioned as a panacea to ecological crises, enabling current forms of overconsumption to continue unabated. This is exemplified by former Australian prime minister Scott Morrison's statement that we will resolve climate change through 'technology not taxes.'[79] This approach is far from novel. In 2007, six years after withdrawing from the Kyoto Protocol, which mandated industrialized nations to reduce greenhouse gas emissions, then U.S. President George W. Bush and then Australian prime minister John Howard released a joint statement arguing that 'the development and deployment of low emission technologies will be a key element in addressing the climate challenge,'[80] citing clean coal and carbon capture and storage (CCS) as technological solutions. Fifteen years on, clean coal and CCS have repeatedly failed to demonstrate technical and economic viability.[81] As Kuch illustrates, CCS is framed by a worldview derived from the fossil fuel industries, for whom climate change is a technical issue to resolve technologically rather than by phasing out fossil fuels.[82]

While at first glance, CCS appears to be a sleight of hand employed by the fossil fuel industries and right-wing political leaders to inhibit actions that address ecological crises, it has been embraced by the Intergovernmental Panel on Climate Change Fifth Assessment Report,[83] which centers CCS in conjunction with bioenergy (abbreviated to BECCS) in socio-economic models designed to avert catastrophic climate change. BECCS features in over 100 of the 116 scenarios for avoiding dangerous warming.[84] BECCS theoretically allows significant overshoot of the carbon budget for remaining under 2°C of warming as it produces negative emissions, capturing carbon dioxide from the air in trees, turning these trees into pellets that are then burnt, and capturing the carbon emissions and storing them underground, thereby reducing atmospheric CO_2 levels. Relying on problematic (and probably inaccurate) forecasts for significant negative emissions in the second half of the 21st-century allows governments to delay reducing emissions now

Morozov productively outlines how solutionism exemplifies a desire to solve problems that do not meaningfully exist, as epitomized by smart fridges or bin cameras. While we concur with the critique of these technologies as needlessly extending corporate dataveillance, our critique of technological solutionism instead addresses how this logic adversely impacts contemporary responses to urgent ecological and social justice issues.

79 'PM Defends his "Technology Not Taxes" Approach to Cutting Emissions', *ABC News*, 23 April 2021, https://www.abc.net.au/news/2021-04-23/pm-defends-his-technology-not-taxes-approach-to-emissions/13315616.
80 George W. Bush and John Howard, *Joint Statement on Climate Change and Energy by President Bush and Australian Prime Minister John Howard*, 4 September 2007, https://georgewbush-whitehouse.archives.gov/news/releases/2007/09/20070904-8.html.
81 Kevin Anderson and Glen Peters, 'The Trouble with Negative Emissions', *Science* 354. 6309 (2016): 182–3.
82 Declan Kuch, '"Fixing" Climate Change through Carbon Capture and Storage: Situating Industrial Risk Cultures', *Futures* 92 (2017): 90–9.
83 IPCC, *Climate Change 2014: Synthesis Report. Contribution of Working Groups I, II and III to the Fifth Assessment Report of the Intergovernmental Panel on Climate Change* [Core Writing Team, Rajendra Pachauri and Leo Meyer (eds)]. IPCC, Geneva: Switzerland, 2014.
84 Hickel, *Less Is More.*

based on a speculative panacea of unrealized future technological innovations.[85] While CCS technology has so far failed to realize efficacy claims, the bioenergy component of BECCS is also problematic, with the land required for biomass in IPCC models typically being one to two times the size of India.[86] In conjunction with the reduction of crop yields in a warming world, this likely compounds the catastrophic food shortages and reductions in biodiversity already being experienced in parts of the global economic periphery.[87]

The issue is not just that technological solutionism (such as BECCS) is unlikely to resolve ecological crises, but also that they are a distraction that actively inhibits the collective social, political, and cultural change that is urgently required by suggesting that technology (including technologies that do not yet exist) will comprehensively 'fix' the ecological crises, so there is little to be gained by citizens demanding action now.[88] In the case of AI, the alleged solutionist silver bullet involves using renewable energy to power data centres. Big Tech companies have embraced this extremely limited definition of sustainability, foregrounding it within promotional materials such as annual environmental reports that publicly portray themselves as leading society towards a sustainable future.[89]

For example, Google's 2020 environmental report declares 'sustainability is one of our core values at Google and we've been a leader on climate change since the company's founding over 20 years ago.'[90] Google claims that they became the first major company to become carbon neutral in 2007 and that by 2020 they had 'neutralized our legacy carbon footprint since our founding, making Google the first major company to be carbon neutral for its entire operating history.' However, the environmental data located at the end of Google's environmental report shows otherwise. Unpacking this data requires a basic grasp of the ways corporations measure and audit emissions. Distinctions are drawn between Scope 1, 2 and 3 emissions;[91] Scope 1 refers to emissions produced by

85   Anderson and Peters, 'The Trouble with Negative Emissions', 182-3; Naomi E. Vaughan and Clair Gough, 'Expert Assessment Concludes Negative Emissions Scenarios May Not Deliver', *Environmental Research Letters* 11.9 (2016).

86   Anderson and Peters, Glen, 'The Trouble with Negative Emissions', 183.

87   Planting trees has also been criticized for employing a reductionist framing that can reduce biodiversity, increase deforestation, deflect attention from phasing out fossil fuels (see Karen D. Holl, and Pedro H. S. Brancalion, 'Tree Planting Is Not a Simple Solution', *Science* 368.6491 (2020): 580–1; Nathalie Seddon, et al. 'Getting the Message Right on Nature-Based Solutions to Climate Change, *Global Change Biology* 27. 8 (2021): 1518–46.) and may not result in net carbon sequestration on decadal timescales (see Nina L. Friggens, Alison J. Hester, Ruth J. Mitchell, Thomas C. Parker, Jens-Arne Subke, and Philip A. Wookey, 'Tree Planting in Organic Soils Does Not Result in Net Carbon Sequestration on Decadal Timescales', *Global Change Biology* 26.9 (2020): 5178–88).

88   Sy Taffel, 'Hopeful Extinctions? Tesla, Technological Solutionism and the Anthropocene', *Culture Unbound: Journal of Current Cultural Research* 10.2 (2018): 163–84.

89   Rianne Riemens, 'Decoupling as Rhetorical Strategy in Google's Green Discourse', AoIR Selected Papers of Internet Research, 2021.

90   Google, 'Google Environmental Report 2020', 2021, https://www.gstatic.com/gumdrop/sustainability/google-2019-environmental-report.pdf

91   Janet Ranganathan, Laurent Corbier, P. Bhatia, Simon Schmitz, Peter Gage, and Kjell Oren, 'The Greenhouse Gas Protocol: A Corporate Accounting and Reporting Standard (Revised Edition)',

directly owned sources, such as onsite furnaces, while Scope 2 covers the GHG emissions associated with purchased electricity and other utilities. Scope 3 emissions are usually the most significant in terms of overall volume, they include all the emissions associated with those that the company is indirectly responsible for, all the way up and down its supply chain.

Whereas Google's total reported emissions for 2019 were 17,646,902 tCO2e—the majority of which are Scope 3 emissions, whose sources are of indeterminate origin within the document, but which almost certainly arise from the production of hardware and infrastructure[92]—Google's emissions reductions arising from onsite renewable installations, power purchase agreements with third-party providers and carbon offset projects totalled 5,725,635 tCO2e.[93] Basic arithmetic demonstrates that net emissions far exceed mitigation, Google was not carbon neutral in 2019, let alone counteracting the corporation's historical carbon footprint as the Environmental Report claims. Google's declaration of carbon neutrality only includes their negligible direct emissions and more substantial electricity usage (Scope 1 and 2 emissions), and simply ignore the vast carbon footprint associated with producing hardware and infrastructure. Ergo Google's claims surrounding carbon neutrality are a straightforward case of greenwashing through a strategy of selective disclosure,[94] whereby a company selectively highlights positive elements of their environmental performance in order to misleadingly portray themselves.

In comparison to Google, Apple deserves praise for including their supply chain (Scope 3 emissions) within their carbon footprint, and for moving to make their entire business carbon neutral within a decade. However, despite first appearances, Apple still falls short of genuinely sustainable action. Between 2016 and 2020 electricity use at Apple's corporate facilities (primarily data centers) almost doubled, rising from 1,420,000 MWh to 2,580,000 MWh.[95] Although during this period Apple increased renewable electricity usage to cover this increase, there are two reasons why this cannot reasonably be considered sustainable. Firstly, in the USA, where approximately 80 percent of Apple's corporate electricity usage occurs, over 60 percent of electricity generation was from fossil fuels in 2021.[96] While decarbonization urgently requires replacing fossil fuels with renewable energy, in Apple's case, instead of replacing existing fossil fuel generation,

Washington, DC: World Resources Institute and World Business Council for Sustainable Development, 2004.

92   While Google's environmental data does not break down scope three into categories, Apple's 2021 Environmental Progress Report (2021b, 67) does, finding that manufacturing is 16,100,000 of the company's total carbon footprint of 22,600,000 tCO2e—71 percent of the total.

93   Google, 'Google Environmental Report 2020', 2021, https://www.gstatic.com/gumdrop/sustainability/google-2019-environmental-report.pdf.

94   Netto de Freitas, Sebastião Vieira, Marcos Felipe Falcão Sobral, Ana Regina Bezerra Ribeiro, and Gleibson Robert da Luz Soares, 'Concepts and Forms of Greenwashing: A Systematic Review', *Environmental Sciences Europe*, 32.19 (2020).

95   Apple, *Environmental Progress Report*, April 2021, https://www.apple.com/environment/pdf/Apple_Environmental_Progress_Report_2021.pdf.

96   U.S. Energy Information Administration, *Electricity Explained, Electricity in the United States*, July 2022, https://www.eia.gov/energyexplained/electricity/electricity-in-the-us.php.

vast amounts of renewable energy are required to cover the rapid growth in electricity usage associated with data centres.[97]

The history of energy is often narrativized as the successive dominance of coal, then oil, then gas. What this periodization obscures is the fact that these sources have supplemented, rather than replaced, one another. Since the first IPCC report in 1990, coal use has increased slightly, oil and gas use has nearly doubled, and by 2019 solar and wind combined provided just 2.6 percent of global energy.[98] Transitioning away from fossil fuels within the time required to avoid global warming above 2 degrees is a monumental task, one that means the additive logic of the energy mix since the industrial revolution must be supplanted by one whereby the energy currently provided by fossil fuels is rapidly replaced by renewables. In this context, alongside the need for growth in energy use among non-OECD nations in the global periphery and semi-periphery where electricity blackouts are common and billions lack internet access, rapid growth in electricity demand within affluent nations in the economic core cannot be considered just nor 'ethical.'

The second issue is that alongside GHG emissions, material footprint is a pressing ecological issue and solar panels and wind turbines require many of the materials also required for digital hardware such as highly-purified silicon, rare earth minerals, lithium, and cobalt. Accepting the finitude of these resources, and the inequitably experienced social and environmental harms associated with their extraction, entails realizing that while energy sources such as the sun and the wind are renewable, the technological means of converting them into electricity is not. Solutionists contend that further speculative technologies, such as deep-sea[99] or comet mining[100] will resolve the scarcity of terrestrial materials required for green capitalism. However, given both the multi-decadal timescales involved and the fact that ventures such as deep-sea mining will cause significant environmental harms, these claims should not distract us from the urgent task of reducing emissions, material usage and ultimately consumption.

Far from genuinely resolving problems, technological solutionism provides an extremely narrow focus that ignores the broader context of EUE and serves, instead to greenwash corporate communications. The neoliberal technical fix is designed to preserve existing

---

97   Apple has also been active in challenging right-to-repair movements and engaging in strategies of planned obsolescence to drive ongoing consumption of its devices leading to more mineral extraction and waste creation. See Lisa Vonk, 'Paying Attention to Waste: Apple's Circular Economy', *Continuum* 32.6 (2018): 745–57; Bedford, Mann, Walters, and Foth, 'A post-Capitalocentric Critique of Digital Technology and Environmental Harm: New Directions at the Intersection of Digital and Green Criminology'; Sy Taffel, 'AirPods and the Earth: Digital Technologies, Planned Obsolescence and the Capitalocene', *Environment and Planning E: Nature and Space*, 2022.

98   Hannah Ritchie and Max Roser, *Energy Mix*, 2021, https://ourworldindata.org/energy-mix.

99   Laura Bedford, Monique Mann, Reece Walters, and Marcus Foth, 'A Post-capitalocentric Critique of Digital Technology and Environmental Harm: New Directions at the Intersection of Digital and Green Criminology in 'Beyond Cybercrime: New perspectives on crime, harm and digital technologies', *International Journal for Crime, Justice and Social Democracy (Special Issue)*, 11.1 (2022): 167–81.

100   Aaron Bastani, *Fully Automated Luxury Communism*, London: Verso Books, 2020.

systems of power and privilege by positing technical fixes that maintain a growth-orientated capitalist model which is fundamentally unethical and at odds with ecological justice.

Conclusion

This chapter forms a damning critique that 'ethical' and 'green' AI can render current AI systems ethical and just, especially where ethical interventions are largely limited to mathematically addressable technical fixes to make AI systems more 'fair', 'accountable' and 'transparent.'[101] Instead, we must take action to remedy ecological harms associated with AI that address the deeply unjust, unsustainable and inequitable socio-economic system in which AI is entangled.[102] Fundamentally, according to the normative model of social ethics present within political ecology, AI cannot be deemed ethical while it is complicit in ecocide. We therefore conclude by outlining emerging postcapitalist approaches that re-envision and prefigure less ecologically destructive and more 'ethical' sociotechnical systems.

The structure of capitalist economies requires compound growth of at least 2 to 3 percent GDP per annum.[103] Economic growth strongly correlates with material footprint and greenhouse gas emissions. While widespread adoption of renewable energy enables the decoupling of greenhouse gas emissions from GDP, the underlying correlation between energy and GDP remains, and 'renewable' energy still requires significant unrenewable materials. This means that the inevitable quest for infinite growth under a capitalist mode of production is impossible on a materially finite planet. Consequently, postcapitalist positions broadly concur on the necessity of supplanting and replacing GDP as a measure of socioeconomic wellbeing.[104] GDP is a measure of economic exchange value—the sum of monetary transactions within nation states—and has been widely criticized for valuing things that are destructive, including coal burning power stations, producing nuclear weapons and increased hospital admissions. At the same time GDP fails to value things that do not generate incorporate exchange value, including clean air, biodiversity, unpaid domestic labour, and commons-based digital ventures such as Wikipedia. Equally, GDP fails to account for spectacular levels of inequality within nation states, so employing GDP as an indicator of social progress fails to recognize that since the 1970s, within developed economies, growth has almost exclusively accrued among the wealthiest while poverty

101 Thilo Hagendorff, 'The Ethics of AI Ethics: An Evaluation of Guidelines', *Minds & Machines* 30, 2020: 99–120.
102 Manu V. Mathai, Cindy Isenhour, Dimitris Stevis, Philip Vergragt, Magnus Bengtsson, Sylvia Lorek, Lars Fogh Mortensen et al., 'The Political Economy of (un) Sustainable Production and Consumption: A Multidisciplinary Synthesis for Research and Action', *Resources, Conservation and Recycling* 167 (2021): 105265.
103 David Harvey, *The Enigma of Capital and the Crises of Capitalism*, London: Profile Books, 2010.
104 Giorgos Kallis, *Degrowth*, Newcastle-Upon-Tyne: Agenda Publishing, 2018; Brian Massumi, *99 Theses on the Revaluation of Value: A Postcapitalist Manifesto*, Minneapolis: University of Minnesota Press, 2018; Alf Hornborg, 'Energy, Space, and Movement: Toward a Framework for Theorizing Energy Justice', *Geografiska Annaler: Series B, Human Geography* 102.1 (2020): 8–20; Hickel, *Less Is More*; Tim Jackson, *Post Growth: Life After Capitalism*, Cambridge: Polity, 2020.

levels have steadily risen.[105] Postcapitalist arguments are thus clear that GDP, with its focus on exchange value, is an inadequate measure for evaluating what matters in life.

While there has been significant debate within political ecology surrounding the merits and potential shortcomings of degrowth, ecomodernist and ecosocialist approaches,[106] both eco-socialists[107] and proponents of degrowth[108] argue for a decommodification of the relationships between humans and ecosystems and emphasize that the need for an economy based on use value. Nevertheless, when discussing technology there are tensions between eco-socialist positions which advocate for democratic centralizations such as state-funded national digital public services and infrastructures[109] or platform socialism,[110] and degrowth approaches that emphasize conviviality as a means of creating non-alienated technologies that draw upon forms of communing,[111] including the free/open source software and peer-to-peer movements.[112] Rather than advocating for any specific 'solution' we briefly highlight this diversity of postcapitalist approaches in order to advance dialogue and solidarity between those involved in promoting a range of ecosystem-centred alternatives to technological solutionism and hyper-efficient 'green' capitalism.

As it stands, AI and data centers exhibit network effects and economies of scale that lead towards the immense centralization associated with hyperscale data centers and this in turn produces oligopolistic corporate control over these systems and infrastructures.[113] Although AI, the internet and computers were all developed within capitalist economies, the current, corporate-dominated model of AI infrastructure is not inevitable. Indeed, a key contention of postcapitalist approaches is that altering the governance of technologies can transform their functioning in ways that markedly reduce ecosystem harms and social inequalities. Platform socialists argue that current asymmetries of power between corporations, and ecosystems (including humans) can be meaningfully addressed by

---

105 Thomas Piketty, *Capital in the Twenty-first Century*, Cambridge: Harvard University Press, 2018.
106 See for example, Paul Robbins, 'Is Less More...or Is More Less? Scaling the Political Ecologies of the Future', *Political Geography* 76 (2020): 102018; Erik Gómez-Baggethun, 'More Is More: Scaling Political Ecology within Limits to Growth', *Political Geography* 76 (2020): 102095.
107 See for example, Joel Kovel, *The Enemy of Nature: The End of Capitalism or the End of the World?*, London: Zed Books, 2007.
108 Hickel, *Less Is More*.
109 Jathan Sadowski, Salomé Viljoen, and Meredith Whittaker, 'Everyone Should Decide How Their Digital Data are Used—Not Just Tech Companies', *Nature* 595 (2021): 169–71.
110 Srnicek, *Platform Capitalism*; James Muldoon, *Platform Socialism: How to Reclaim our Digital Future from Big Tech*, London: Pluto Press, 2022.
111 Christian Kerschner, Petra Wächter, Linda Nierling, and Melf-Hinrich Ehlers, 'Degrowth and Technology: Towards Feasible, Viable, Appropriate and Convivial Imaginaries', *Journal of Cleaner Production* 197 (2018): 1619–36; Beinsteiner, Andreas, 'Conviviality, the Internet, and AI. Ivan Illich, Bernard Stiegler, and the Question Concerning Information-technological Self-limitation', *Open Cultural Studies* 4.1 (2020): 131–42.
112 Vasilis Kostakis, Kostas Latoufis, Minas Liarokapis, and Michel Bauwens, 'The Convergence of Digital Commons with Local Manufacturing From a Degrowth Perspective: Two Illustrative Cases', *Journal of Cleaner Production* 197 (2018): 1684–93.
113 Albert-László Barabási and Albert, Réka, 'Emergence of Scaling in Random Networks', *Science*, 286.5439 (1999): 509–12; Srnicek, *Platform Capitalism*.

centralized public service models, such as those used in many nations for healthcare, telecommunication, sewage systems and other forms of infrastructure. Where a 'natural monopoly'[114] occurs, a use-value led approach suggests managing infrastructure as a socialised public good, rather than as private commodities. Elsewhere, cooperatives, federated, and distributed peer-to-peer systems, and other forms of digital commons suggest decentralized alternatives. Further, moving away from exchange value as a measure of wealth would entail that numerous harmful forms of AI would no longer be deemed useful or valuable.

Eliminating harmful models of capitalist surveillance designed to nudge citizens to engage in acts of unsustainable consumption, and corporate hoarding of as much data as possible in the hope that there will eventually be a way to monetize it,[115] would enable significant reductions in data storage and computational processing. This would go some way toward reducing the current social and environmental harms AI incurs, while affording growth in those areas where AI can support the healing of ecosystems and communities rather than benefit the private interests of those who control technology and associated infrastructure. Within the context of data/digital colonialism,[116] a key component of this change must involve the decolonization of data[117] and enhanced technological sovereignty,[118] enabling individuals and communities to utilize their data for their own benefit. However, decolonization must also go beyond data to address EUE.

It is critical to highlight the role of AI in the current extractivist, capitalist system, a system that is causing a global ecological collapse through rapacious overconsumption predicated upon spectacular levels of social inequality within and between regions of the globe, and which can be considered neither just nor ethical. Alongside addressing climate and ecological debt, what is urgently required is a rapid decommodification of the economic system in the economic core. This will enable those living outside the core to reinstitute sovereignty over their resources, technology, energy, and land. While there are contentious debates about the appropriate ways to move beyond capitalism, a starting point is acknowledging that we can. A political ecology perspective requires us to strengthen our understanding of the possible roles of AI in the process of postcapitalist transition and to develop a praxis around 'AI ethics' and justice that incorporates these broad aims. We need much more than an ethical plaster to cover the flawed structures and systemic failures we face on a global scale.

114 Nicholas Garnham, 'Editorial', *Media, Culture & Society* 14.3 (1992): 339–42.
115 Jathan Sadowski, 'When Data Is Capital: Datafication, Accumulation, and Extraction', *Big Data & Society* 6.1 (2019):1 -12.
116 Nick Couldry and Ulises A. Mejias, 'Data Colonialism: Rethinking Big Data's Relation to the Contemporary Subject', *Television & New Media* 20.4 (2018): 336–49; Monique Mann and Angela Daly, '(Big) Data and the North-in-South: Australia's Informational Imperialism and Digital Colonialism', *Television & New Media* 20.4 (2019): 379–95.
117 Tahu Kukutai and John Taylor (eds), *Indigenous Data Sovereignty: Toward an Agenda*. Canberra: ANU Press, 2016.
118 Monique Mann, Peta Mitchell, Marcus Foth, and Irina Anastasiu, '#BlockSidewalk to Barcelona: Technological Sovereignty and the Social Licence to Operate Smart Cities', *Journal of the Association for Information Science and Technology* 71.9 (2020): 1103–15.

Funding Disclosure

The authors have received no external funding for this article and have no financial conflicts of interest to disclose

References

ABC News, 'PM defends his "technology not taxes" approach to cutting emissions', *ABC News*, 23 April 2021, https://www.abc.net.au/news/2021-04-23/pm-defends-his-technology-not-taxes-approach-to-emissions/13315616.

Al Qundus, Jamal, Dabbour, Kossai, Gupta, Shivam, Meissonier, Régis, and Paschke, Adrian. 'Wireless Sensor Network for AI-based Flood Disaster Detection', *Annals of Operations Research*, 7 August 2020: 1–23.

Amoore, Louise. *Cloud Ethics: Algorithms and the Attributes of Ourselves and Others*, Durham: Duke University Press, 2020.

Anderson, Kevin and Peters, Glen. 'The Trouble with Negative Emissions', *Science* 354. 6309 (2016): 182–3.

Andrae, Anders, S.E. 'Hypotheses for Primary Energy Use, Electricity Use and CO2 Emissions of Global Computing and its Shares of the Total Between 2020 and 2030', *WSEAS Transactions on Power Systems* 15 (2020): 50–9.

Andrejevic, Mark. *Automated Media*, New York: Routledge, 2020.

Apple. *iPhone 13 Product Environmental Report*, 14 September 2021, https://www.apple.com/environment/pdf/products/iphone/iPhone_13_PER_Sept2021.pdf.

——. *Environmental Progress Report*, April 2021, https://www.apple.com/environment/pdf/Apple_Environmental_Progress_Report_2021.pdf.

Barabási, Albert-László and Albert, Réka. 'Emergence of Scaling in Random Networks', *Science* 286.5439 (1999): 509–12.

Barbrook, Richard and Cameron, Andy. 'The Californian Ideology', *Science as Culture* 6.1 (1996): 44–72.

Barnes, Elizabeh A., Hurrell, James W., Ebert-Uphoff, Imme., Anderson, Chuck and Anderson, David. 'Viewing Forced Climate Patterns Through an AI Lens', *Geophysical Research Letters*, 46.22 (2019): 13389–98.

Barr, Jeff. *Amazon EC2 Update—Inf1 Instances with AWS Inferentia Chips for High Performance Cost-Effective Inferencing*, 3 December 2019, https://aws.amazon.com/blogs/aws/amazon-ec2-update-inf1-instances-with-aws-inferentia-chips-for-high-performance-cost-effective-inferencing/.

Bashroush, Rabih and Lawrence, Andy. *Beyond Pue: Tackling Its Wasted Terawatts*, Uptime Institute, January 2020, https://uptimeinstitute.com/beyond-pue-tackling-wasted-terawatts.

Bastani, Aaron. *Fully Automated Luxury Communism*, London: Verso Books, 2020.

Bedford, Laura, Mann, Monique, Walters, Reece, and Foth, Marcus. 'A Post-capitalocentric Critique of Digital Technology and Environmental Harm: New Directions at the Intersection of Digital and Green Criminology, in *Beyond Cybercrime: New perspectives on crime, harm and digital technologies, International Journal for Crime, Justice and Social Democracy (Special Issue)*, 11.1 (2022): 167–81.

Beer, David. *The Data Gaze: Capitalism, Power and Perception*, Newbury Park: Sage, 2018.

Beinsteiner, Andreas. 'Conviviality, the Internet, and AI. Ivan Illich, Bernard Stiegler, and the Question Concerning Information-technological Self-limitation', *Open Cultural Studies* 4.1 (2020): 131–42.

Beiser, Vince. *The World in a Grain: The Story of Sand and How It Transformed Civilization*. New York: Riverhead Books, 2018.

Bender E.M., Gebru, Timnit, McMillan-Major, Angelina, and Shmitchell, Shmargaret. 'On the Dangers of Stochastic Parrots: Can Language Models Be Too Big??' *Proceedings of the 2021 ACM Conference on Fairness, Accountability, and Transparency*, 1 March 2021, 610–23.

Benkler, Yochai. 'Don't Let Industry Write the Rules for AI', *Nature* 569.7754 (2019): 161–2.

Bergvall-Kåreborn, Birgitta and Howcroft, Debra. 'Amazon Mechanical Turk and the Commodification of Labour', *New Technology, Work and Employment* 29.3 (2014): 213–23.

Bonneuil, Christophe and Fressoz, Jean-Baptiste. *The Shock of the Anthropocene: The Earth, History and Us*, London: Verso Books, 2016.

Brady, Gemma A., Kapur, Nikil, Summers, Jonathan L., and Thompson, Harvey M. 'A Case Study and Critical Assessment in Calculating Power Usage Effectiveness for a Data Centre', *Energy Conversion and Management* 76 (2013): 155–61.

Bridle, James. *New Dark Age: Technology and the End of the Future*, London: Verso Books, 2018.

Bringezu, Stefan. 'Possible Target Corridor for Sustainable Use of Global Material Resources', *Resources* 4.1 (2015): 25–54.

Bryant, Raymond L. and Jarosz, Lucy. 'Ethics in Political Ecology: A Special Issue of Political Geography: Introduction: Thinking About Ethics in Political Ecology', *Political Geography* 23. 7 (2004): 807–12.

Bunker, Stephan G. 'Raw Materials and the Global Economy', *Society and Natural Resources* 9.4 (1996): 419–29.

Bush, George W. and Howard, John. *Joint Statement on Climate Change and Energy by President Bush and Australian Prime Minister John Howard*, 4 September 2007, https://georgewbush-whitehouse. archives.gov/news/releases/2007/09/20070904-8.html.

Chang, Li-Chiu, Fi-John Chang, Shun-Nien Yang, Fong-He Tsai, Ting-Hua Chang, and Edwin E. Herricks. 'Self-Organizing Maps of Typhoon Tracks Allow for Flood Forecasts up to Two Days in Advance', *Nature Communications* 11.1 (2020): 1983.

Couldry, Nick, and Mejias, Ulises A. *The Costs of Connection: How Data Is Colonizing Human Life and Appropriating It for Capitalism*, Stanford: Stanford University Press, 2019.

———. 'Data Colonialism: Rethinking Big Data's Relation to the Contemporary Subject', *Television & New Media* 20.4 (2018): 336–49.

Crawford, Kate. 'The Atlas of AI: Power Politics and the Planetary Costs of Artificial Intelligence', New Haven: Yale University Press, 2021.

Daly Angela, Hagendorff, Thilo, Hui, Li, Mann, Monique, Marda, Vidushi, Wagner, Ben, Wei Wang, Wayne. 'AI, Governance and Ethics: Global Perspectives' in Pollicino, Oreste and de Gregorio, Giovanni (eds) *Constitutional Challenges in the Algorithmic Society*, Cambridge: Cambridge University Press, 2021.

Daly, Angela, Devitt, S, Kate, and Mann, Monique. 'AI Ethics Needs Good Data' in Pieter Verdegem (ed) *AI for Everyone? Critical Perspectives*, London: University of Westminster Press, 2021.

de Freitas Netto, Sebastião Vieira, Sobral, Marcos Felipe Falcão, Ribeiro, Ana Regina Bezerra, and Soares, Gleibson Robert da Luz. 'Concepts and Forms of Greenwashing: A Systematic Review', *Environmental Sciences Europe* 32.1 (2020): 1–12.

Delmas, Magali A., and Cuerel Burbano, Vanessa. 'The Drivers of Greenwashing', *California Management Review* 54.1 (2011): 64–87.

Dieter, Cheryl A., Maupin, Molly A., Caldwell, Rodney R., Harris, Melissa A., Ivahnenko, Tamara I., Lovelace, John K., Barber, Nancy L., and Linsey, Kristin S. *Estimated Use of Water in the United States in 2015*, Reston: U.S. Geological Survey, 2018.

Dorninger, Christian, Hornborg, Alf, Abson, David J., Von Wehrden, Henrik, Schaffartzik, Anke, Giljum, Stefan, Engler, John-Oliver, et al. 'Global Patterns of Ecologically Unequal Exchange: Implications for Sustainability in the 21st Century', *Ecological Economics* 179 (2021): 106824.

'The World's Most Valuable Resource Is No Longer Oil, but Data', *The Economist*, 6 May 2017, https://www.economist.com/leaders/2017/05/06/the-worlds-most-valuable-resource-is-no-longer-oil-but-data.

Eubanks, Virginia. *Automating Inequality: How High-Tech Tools Profile, Police, and Punish the Poor*, New York: St. Martin's Press, 2018.

Forti, Vanessa, Balde, Cornelis P., Kuehr, Ruediger, and Bel, Garam. *The Global E-Waste Monitor 2020: Quantities, Flows and the Circular Economy Potential*, Bonn, Geneva and Rotterdam: United Nations University/United Nations Institute for Training and Research, International Telecommunication Union, and International Solid Waste Association, 2020.

Foster, John Bellamy, Clark, Brett, and York, Richard. 'Capitalism and the Curse of Energy Efficiency', *Monthly Review* 62.6 (2010): 1–12.

Friggens, Nina L., Hester, Alison J., Mitchell, Ruth J., Parker, Thomas C., Subke, Jens-Arne, and Wookey, Philip A. 'Tree Planting in Organic Soils Does Not Result in Net Carbon Sequestration on Decadal Timescales', *Global Change Biology* 26.9 (2020): 5178–88.

Garnham, Nicholas. 'Editorial', *Media, Culture & Society* 14.3 (1992): 339–42.

Gómez-Baggethun, Erik. 'More Is More: Scaling Political Ecology within Limits to Growth', *Political Geography* 76 (2020): 102095.

Google. 'Google Environmental Report 2020', 2020, https://www.gstatic.com/gumdrop/sustainability/google-2019-environmental-report.pdf.

Hagendorff, Thilo. 'The Ethics of AI Ethics: An Evaluation of Guidelines', *Minds & Machines* 30 (2020): 99–12.

Harvey, David. *The Enigma of Capital and the Crises of Capitalism.* London: Profile Books, 2010.

Hickel, Jason. *Less Is More: How Degrowth Will Save the World*, New York: Penguin Random House, 2020.

Hickel, Jason, and Kallis, Giorgos. 'Is Green Growth Possible?', *New Political Economy* (2019): 1–18.

Higgins, Polly. *Eradicating Ecocide: Exposing the Corporate and Political Practices Destroying the Planet and Proposing the Laws to Eradicate Ecocide*, London: Shepard-Walwyn, 2016.

Hogan, Mél. 'Data Flows and Water Woes: The Utah Data Center', *Big Data & Society* 2(2): (2015): 1–12.

——. 'Big Data Ecologies', *Ephemera* 18(3) (2018): 631–57.

Hogan, Mél, and Asta Vonderau. 'The Nature of Data Centers', *Culture Machine* 18 (2019) 1–4.

Holl, Karen D., and Brancalion, Pedro H. S. 'Tree Planting Is Not a Simple Solution', *Science* 368.6491 (2020): 580–1.

Hornborg, Alf. 'Towards an Ecological Theory of Unequal Exchange: Articulating World System Theory and Ecological Economics', *Ecological Economics* 25.1 (1998): 127–36.

——. *The Power of the Machine: Global Inequalities of Economy, Technology, and Environment*,. Lanham: Altamira Press, 2001.

——. 'The Political Ecology of the Technocene', *The Anthropocene and the Global Environmental Crisis: Rethinking Modernity in a New Epoch*, (2015): 177–83.

——. 'Energy, Space, and Movement: Toward a Framework for Theorizing Energy Justice', *Geografiska Annaler: Series B, Human Geography* 102.1 (2020): 8–20.

Hornborg, Alf and Martinez-Alier, Joan. 'Ecologically Unequal Exchange and Ecological Debt', *Journal of Political Ecology* 23.1(2016): 328–33.

Huntingford, Chris, Jeffers, Elizabeth S., Bonsall, Michael B., Christensen, Hannah M., Lees, Thomas, and Yang, Hui. 'Machine Learning and Artificial Intelligence to Aid Climate Change Research and Preparedness', *Environmental Research Letters* 14.12 (2019): 124007.

Jackson, Tim. *Post Growth: Life After Capitalism*, Cambridge: Polity, 2020.

Jevons, William Stanley. (1865) *The Coal Question*, 3rd edition. New York: Augustus M. Kelley, 1965.

Jiao, Pengcheng, and Alavi, Amir H. 'Artificial Intelligence in Seismology: Advent, Performance and Future Trends', *Geoscience Frontiers* 11.3 (2020): 739–44.

Kallis, Giorgos. *Degrowth*, Newcastle-Upon-Tyne: Agenda Publishing, 2018.

Keane, Pearse A., and Topol, Eric J. 'With an Eye to AI and Autonomous Diagnosis', *Npj Digital Medicine* 1.1 (2018): 40.

Kerschner, Christian, Wächter, Petra, Nierling, Linda, and Ehlers, Melf-Hinrich, 'Degrowth and Technology: Towards Feasible, Viable, Appropriate and Convivial Imaginaries', *Journal of Cleaner Production*, 197 (2018): 1619–36.

Klinger, Julie Michelle. *Rare Earth Frontiers*, Ithaca, London: Cornell University Press, 2017.

Koppelaar, Rembrandt H. E. M., and Koppelaar, Hendrik. 'The Ore Grade and Depth Influence on Copper Energy Inputs', *BioPhysical Economics and Resource Quality* 1.2 (2016): 1–16.

Kostakis, Vasilis, Latoufis, Kostas, Liarokapis, Minas, and Bauwens, Michel. 'The Convergence of Digital Commons with Local Manufacturing from a Degrowth Perspective: Two Illustrative Cases', *Journal of Cleaner Production* 197 (2018): 1684–93.

Kostakis, Vasilis, Roos, Andreas and Bauwens, Michel. 'Towards a Political Ecology of the Digital Economy: Socio-Environmental Implications of Two Competing Value Models', *Environmental Innovation and Societal Transitions* 18 (2016): 82–100.

Kovel, Joel. *The Enemy of Nature: The End of Capitalism or the End of the World?*, London: Zed Books, 2007.

Kuch, Declan. '"Fixing" Climate Change through Carbon Capture and Storage: Situating Industrial Risk Cultures', *Futures* 92 (2017): 90–99.

Kukutai, Tahu, and Taylor, John (eds). *Indigenous Data Sovereignty: Toward an Agenda*, Canberra: ANU press, 2016.

Lacoste, Alexandre, Luccioni, Alexandra, Schmidt, Victor, and Dandres, Thomas. 'Quantifying the Carbon Emissions of Machine Learning.' arXiv preprint arXiv:1910.09700, (2019).

Leopold, George. 'Aws to Offer Nvidia's T4 Gpus for Ai Inferencing', *HPC Wire*, 19 March 2019, https://www.hpcwire.com/2019/03/19/aws-upgrades-its-gpu-backed-ai-inference-platform/.

Malm, Andreas, and Hornborg, Alf. 'The Geology of Mankind? A Critique of the Anthropocene Narrative', *The Anthropocene Review* 1.1 (2014): 62–9.

Mann, Monique and Daly, Angela. '(Big) Data and the North-in-South: Australia's Informational Imperialism and Digital Colonialism', *Television & New Media* 20.4 (2019): 379–95.

Mann, Monique, Mitchell, Peta, Foth, Marcus, and Anastasiu, Irina. '#BlockSidewalk to Barcelona: Technological Sovereignty and the Social Licence to Operate Smart Cities', *Journal of the Association for Information Science and Technology* 71.9 (2020): 1103–15.

Masanet, Eric, Shehabi, Arman, Lei, Nuoa, Smith, Sarah, and Koomey, Jonathan. 'Recalibrating Global Data Center Energy-Use Estimates', *Science* 367.6481 (2020): 984–6.

Massumi, Brian. *99 Theses on the Revaluation of Value: A Postcapitalist Manifesto*, Minneapolis: University of Minnesota Press, 2018.

Mathai, Manu V., Isenhour, Cindy, Stevis, Dimitris, Vergragt, Philip, Bengtsson, Magnus, Lorek, Sylvia, Fogh Mortensen, Lars, et al. 'The Political Economy of (un) Sustainable Production and Consumption: A Multidisciplinary Synthesis for Research and Action', *Resources, Conservation and Recycling* 167 (2021): 105265.

Moore, Jason W. *Anthropocene or Capitalocene?: Nature, History, and the Crisis of Capitalism*. Oakland: Pm Press, 2016.

Morozov, Evgeny. *To Save Everything, Click Here: The Folly of Technological Solutionism*, London: Penguin, 2014.

Muldoon, James. *'Platform Socialism': How to Reclaim our Digital Future from Big Tech*, London: Pluto Press, 2022.

Mytton, David. 'Data Centre Water Consumption', *Npj Clean Water* 4.1 (2021): 1–6.

Neilson, Brett, and Rossiter, Ned. 'Automating Labour and the Spatial Politics of Data Centre Technologies', iIn Mascha Will-Zocholl and Caroline Roth-Ebner (eds) *Topologies of Digital Work*, London: Palgrave Macmillan, Cham, 2021, pp. 77–101.

Niarchos, Nicholas. 'The Dark Side of Congo's Cobalt Rush', *The New Yorker*, 2021. https://www.newyorker.com/magazine/2021/05/31/the-dark-side-of-congos-cobalt-rush.

Noble, Safiya Umoja. *Algorithms of Oppression: How Search Engines Reinforce Racism*. New York: NYU Press, 2018.

Nost, Eric, and Goldstein, Jenny Elaine. 'A Political Ecology of Data', *Environment and Planning E: Nature and Space* (2021): 25148486211043503.

Nost, Eric, and Colven, Emma. 'Earth for AI: A Political Ecology of Data-Driven Climate Initiatives', *Geoforum* 130 (2022): 23–34.

Patel, Raj, and Moore, Jason W. *A History of the World in Seven Cheap Things: A Guide to Capitalism, Nature, and the Future of the Planet*, New York: Verso, 2017.

Patterson, David, Gonzalez, Joseph, Le, Quoc, Liang, Chen, Munguia, Lluis-Miquel, Rothchild, Daniel, So, David, Texier, Maud, and Dean, Jeff. 'Carbon Emissions and Large Neural Network Training', arXiv preprint arXiv:2104.10350, 2021.

Phan, Thao, and Wark, Scott. 'What Personalisation Can Do for You! Or: How to do Racial Discrimination without "Race".' *Culture machine* 20 (2021): 1–29.

Pickren, Graham. 'Geographies of E-Waste: Towards a Political Ecology Approach to E-Waste and Digital Technologies', *Geography Compass* 8.2 (2014): 111–24.

Piketty, Thomas. *Capital in the Twenty-first Century*, Cambrdige: Harvard University Press, 2018.

Ranganathan, Janet, Corbier, Laurent, Bhatia, P., Schmitz, Simon, Gage, Peter, and Oren, Kjell. 'The Greenhouse Gas Protocol: A Corporate Accounting and Reporting Standard (revised edition)', Washington, DC: World Resources Institute and World Business Council for Sustainable Development, 2004.

Riemens, Rianne. 'Decoupling as Rhetorical Strategy in Google's Green Discourse', AoIR Selected Papers of Internet Research, 2021.

Ritchie, Hannah and Roser, Max. *Energy Mix*, 2021, https://ourworldindata.org/energy-mix.

Robbins, Paul. 'Is Less More...or Is More Less? Scaling the Political Ecologies of the Future', *Political Geography* 76 (2020): 102018.

Sadowski, Jathan. 'When Data Is Capital: Datafication, Accumulation, and Extraction', *Big Data & Society* 6.1 (2019): 1-12.

——. 'The Internet of Landlords: Digital Platforms and New Mechanisms of Rentier Capitalism', *Antipode* 52 (2020): 562–80.

Sadowski, Jathan, Viljoen, Salomé, and Whittaker, Meredith. 'Everyone Should Decide How their Digital Data are Used—Not Just Tech Companies', *Nature* 595 (2021): 169–171.

Sanyé-Mengual, Esther, Secchi, Michaela, Corrado, Sara, Beylot, Antoine, and Sala, Serenella. 'Assessing the Decoupling of Economic Growth from Environmental Impacts in the European Union: A Consumption-based Approach', *Journal of Cleaner Production* 236 (2019): 117535.

Schwartz, Roy, Dodge, Jesse, Smith, Noah A., and Etzioni, Oren. 'Green AI', *Communications of the ACM* 63.12 (2020): 54–63.

Seddon, Nathalie, Smith, Alison, Smith, Pete, Key, Isabel, Chausson, Alexandre, Girardin, Cécile, House, Jo, Srivastava, Shilpi, and Turner, Beth. 'Getting the Message Right on Nature-Based Solutions to Climate Change', *Global Change Biology* 27.8 (2021): 1518–46.

Shehabi, Arman, Smith, Sarah J., Masanet, Eric, and Koomey, Jonathan. 'Data Center Growth in the United States: Decoupling the Demand for Services from Electricity Use', *Environmental Research Letters* 13.12 (2018): 124030.

Shehabi, Arman, Smith, Sarah, Sartor, Dale, Brown, Richard, Herrlin, Magnus, Koomey, Jonathan, Masanet, Eric, Horner, Nathaniel, Azevedo, Inês, and Lintner, William. *United States Data Center Energy Usage Report*, U.S. Department of Energy Office of Scientific and Technical Information, 2016, https://www.osti.gov/biblio/1372902/.

Shell. *Artificial Intelligence*, 2021, https://www.shell.com/energy-and-innovation/digitalisation/digital-technologies/shell-ai.html.

Siddik, Md Abu Bakar, Shehabi, Arman, and Marston, Landon. 'The Environmental Footprint of Data Centers in the United States', *Environmental Research Letters* 16.6 (2021): 064017.

Sluis Katarina, and Li, Fei-Fei. *Where Did ImageNet Come From?*, 2019, https://unthinking.photography/articles/where-did-imagenet-come-from.

Srnicek, Nick. *Platform Capitalism*, Cambridge: Polity, 2016.

Starosielski, Nicole. 'Thermocultures of Geological Media', *Cultural Politics* 12.3 (2016): 293–309.

Stiegler, Bernard. *Automatic Society: The Future of Work*, Cambridge: Polity, 2017.

Strubell, Emma, Ananya Ganesh, and Andrew McCallum. 'Energy and Policy Considerations for Deep Learning in Nlp', arXiv preprint arXiv:1906.02243, 2019.

Swinhoe, Dan. 'Microsoft, Amazon, and Google Operate Half the World's 600 Hyperscale Data Centers,', 2021, https://www.datacenterdynamics.com/en/news/microsoft-amazon-and-google-operate-half-the-worlds-600-hyperscale-data-centers/.

Taffel, Sy. 'Hopeful Extinctions? Tesla, Technological Solutionism and the Anthropocene', *Culture Unbound: Journal of Current Cultural Research* 10.2 (2018): 163–84.

——. *Digital Media Ecologies*, New York and London: Bloomsbury, 2019.

——. 'Data and Oil: Metaphor, Materiality and Metabolic Rifts', *New Media & Society* (2021).

——. 'AirPods and the Earth: Digital Technologies, Planned Obsolescence and the Capitalocene', *Environment and Planning E: Nature and Space*, 2022.

Ursin, Frank, Timmermann, Cristian, Orzechowski, Marcin, and Steger, Florian. 'Diagnosing Diabetic Retinopathy with Artificial Intelligence: What Information Should Be Included to Ensure Ethical Informed Consent?' [In English]. Original Research. *Frontiers in Medicine* 8.1108 (2021). 1–6.

U.S. Energy Information Administration. *What is U.S. Electricity Generation by Energy Source?*, June 2022, https://www.eia.gov/tools/faqs/faq.php?id=427&t=3.

van Wynsberghe, Aimee. 'Sustainable AI: AI for Sustainability and the Sustainability of AI', *AI and Ethics* (2021): 1–6.

Vaughan, Naomi E., and Gough, Clair. 'Expert Assessment Concludes Negative Emissions Scenarios May Not Deliver', *Environmental Research Letters* 11.9 (2016): 095003.

Vonk, Lisa. 'Paying Attention to Waste: Apple's Circular Economy', *Continuum* 32.6 (2018): 745–57.

Vopson, Melvin M. 'The Information Catastrophe', *AIP Advances* 10.8 (2020): 085014.

Wagner, Ben. 'Ethics as an Escape from Regulation. From 'Ethics-Washing' to Ethics-Shopping?' in *Being Profiled*, Amsterdam: Amsterdam University Press, 2018, pp. 84–9.

Walker, Peter A. 'Political Ecology: Where is the Politics?.' *Progress in Human geography* 31.3 (2007): 363–69.

Wiedmann, Thomas O., Schandl, Heinz, Lenzen, Manfred, Moran, Daniel, Suh, Sangwon, West, James, and Kanemoto, Keiichiro. 'The Material Footprint of Nations', proceedings of the National Academy of Sciences 112.20 (2015): 6271–6.

Zhang, John, and Hoshino, Kazunori. *Molecular Sensors and Nanodevices* 2nd edition. Cambridge: Academic Press, 2019.

EVERYDAY AI ETHICS: FROM THE GLOBAL TO LOCAL THROUGH FACIAL RECOGNITION

ANGELA DALY

Introduction

Prominent discussions on AI ethics frameworks and other initiatives take place at the international or national level, and especially those from the human rights approach may claim a universal or global application and significance.[1] Outside of prominent countries such as those in North America, Europe, and East Asia,[2] national—and within even the 'prominent countries', subnational (e.g. devolved regional or provincial administrations), and local level— discussions and activities around AI ethics have received less attention and instead are often overlooked in favor of supposedly more impactful, 'higher-level' discussions. However, this is a problem, as these higher-level discussions do not make much sense unless we have an understanding of how AI is encountered, negotiated, and contested on local levels.[3]

Even within such prominent countries and regions, more local AI ethics discussions and practices may be overlooked or deemed less relevant and impactful for researchers, and possibly inconvenient for policy makers and corporations. Looking at the U.K. context where I am now based and which this chapter relates to, 'impact' in academia means 'the demonstrable contribution that excellent research makes to society and the economy.'[4] Research impact policy in the U.K. has led to research critical of government policy receiving lower scores than other kinds of policy-related research, and has been perceived by some academics 'to bias research funding towards the interests of political ideology and big business.'[5] The apparent national and international importance of certain AI ethics activities seem also to have attracted research and other forms of funding, at least partly on this presumably 'impactful' basis and the ensuing 'economy of virtue' whereby AI ethics is funded by Big Tech and produces output for Big Tech's consumption.[6]

Indeed, while I hold research projects funded by UK Research and Innovation (UKRI) on automation and AI topics, I am writing this paper on an 'unfunded' basis as it does not fit with

---

1   Pak-Hang Wong, 'Cultural Differences as Excuses? Human Rights and Cultural Values in Global Ethics and Governance of AI', *Philosophy and Technology* 33 (2020): 705–715.
2   Seán ÓhÉigeartaigh, Jess Whittlestone, Yang Liu, Yi Zeng and Zhe Liu, 'Overcoming Barriers to Cross-cultural Cooperation in AI Ethics and Governance', *Philosophy and Technology* 33 (2020): 571–593.
3   I thank Xaroula Kerasidou for this point.
4   UKRI Economic and Social Research Council, 'Defining Impact', https://www.ukri.org/councils/esrc/impact-toolkit-for-economic-and-social-sciences/defining-impact/.
5   Jennifer Chubb and Mark Reed, 'The Politics of Research Impact: Academic Perceptions of the Implications for Research Funding, Motivation and Quality', *British Politics* 13 (2018): 302.
6   Thao Phan, Jake Goldenfein, Monique Mann and Declan Kuch, 'Economies of Virtue: The Circulation of 'Ethics' in Big Tech', *Science as Culture* 31.1 (2022): 121–35.

the scope of these other projects. The UKRI is the U.K.'s public research funding body, but has a strong emphasis on 'commercialisation' guided by policies which lead to, as Finn puts it, 'a commodification of domestic UK innovation.'[7] Other work I've done on facial recognition and Scotland has also been during my non externally-funded research time allocated by my university employer and during my own time outside of official working hours. I believe this says something about competitive funding priorities in academic research that critical work on facial recognition in a more localized context of Scotland is not as attractive as research aiming to facilitate uses of AI and automation in health and manufacturing in the U.K. (for which I have received funding). This insight adds to those identified by other authors in this collection such as corporate priorities, government priorities and gender (and likely other) imbalances in who receives funding.[8] However, this contribution also bears out Edwards' view that unfunded research is 'a space in which to confront and address the tensions generated by forms of academic identity pulling in different directions.'[9] In my case, this meant giving me the opportunity to make 'a creative and intellectually-driven contribution to knowledge'[10] and resist my own neoliberal success in AI grant generation!

This paper also looks critically at AI ethics in the U.K. As mentioned above, critiques of U.K. government policy may score lower in research impact compared to other policy-oriented research. The U.K. government has invested heavily in AI, including in governance and policy aspects, supporting directly or indirectly a constellation of actors and initiatives such as the Alan Turing Institute, the Digital Catapult, and the Centre for Data Ethics and Innovation. The Ada Lovelace Institute, while ostensibly independent, was established 'in collaboration' with a number of U.K. government-funded bodies, including the Alan Turing Institute, and has received funding from UKRI. The U.K. has been active as a nation-state in global AI governance discussions as well as domestically with its own National AI Strategy, and more recently a policy paper outlining its 'pro-innovation approach to regulating AI,' which eschews legally binding norms in the process.[11] The U.K.'s current AI approach is underpinning by a number of themes including a prioritising of 'innovation' and a cleavage with the European Union's approach to data protection, moving closer to that of the U.S., both related to the U.K.'s post-Brexit geopolitical and economic stance.[12] Ossewaarde and Gulenc find the British AI approach to be digitally utopian, technologically solutionist and leveraging British imperialism and leadership in the Industrial Revolution to project

---

7   Mike Finn, *British Universities in the Brexit Moment: Political, Economic and Cultural Implications*, Bingley: Emerald Publishing, 2018, p. 97.
8   See Cath & Keyes, Pink, & Richardson in this collection.
9   Rosalind Edwards, 'Why do Academics do Unfunded Research? Resistance, Compliance and Identity in the UK Neo-liberal University', *Studies in Higher Education*, 47.4 (2022): 912.
10   Edwards, 'Why do academics do unfunded research?', 912.
11   U.K. Government, 'National AI Strategy', 21 September 2021, https://www.gov.uk/government/publications/national-ai-strategy; U.K. Government, 'Establishing a pro-innovation approach to regulating AI', 20 July 2022, https://www.gov.uk/government/publications/establishing-a-pro-innovation-approach-to-regulating-ai.
12   Emre Kazim, Denise Almeida, Nigel Kingsman, Charles Kerrigan, Adriano Koshiyama, Elizabeth Lomas and Airlie Hilliard, 'Innovation and Opportunity: Review of the UK's National AI Strategy', *Discover Artificial Intelligence* 1.14 (2021): 1–10.

the U.K. as a neo-imperial post-Brexit 'world leader' in AI in the future, while glossing over the potentially de-democratizing 'dark side' of AI.[13]

Furthermore, Ossewaarde and Gulenc identify a strong technocratic character to the U.K.'s AI policy.[14] The very people involved in AI governance and ethics discussions and formulating any principles or rules are often 'technically oriented' experts, far removed from ordinary people and their experiences, therefore rendering AI governance a hitherto 'elitist project.'[15] AI ethics are also 'primarily shaped by men,' exhibit a more general 'lack of diversity,'[16] and are usually 'framed by means of Western values, contexts, and concerns.'[17]

I want to turn attention away from this somewhat elitist affair of devising high level (in various senses) AI principles to looking more at localized, everyday encounters with AI technologies and AI ethics which are manifesting in different parts of the world in response to actual problems with AI. I do this through the lens of a particular application of AI, in the form of facial recognition cameras and software, especially when used by law enforcement. This is a concrete example of localized engagements with AI and the formation of resistance which have led to forms of localized governance of AI in some places including the U.K.. Despite the lofty ideals and potential for large scale impact that more global initiatives on AI ethics and governance promise, and despite a more global approach probably being more appropriate for a globalized, transnational technology such as AI and applications including facial recognition, it is the everyday, localized encounter with AI technologies and AI ethics I consider in this chapter. The local and everyday have been largely overlooked and neglected by much of the AI ethics literature and activity to date, possibly due to the less 'impactful' perception of such encounters. Yet without an understanding of these local encounters, high-level AI ethics remain abstract, adrift, and often apolitical.

In any event, these everyday encounters are impactful in other ways when individuals and communities negotiate and contest certain AI uses in ways that may lead to change as policymakers and the law may respond to their wishes. This is clearly impactful in localities where it takes place but lacks acknowledgement and and may contrast with claims, whether implicit or explicit, to universality that conventional high-level AI ethics initiatives contain, and is incentivized by impact in academic research.[18] In the case of facial recognition at least, and perhaps more broadly, more AI 'ethical' attention given to this application in its local and everyday encounters can highlight or serve forms of activism, resistance, or critique, whereas ethical attention that aims at the more abstracted, higher or 'universal' level is frequently more in service of forces of capital and political power.[19]

13   Marinus Ossewaarde and Erdener Gulenc, 'National Varieties of Artificial Intelligence Discourses: Myth, Utopianism, and Solutionism in West European Policy Expectations', *Computer* 53.11 (2020): 53–61.
14   Ossewaarde and Gulenc, 'National Varieties of Artificial Intelligence Discourses'.
15   Thilo Hagendorff, 'Blind Spots in AI ethics', *AI Ethics* (2021).
16   Thilo Hagendorff, 'The Ethics of AI Ethics: An Evaluation of Guidelines', *Minds & Machines* 30 (2020), 99–120, 105.
17   Hagendorff, 'Blind Spots in AI ethics'.
18   I thank Jake Goldenfein for this point.
19   I thank Jake Goldenfein for this point.

I start by considering the ways in which AI is an everyday technology already. I concentrate on facial recognition as an example of everyday AI that has invoked contestations over its use, and in some places resulted in curbs on it, with a particular focus on the U.K. Overall, this shows that a key point of encounter with AI, and thus a key site of ethical, legal, and political interrogation, is and must be the point at which individuals and communities engage with, and in some cases such as facial recognition, contest AI.[20] Moving beyond the technocratic high level AI ethics norm formation, a consideration of these everyday encounters, including protest, social movements, and legal mobilization through litigation must be part of the AI ethics discussion, especially when, as in the case of the U.K., the everyday paints a different picture to the imaginaries of the U.K.'s high level AI strategies and policies.

AI as an Everyday Technology

AI is becoming an everyday technology throughout the world, although it is often not considered in this way. The idea of the everyday in AI, and people's everyday practices and experiences of AI, has been considered by some authors, including Burgess, Mitchell, and Highfield, who have aimed to:

> get beyond the current hype and anxieties around self-driving cars, algorithms and robotics, and to achieve a more precise and grounded understanding of exactly what might be meant by automation, how and with what effects it is becoming entangled with everyday life and how investigating these relationships also helps us understanding processes of media change in society more broadly.[21]

Further, Pink et al. recognize:

> [d]iscussion of these automated technologies is often shrouded with narratives which highlight extreme and spectacular examples, rather than the ordinary mundane realities that characterise the overwhelming majority of people's actual encounters with them.[22]

As AI is penetrating our everyday lives, albeit in different ways and different contexts, this focus on the quotidian departs from much of the literature and other discussions on AI,[23] which concentrates on the more global or abstracted levels—and also often occurs at a more elite level, as identified by Hagendorff above. It is the everyday where encounters with AI occur, even if that everyday encounter may look different in different scenarios.

However, it is also the everyday where people can fight back against technologies, including AI and automation, despite the passivity often implied by debate and literature. For Pink et al:

20 I thank Jake Goldenfein for this point.
21 Jean Burgess, Peta Mitchell and Tim Highfield, 'Automating the Digital Everyday: An Introduction', *Media International Australia*, 166.1 (2018): 6-10, 6.
22 Pink, Ruckenstein, Berg and Lupton, 'Everyday Automation: Setting a Research Agenda'.
23 See for example, Anna Jobin, Marcello Ienca and Effy Vayena, 'The Global Landscape of AI Ethics Guidelines', *Nature Machine Intelligence* 1 (2019): 389–99.

> The ordinary citizen is represented as passively in thrall to manipulation and exploitation of the proponents of the digital data economy. Yet, the automation logic is not the same everywhere—nor does it operate with the same kind of intensity on every occasion of use or every geographical location. People can and do resist[...][24]

As well as the encounter with AI for many if not most people being primarily on this everyday, localized level, much of the AI governance with 'bite' is also happening at this level, and, I argue, it has been overlooked by much of the AI debates to date. This governance can be shaped by individuals and communities encountering AI, negotiating it and in some cases resisting it, as they do with other data-driven surveillance technologies.[25] It is this which I turn to later, by looking at how AI ethics is playing out at a grounded, local level, and how this relates, or not, to the 'higher-level' discussions and formulations of AI ethics, through the lens of facial recognition. First, I consider what an everyday law and ethics of AI means by engaging with ideas of the everyday from legal studies.

Turning from AI Ethics to Law to the Everyday

Considerations of law- and norm-making need to be brought into this idea of everyday AI, as in some cases everyday negotiations and contestations of norms address AI ethics in more impactful or satisfactory ways than the higher level, abstracted AI ethics activities we have seen in recent years.

The turn to such high-level ethics initiatives in AI has been criticized by Wagner as 'ethics washing' since the ethics statements and initiatives usually lack legal or other forms of enforceability and accountability in their implementation.[26] So, instead of being a complement for binding rights and responsibilities, they are a substitute for them. It is important to note that ethics is used in a specific way in the context of AI governance—i.e., to promote lists of non-binding norms often by nation-states and large corporations—and critiques of ethics relate to that specific situation and use, but ethics has a broader meaning since law and other normative schemes are also manifestations of applied ethics.[27]

Yet legal enforceability of AI norms is not necessarily sufficient or appropriate alone to address issues pertaining to the unenforceability of AI ethics principles, since the content of those norms as well as their enforceability needs to be 'good.'[28] The Trump Administration in the U.S.

---

24   Pink, Ruckenstein, Berg and Lupton, 'Everyday Automation: Setting a Research Agenda', 8.
25   Alex Jiahong Lu, 'Toward Everyday Negotiation and Resistance Under Data-Driven Surveillance', *Interactions* 29.2 (2022).
26   Ben Wagner, 'Ethics as an Escape from Regulation: From 'Ethics-Washing' to Ethics-Shopping?', in Emre Bayamlioglu, Irina Baraliuc, Liisa Janssens and Mireille Hildebrandt (eds) *Being Profiled: Cogitas Ergo Sum: 10 Years of Profiling the European Citizen*, Amsterdam: Amsterdam University Press, 2018, pp. 84–9.
27   Elettra Bietti, 'From Ethics Washing to Ethics Bashing: A View on Tech Ethics from Within Moral Philosophy', Proceedings of ACM FAT* Conference, 2020, https://ssrn.com/abstract=3513182.
28   Angela Daly, S. Kate Devitt and Monique Mann, 'AI Ethics Needs Good Data', in Pieter Verdegem (ed) *AI for Everyone? Critical Perspectives*, London: University of Westminster Press, 2021.

adopted legally binding Executive Orders on AI, which mandated a deregulatory approach to the technology, an outcome with which critics of non-binding AI ethics are unlikely to seek or be satisfied.[29] In any event, there are few legally enforceable AI ethics/governance initiatives, and those that do exist are not at the international level, but regional or national level instead.

At the international level, UNESCO member states recently adopted its Recommendation on the Ethics of Artificial Intelligence. This is significant since it is the first global standard on the topic, however it is not binding on signatory states, and it is merely 'recommended' that member states implement it on a 'voluntary basis' in their respective domestic jurisdictions.[30] Much attention so far has been paid to efforts in the European Union (E.U.) to formulate its own legislation on AI, the E.U. AI Act, which is currently under discussion at the time of writing,[31] and is notable as the first major attempt by a leading global jurisdiction to regulate AI in a binding way, albeit one as it currently stands that will not outlaw completely law enforcement use of facial recognition.[32]

Here, though, I want to look at more everyday understandings, negotiations, and resistance of AI ethics norms and law, at the local or microcosmic rather than national or international level. In doing this, I seek to connect with scholarship on 'everyday law' or 'legal socialisation' in how people experience, form and respect (legal) norms,[33] or as Sarat and Kearns put it, 'how law's consumers produce their own law and, in so doing, transform and reproduce state law.'[34] This is because these understandings, negotiations, and resistances to AI uses—especially by the state and corporations—emanating from individuals and communities give us a sense of what AI uses people notice and what they find acceptable/unacceptable, which may in turn influence state law and corporate practices. Facial recognition technology is notable as its use has provoked physical protests in various parts of the world, in different contexts, and its use has formed the basis of litigation and policy change in the U.K.

---

29   Angela Daly, Thilo Hagendorff, Li Hui, Monique Mann, Vidushi Marda, Ben Wagner and Wayne Wei Wang, 'AI, Governance and Ethics: Global Perspectives' in Hans Micklitz, Oreste Pollicino, Amnon Reichman, Andrea Simoncini, Giovanni Sartor and Giovanni De Gregorio (eds) *Constitutional Challenges in the Algorithmic Society*, Cambridge: Cambridge University Press, 2022.
30   UNESCO, 'UNESCO member states adopt the first ever global agreement on the Ethics of Artificial Intelligence', 25 November 2021, *https://en.unesco.org/news/unesco-member-states-adopt-first-ever-global-agreement-ethics-artificial-intelligence*.
31   See for example, Michael Veale and Frederik Zuiderveen Borgesius, 'Demystifying the Draft EU Artificial Intelligence Act—Analysing the Good, the Bad, and the Unclear Elements of the Proposed Approach', *Computer Law Review International* 22.4 (2021): 97–112.
32   Leigh McGowran, 'The Issues with the EU's Draft Regulation on Facial Recognition AI', *Silicon Republic*, 17 May 2022, https://www.siliconrepublic.com/enterprise/the-issues-with-the-eus-draft-regulation-on-facial-recognition-ai.
33   See for example, Patricia Ewick and Susan Silbey, *The Common Place of Law: Stories from Everyday Life,* Chicago: University of Chicago Press, 1998; Richard Moule, George Burruss, Faith Gifford, Megan Parry and Bryanna Fox, 'Legal Socialization and Subcultural Norms: Examining Linkages Between Perceptions of Procedural Justice, Legal Cynicism, and the Code of the Street', *Journal of Criminal Justice* 61 (2019): 26–39.
34   Austin Sarat and Thomas Kearns (eds) *Law in Everyday Life*. Ann Arbor: University of Michigan Press, 1995, p. 9.

On this point, I also want to link this discussion of everyday law to how law interacts with social movements and protest, an area understudied both by social movement scholars and legal scholars.[35] This is significant for facial recognition as protest and campaigning have built up pressure, resulting in prohibitions or moratoriums on the practice, and contested its use through litigation. This also connects with the work done on 'data activism' by Milan and others, 'which critically engages with the manifold impact of data on social life' and includes 'for instance, socio-technical practices that provide counter-hegemonic responses to the discrimination, social exclusion and privacy infringement that go hand in hand with big data'.[36] Data activism has a particular emphasis on the 'grassroots contentious processes [vis-à-vis datafication] expressed by laypersons, nongovernmental organizations and social movement networks alike.'[37] Opposition to facial recognition both in social movement responses and legislation and policy responses constitute what Kazansky terms 'resistance to data-driven surveillance.'[38] Yet protest, social movements, and law/policy change have rarely been viewed in concert in the literature in this area on new technologies, especially AI.

I introduce these concepts as a backdrop for my inquiry into facial recognition as an everyday AI technology creeping into the lives of people around the world, and as a site of social movement data activist contestations that interact with the law and ethics of AI. More theoretical and empirical work is warranted on AI, activism, and ethics (including law) to give a deeper understanding, especially from the quotidian perspective of how normal, everyday people encounter and engage with these issues. Here I seek to introduce these topics, but more work could be done directly e.g. with those who influence, negotiate and in particular resist facial recognition from everyday perspectives and who are not typically involved in the 'higher level' AI ethics initiatives and norm forming.

Everyday AI law, ethics and protest is already a practical reality, as we see through examples such as demonstrations in England against the Department of Education about unfair outcomes in school leaving results in 2020 when they were determined by an algorithm (as traditional exams were cancelled due to the COVID-19 pandemic), at which young people chanted and held up placards saying 'Fuck the Algorithm'. Kaun considers this as an example of Willim's 'mundanization' of digital technologies i.e., 'developing everyday understandings of complex technologies that have implications for our everyday lives'.[39] The use of algorithms

---

35   Michael McCann, 'Law and Social Movements: Contemporary Perspectives', *Annual Review of Law and Social Science* 2.1 (2006): 17–38.

36   Becky Kazansky, Guillen Torres, Lonneke van der Velden, Kersti Wissenbach, and Stefania Milan, 'Data for the Social Good: Towards a Data-Activist Research Agenda', in Angela Daly, S. Kate Devitt and Monique Mann (eds), *Good Data*, Amsterdam: Institute of Network Cultures, 2019, 246.

37   Davide Beraldo and Stefania Milan, 'From Data Politics to the Contentious Politics of Data', *Big Data & Society'* 6.2 (2019): 2.

38   Becky Kazansky, '"It Depends on your Threat Model": The Anticipatory Dimensions of Resistance to Data-driven Surveillance', *Big Data & Society* 8.1 (2021): 1. See also Lu, 'Toward Everyday Negotiation and Resistance Under Data-Driven Surveillance'.

39   Anne Kaun, 'Suing the Algorithm: The Mundanization of Automated Decision-making in Public Services Through Litigation*', Information, Communication & Society* (2021); Robert Willim, 'Imperfect imaginaries: Digitisation, mundanisation, and the ungraspable' in Gertraud Koch (ed), *Digitisation: Theories and Concepts for Empirical Cultural Research*, Abingdon: Routledge, 2017.

in the public sector has provoked broader controversies, such as the RoboDebt welfare surveillance scandal in Australia.[40] Further examples of everyday AI ethics be found during the 2020-2021 Indian farmers' protests where farmers understood the connections between plans for conglomerate Jio (which among many other business activities, operates a mobile network) to enter the agri-tech sector and use AI-powered trading platforms for farmers to consolidate its power, and many such farmers boycotted the operator by transferring their mobile service to a competitor.[41]

These examples demonstrate that contestations over AI already occur in people's everyday lives, and provoke localized action, including in the form of protest, which can lead to law and policy change. These everyday encounters with AI and its politics bring AI ethics (back) from distant policymakers and political and corporate elites to individuals and communities, recognizing their/our agency in negotiating and resisting technology applications. These contestations and resistances can address the enforceability gap critiqued by Wagner's 'ethics washing' by provoking action and change to curb uses of AI on a grounded, local level, compared to the lofty and at times elitist AI ethics initiatives, which often lack 'bite' and tend not to prohibit or severely restrict certain AI uses and applications.

Facial Recognition as Everyday AI

Here I want to focus on the application of AI in the form of facial recognition, and the everyday encounters people have had with it in different parts of the world that in some cases have given rise to everyday AI law and ethics. I concentrate on the U.K. experience of facial recognition, as it is the geographical location with which I am most familiar, and one in which we have experienced protest, policy, and legal events relating to everyday facial recognition use, as well as differing approaches in different parts of the U.K. to facial recognition use, which can be juxtaposed with the 'pro-innovation' and neo-imperialist high-level U.K. AI policy.

Facial recognition is a technology which identifies an individual from a digital image, usually by comparing the features of that person's face to stored biometric images of faces in a database. Facial recognition can be 'live' when this image capture and analysis is done in real time, such as by a 'smart' CCTV camera in a public place, using AI. Controversies have surrounded facial recognition for its inaccuracies, especially in identifying women compared to men and people of color compared to white people, with 'darker-skinned females the most misclassified group.'[42] Furthermore, the conditions in which facial recognition technologies are being researched, developed, and trialed are proving controversial: such as Chinese

---

40   Monique Mann, 'Social (In)security and Social (In)justice: Automation in the Australian Welfare System' in *Artificial Intelligence: Human Rights, Social Justice and Development: Global Information Society Watch 2019 Report*, 2019, pp. 68–72.

41   Tulsi Parida and Aparna Ashok, 'Consolidating Power in the Name of Progress: Techno-solutionism and Farmer Protests in India' in Frederike Kaltheuner (ed), *Fake AI*, Manchester: Meatspace Press, 2021, pp. 161–9.

42   Joy Buolamwini and Timnit Gebru, 'Gender Shades: Intersectional Accuracy Disparities in Commercial Gender Classification' in Proceedings of the 1st Conference on Fairness, Accountability and Transparency, PMLR 81, 2018, 1.

facial recognition products used against Uyghurs and other ethnic minorities in Xinjiang/ East Turkestan;[43] and Clearview AI in the west which has scraped photos from social media without users' knowledge or permission, and whose product is used by law enforcement in the U.S. and possibly Europe.[44] Recently, these scraping processes by Clearview have attracted data protection infringement decisions and fines in the E.U., U.K., and Australia.[45]

Facial recognition has been implemented in a wide variety of social, political, and economic contexts throughout the world, in both authoritarian regimes and (supposed) liberal democracies. Accordingly, it is becoming an everyday AI technology, encountered by the general public as they go about their business, especially in public places. Importantly, these everyday encounters with facial recognition have led to processes of negotiation and outright resistance in some cases from the general public. Facial recognition has been an object for social movement mobilizations, either specifically against the use of this surveillance technology, or as part of broader protests. Facial recognition has also seen the mobilisation of everyday law against it, and led to questions as to how state law addresses it.

Facial recognition and CCTV cameras have been the site of protest and actual destruction in various locations globally. During protests in Iran in 2019 against government increases to petrol prices,[46] footage emerged of protestors disabling and destroying CCTV cameras in different locations in the country, including Shiraz and Tehran.[47] In more recent protests in the Khuzestan province in 2021, there is also footage which appears to show similar attacks on CCTV cameras.[48] There is an extensive surveillance infrastructure in Iran and in particular since the 2019 protests, after which, according to Akbari, 'CCTV cameras became compulsory in cafes, universities, and even kindergartens. Traffic control cameras mushroomed in big cities,' with 'the government actively us[ing] CCTV/traffic cameras' footage in tackling political dissent.'[49]

Also in 2019, suspected facial recognition CCTV cameras were the target of protestors against the extradition bill and national security law in Hong Kong, where a 'lack of trust

43   Angela Daly, 'Algorithmic Oppression with Chinese Characteristics: AI Against Xinjiang's Uyghurs' in *Artificial Intelligence: Human Rights, Social Justice and Development: Global Information Society Watch 2019 Report,* 2019, pp. 108–12.
44   Isadora Neroni Rezende, 'Facial Recognition in Police Hands: Assessing the 'Clearview case' from a European Perspective', *New Journal of European Criminal Law* 11.3 (2020): 375–89.
45   Melissa Heikkilä, 'The Walls are Closing in on Clearview AI', *MIT Technology Review*, 24 May 2022, https://www.technologyreview.com/2022/05/24/1052653/clearview-ai-data-privacy-uk/.
46   Afshin Shahi and Ehsan Abdoh-Tabrizi, 'Iran's 2019–2020 Demonstrations: The Changing Dynamics of Political Protests in Iran', *Asian Affairs* 51.1 (2020): 1–41.
47   See for example, @DrParchizadeh, 'Protesters in Tehran sabotage the police CCTV so that they can't be identified, arrested and killed by the regime. #IranProtests', Twitter post, 16 November 2019, 4:25PM, https://twitter.com/DrParchizadeh/status/1195739605460496385.
48   @javidirani30, 'Last night, Monday, July 19th, Ahwazi youths in Alavi alley disabled CCTV cameras #Khuzestan #IranProtests', Twitter post, 20 July 2021, 8:45AM, https://twitter.com/javidirani30/status/1417390100720279569.
49   Azadeh Akbari, 'The Threat of Automating Control: Surveillance of Women's Clothing in Iran', in Aleš Završnik and Vasja Badalič (eds) *Automating Crime Prevention, Surveillance, and Military Operations*, Cham: Springer, 2021, 186.

in technology persists'.[50] Not only did were 'face masks, umbrellas and lasers ... routinely used by demonstrators to blind CCTV cameras ... thereby render[ing] facial recognition ineffective',[51] protestors 'also took down new 'smart' lampposts, where their full technological capabilities have not been disclosed, installed by the Government during a protest against surveillance and increasing prevalence of facial recognition technologies.[52]

Protestors not only took down the lampposts but also 'dissected' them by opening up their 'black boxes' to see exactly what components and equipment was inside, including whether facial recognition equipment was contained within, as the Hong Kong government had claimed that the lampposts merely monitored air quality and traffic.[53] Some smart lampposts did have cameras inside them and while it seems that these cameras did not have facial recognition capacity, independent experts considered that it would not be difficult to modify the cameras to include such capabilities.[54] In any event, the Hong Kong authorities decided not to activate certain features of the smart lampposts due to privacy concerns.

In both the Iranian and Hong Kong examples, the possibility or reality of facial recognition technologies in public places has prompted protests and mobilizations, which can be conceptualized as part of broader movements responding to material circumstances and against state power. However, significant in both movements is the popular suspicion and physical targeting of (possible) facial recognition CCTV, which demonstrate forms of citizen resistance against aspects of the digital data (political) economy. In the case of Hong Kong, this contributed to the Hong Kong authorities deciding not to implement certain aspects of the smart lampposts, which in the context of the National Security Law was a notable and rare positive response to the protestors' concerns, and also demonstrates government responsiveness to citizen concerns in the general context of top-down smart city initiatives such as that of Hong Kong.[55]

Facial Recognition, Everyday AI Law and Ethics in the U.K.

Facial recognition as everyday AI, and contestations around it, have been prominent in the U.K., and mobilization against facial recognition has resulted in litigation and policy change, and divergence between the approaches in different parts of the U.K. Live facial recognition technology has been used in different parts of the U.K. to police public places, to mounting levels of controversy and legal challenge. For these reasons, I consider it an interesting case

50   Janis Wong, 'Protests Decentralised: How Technology Enabled Civil Disobedience by Hong Kong Anti-
      extradition Bill Protesters', *LawArXiv*, 2020, https://osf.io/preprints/lawarxiv/efvwn/.
51   Manoj Kewalramani and Rohan Seth, 'Networked Protests & State Responses: The Case of Hong Kong
      2019–2020', Takshashila Discussion Document 2020-03, 2020, https://ssrn.com/abstract=3580591.
52   Wong, 'Protests Decentralised', 6.
53   'Hong Kong: Anti-surveillance Protestors Tear Down 'Smart' Lamp-post', *Guardian*, 26 August 2019,
      https://www.theguardian.com/world/video/2019/aug/26/hong-kong-anti-surveillance-protesters-tear-
      down-smart-lamp-post-video.
54   Sean Gleeson, 'How Smart are Hong Kong's Lampposts?', *AFP Fact Check*, 4 September 2019, https://
      factcheck.afp.com/how-smart-are-hong-kongs-lampposts.
55   Kevin Leung and H.Y. Lee, 'Implementing the Smart City: Who Has a Say? Some Insights from Hong
      Kong', *International Journal of Urban Sciences*, 2021, 1–25.

study of everyday AI ethics (and law), and how activities from individuals and communities at a more localized level in encountering, negotiating and resisting AI can be impactful for governing AI more generally. Furthermore, the differences in approach to facial recognition within the U.K. also demonstrate the importance of looking at the local level as well as the national, continental, and international. As mentioned above, the U.K. has a pro-innovation techno-solutionist approach to AI at the 'high' level, but the 'dark side' of AI and democratic contestations around it are only clear if we look at these more localized encounters between facial recognition and the general public. Contestations around facial recognition resulting in law and policy change can also be seen in the U.S., where some municipalities have prohibited police use of facial recognition, including San Francisco, which was the first to do so.[56] Two states, Virginia and Vermont, have also banned police use of facial recognition throughout their territory.[57] Local-level mobilization against problematic uses of AI such as live facial recognition can lead to prohibitions, and in a snowballing effect can circulate to inspire prohibitions elsewhere, forming bottom-up and more critical norms around AI in distinction to the top-down but often toothless AI ethics initiatives.

There is a recent history of proposals to use and actual uses of facial recognition technology, especially by the police and law enforcement, in controversial contexts within the U.K., even in Scotland, which more recently introduced a moratorium on these uses. For example, the Scottish Professional Football League (SPFL) intended to introduce facial recognition technology in Scottish (soccer) football stadiums as far back as 2016, in a context of heightened surveillance of football fans using cameras and worsening relationships between fans and the police.[58] Various supporters' groups spoke out against the plans, including by unveiling anti-facial recognition banners at matches.[59] Police Scotland also signalled that they wanted to use live facial recognition in their broader activities, not just vis-à-vis football fans, and Glasgow, Scotland's largest city, bought facial recognition–enabled cameras for the city center in 2015, but these have not been used due to privacy and human rights concerns.[60] In both cases, pressure and concern from those against whom the technology would be used caused public authorities to reconsider and refrain from using facial recognition, although in the latter case this also involves a waste of public money in buying technology that has never been used. This is ironic given the ways in which the police have been encouraged to turn to private tech providers such as facial

56   Dave Lee, 'San Francisco is First US City to Ban Facial Recognition', *BBC*, 15 May 2019, https://www. bbc.co.uk/news/technology-48276660.

57   Todd Feathers, 'Facial Recognition Is Racist. Why Aren't More Cities Banning It?', *Vice*, 25 May 2021, https://www.vice.com/en/article/4avx3m/facial-recognition-is-racist-why-arent-more-cities-banning-it.

58   Niall Hamilton-Smith, Maureen McBride and Colin Atkinson, 'Lights, Camera, Provocation? Exploring Experiences of Surveillance in the Policing of Scottish Football', *Policing and Society* 31.2 (2021): 179–94.

59   Graham Ruthven, 'The Criminalization of Scottish Soccer Fans', *Vice*, 23 February 2016, https://www. vice.com/en/article/9apyad/the-criminalization-of-scottish-soccer-fans.

60   Marcello Mega, 'Cops Fear Gangsters are Evading Law as Glasgow's Facial Recognition Cameras Remain Mothballed', *Daily Record*, 11 August 2020, https://www.dailyrecord.co.uk/news/scottish-news/scots-cops-fear-gangsters-evading-22499468.

recognition providers as a supposed cost-cutting exercise in the context of austerity and privatization.[61]

During 2020, the Scottish Parliament's Justice Sub-Committee considered police use of facial recognition technology. A consultation process was held to which I along with various other academics, and civil society groups contributed, most of us contesting the use of facial recognition by police, and pointing to discriminatory aspects of it and prohibitions in other places especially US cities. The Committee concluded that there was 'no justifiable basis for Police Scotland to invest in this technology', principally due to the gender and racial discrimination the technology implicates.[62] Since then, there has been a moratorium on the use of live facial recognition technology by police in Scotland.

This contrasts with the approach taken in England and Wales - which are the same jurisdiction, Scotland and Northern Ireland each being the other two jurisdictions which make up the U.K.. According to Big Brother Watch:

> Police forces in the U.K. have rolled out automatic facial recognition at a pace unlike any other democratic nation in the world. Leicestershire Police, South Wales Police and the Metropolitan Police have deployed this technology at shopping centres, festivals, sports events, concerts, community events – and even a peaceful demonstration. One police force even used the surveillance tool to keep innocent people with mental health issues away from a public event.[63]

In London, the Metropolitan Police have used facial recognition at events and in areas with large Black and Minority Ethnic (BAME) populations, such as in Stratford, East London, and at the Notting Hill Carnival in 2016 and 2017, despite the inaccuracies facial recognition produces for Black people. This is also in spite of the already strained relationship between the Met Police and Black communities.[64] Specific surveillance and data-gathering activities have impacted Black communities disproportionately, including the gathering of data for the Met Police's controversial 'Gangs Matrix' database on individuals suspected of gang activity, a majority of whom were Black.[65] The U.K. data protection authority, the Information Commissioner's Office (ICO), found that the matrix was not compliant with data protection law, with the Met Police ordered not to destroy it but to bring it in line with these norms.

---

61   Keren Weitzberg, 'A Very British Problem: The Evolution of Britain's Militarised Policing Industrial Complex', Report for Campaign Against the Arms Trade and Netpol, 2022, https://caat.org.uk/app/uploads/2022/08/A-Very-British-Problem-WEB.pdf.
62   Scottish Parliament Justice Sub-Committee on Policing, 'Facial Recognition: How Policing in Scotland Makes Use of This Technology', SP Paper 678, 1st Report (Session 5), 2020, https://sp-bpr-en-prod-cdnep.azureedge.net/published/JSP/2020/2/11/Facial-recognition--how-policing-in-Scotland-makes-use-of-this-technology/JSPS0520R01.pdf.
63   Big Brother Watch, 'Face Off: The Lawless Growth of Facial Recognition in UK Policing', 2018, http://bigbrotherwatch.org.uk/wp-content/uploads/2018/05/Face-Off-final-digital-1.pdf.
64   See for example, Lisa Long and Remi Joseph-Salisbury, 'Black Mixed-race Men's Perceptions and Experiences of the Police', *Ethnic and Racial Studies* 42.2 (2019): 198–215.
65   Jasbinder Nijjar, 'Police–school Partnerships and the War on Black Youth', *Critical Social Policy* 41.3 (2021): 491–501.

The matrix remains controversial and at the time of writing is subject to another legal challenge led by civil liberties and human rights NGO Liberty, this time on the grounds of infringing racial discrimination law as well as human rights, data protection, and public law principles.[66]

While in the U.K. facial recognition cameras have not been physically attacked, unlike in the Iranian and Hong Kong contexts, they have still provoked a visceral response from at least some members of the public when used in everyday public places. On understanding that facial recognition cameras were deployed in public, some individuals have covered their faces to protect their privacy, with at least one person being fined by the police for doing so.[67] Football fans in Scotland were also prompted to unveil banners specifically against the use of facial recognition in the stadium. These may be seen as part of broader contestations of the 'hyper-militarization' of U.K. police, which Weitzberg identifies as a trend that includes facial recognition use.[68] There is limited support for facial recognition among the public more generally and even scepticism from some parts of the police themselves. A national survey by the Ada Lovelace Institute of public attitudes to facial recognition showed that a majority of the public wanted government restrictions on police use of facial recognition and opposed commercial use of the technology.[69] Urquhart and Miranda's research with frontline U.K. police officers showed also that even the position of police officers was 'mainly one of scepticism and disbelief in the technology.'[70]

Critics of live facial recognition in the U.K. have also mobilized the law, specifically human rights and data protection law, through litigation, resulting in 'the first major successful legal challenge to police use of automated facial recognition technology anywhere in the world.'[71] A civil liberties campaigner, Ed Bridges, challenged South Wales Police's use of live facial recognition, on the basis that it breached the right to privacy, data protection law and equality laws. At first instance, the High Court found that while facial recognition did interfere with the public's rights, its use by the South Wales Police was lawful due to safeguards in the framework governing the use of facial recognition.[72] However, this

---

66   Nadine White, 'Met Police Faces Legal Action Over 'Racist' Gangs Matrix Database', *Independent*, 1 February 2022, https://www.independent.co.uk/news/uk/home-news/met-police-gangs-matrix-database-b2004293.html.
67   Lizzie Dearden, 'Police Stop People for Covering their Faces from Facial Recognition Camera Then Fine Man £90 After he Protested', *The Independent*, 31 January 2019, https://www.independent.co.uk/news/uk/crime/facial-recognition-cameras-technology-london-trial-met-police-face-cover-man-fined-a8756936.html.
68   Weitzberg, 'A Very British Problem'.
69   Ada Lovelace Institute, 'Beyond Face Value: Public Attitudes to Facial Recognition Technology', 2019, https://www.adalovelaceinstitute.org/report/beyond-face-value-public-attitudes-to-facial-recognition-technology/.
70   Lachlan Urquhart and Diana Miranda, 'Policing Faces: The Present and Future of Intelligent Facial Surveillance', *Information & Communications Technology Law* 31.2 (2022): 194-219, 198.
71   Monika Zalnieriute, 'Burning Bridges: The Automated Facial Recognition Technology and Public Space Surveillance in the Modern State', *Science and Technology Law Review*, 22.2 (2021): 284-307, 287.
72   Suneet Sharma, 'Case Law: R (Bridges) v Chief Constable of South Wales Police: The Use of Facial Recognition Software by the Police is Lawful', *Inforrm blog*, 6 September 2019, https://inforrm.org/2019/09/06/case-law-r-bridges-v-chief-constable-of-south-wales-police-the-use-of-facial-

decision was overturned on appeal, with the Court of Appeal finding that the use of live facial recognition did breach human rights, there were 'fundamental deficiencies' in the governing framework and that the police force had not ensured that the software used was unbiased on grounds of race and sex.[73] South Wales Police will not appeal this decision. Yet, as with the ICO's aforementioned decision about the Met Police's Gangs Matrix, the Court of Appeal did not find facial recognition use per se by the police to be illegal in public places, just that there were not appropriate safeguards in place: indeed 'the decision still affirms the role of automated facial recognition in modern policing and law enforcement.'[74]

In light of the above, with live facial recognition use by police in Scotland effectively banned, yet permitted with some limitations in England and Wales, there is a 'North–South Divide' as Lynch has termed it, regarding police use of live facial recognition as an everyday AI application in public places in the UK:

> If you find yourself walking in some parts of London or Wales, for example, live facial recognition technology will now be able to scan your face without consent and you may even be subject to an on-the-spot identity check (particularly if you are a woman or an ethnic minority). In Scotland, however, you will not have to worry about this—at least for now.[75]

However, police use of facial recognition is only part of the picture. There have been other controversial uses of facial recognition in everyday U.K. life, including in Scotland. During 2021, facial recognition technology was used at nine schools in North Ayrshire to facilitate quicker and contactless payment for canteen lunches.[76] The ICO urged the local authority to take a less intrusive approach to ensure compliance with necessity and proportionality requirements, and it seems that the use of facial recognition was suspended shortly after.[77] While this may have nipped facial recognition in schools in the bud in Scotland, a supermarket, the Co-op (which is traditionally considered an ethical retailer) is using live facial recognition in stores in the south of England for safety and security reasons, although this is opposed by digital rights group

recognition-software-by-the-police-is-lawful-suneet-sharma/.

73   Hunton Andrews Kurth, 'UK Court of Appeal Finds Automated Facial Recognition Technology Unlawful in Bridges v South Wales Police' 12 August 2020, https://www.huntonprivacyblog. com/2020/08/12/uk-court-of-appeal-finds-automated-facial-recognition-technology-unlawful-in- bridges-v-south-wales-police/; see also Urquhart and Miranda, 'Policing Faces'.

74   Zalnieriute, 'Burning Bridges'.

75   Euan Lynch, 'The Use of Live Facial Recognition Technology in Scotland: A New North–South Divide?', *UK Human Rights blog*, 25 February 2020, https://ukhumanrightsblog.com/2020/02/25/ the-use-of-live-facial-recognition-technology-in-scotland-a-new-north-south-divide/.

76   Sally Weale, 'ICO to Step In After Schools Use Facial Recognition to Speed Up Lunch Queue', *Guardian*, 18 October 2021, https://www.theguardian.com/education/2021/oct/18/privacy-fears- as-schools-use-facial-recognition-to-speed-up-lunch-queue-ayrshire-technology-payments-uk.

77   Pascale Davies, 'UK Schools Suspend Use of Controversial Facial Recognition Technology', *Euronews*, 25 October 2021, https://www.euronews.com/next/2021/10/18/schools-in-scotland- start-using-facial-recognition-on-children-paying-for-lunch.

Big Brother Watch, which has led a #StopCoopSpying social media campaign.[78] At the time of writing, the Co-op is the subject of a complaint to the ICO by Big Brother Watch and digital rights agency AWO.[79]

Everyday encounters and contestations of facial recognition in the U..K demonstrate how the public meets AI in the form of facial recognition in their quotidian lives, through police deployment in public places, to its use in schools and supermarkets. The most successful influencing of policymakers can be seen in the Scottish Parliament's moratorium on police use of live facial recognition. Legal challenges and use of the ICO's complaints process especially by activists and NGOs have produced some success in reining in facial recognition but are not outright victories. The unwillingness of the ICO or courts to find the highly intrusive use of facial recognition in public places illegal outright demonstrates only partial success in a bottom-up norm forming, although this may also reflect a deference on behalf of these bodies towards the U.K. Parliament which they might find to be the more appropriate body to impose such a ban. Yet we are still waiting for such action, despite such calls bolstered recently by Matthew Ryder QC's Independent Review of the Governance of Biometric Data in England and Wales, who recommended that a new legislative framework for all uses of biometric technologies, and legally binding codes of practice for police and other users of live facial recognition respectively were needed; until these are implemented, all live facial recognition use should cease.[80]

Norms developed in localized contexts can circulate more internationally. Sometimes this is due to circulations of national or global capital, in the cases of laws and policies developed in California in the U.S., and increasingly the effect of European Union law and policy more globally, with the 'Brussels effect' of its governance mechanisms influencing law and policy elsewhere due to the E.U.'s status as the world's largest trading bloc and its active stance in developing and circulating its law and regulation beyond its borders.[81] This may also be the case for the E.U.'s proposed AI Act, which may follow the GDPR in forming a de facto global norm,[82] and one which at the moment, as mentioned above, will not prohibit outright the use of facial recognition, even by law enforcement.

---

78   Asssiah Hamed, 'Co-op Defends Facial Recognition Cameras in Bristol Stores Amid Claims of 'Orwellian'Ssurveillance', *Bristol Post*, 9 December 2021, https://www.bristolpost.co.uk/whats-on/shopping/co-op-defends-facial-recognition-6302476.

79   'Southern Co-operative's Use of Facial Recognition on Customers Prompts Legal Complaint', *Sky News*, 27 July 2022, https://news.sky.com/story/co-ops-use-of-facial-recognition-on-customers-prompts-legal-complaint-12659309.

80   Matthew Ryder, 'Independent Legal Review of the Governance of Biometric Data in England and Wales ('The Ryder Review')', Ada Lovelace Institute, 2022, https://www.adalovelaceinstitute.org/wp-content/uploads/2022/06/The-Ryder-Review-Independent-legal-review-of-the-governance-of-biometric-data-in-England-and-Wales-Ada-Lovelace-Institute-June-2022.pdf.

81   Anu Bradford, *The Brussels Effect: How the European Union Rules the World*. Oxford: Oxford University Press, 2020.

82   Angela Daly, 'Neo-Liberal Business-As-Usual or Post-Surveillance Capitalism With European Characteristics? The EU's General Data Protection Regulation in a Multi-Polar Internet', in Rolien Hoyng and Gladys Pak Lei Chong (eds) *Critiquing Communication Innovation: New Media in a Multipolar World*, East Lansing: Michigan State University Press, 2022 (forthcoming).

Yet, the Scottish example shows how other forms of norm circulation are possible which are not in the service of global capital and power with the local prohibitions on police facial recognition use in other parts of the world being referenced by the Scottish Parliament Justice Sub-Committee in its call for a moratorium on police use of live facial recognition in Scotland. This shows that norms developed locally through negotiation and contestation of AI uses can also circulate more globally and influence activities elsewhere, leading potentially to a snowballing effect of localized AI norms that can be leveraged by social movements, protests, and legal mobilizations in other geographical contexts.

At a 'high level', the U.K. has set out its public research funding approach to AI and its policy intentions as regards a 'light touch' non-binding governance of AI, including facial recognition. This demonstrates a further cleavage with the E.U.'s intention to regulate AI. It can be seen as part of the U.K.'s post-Brexit trajectory, which also involves a distancing from the E.U.'s data protection regime, and accords with Ossewaarde and Gulenc's aforementioned observations of the U.K.'s AI approach as digitally utopian, technologically solutionist, and neo-imperial.[83] Contestations over facial recognition use in practice in individuals' and communities' everyday encounters in British public spaces demonstrate how these logics are perpetuated but also resisted, especially when facial recognition is used as part of the U.K.'s hyper-militarized law enforcement targeting BAME communities. In some cases these mobilizations can lead to litigation (albeit with only limited success so far) and localized policy change, where the opportunities present themselves. Researchers, activists, and others in the U.K. may find limited prospects in influencing the U.K. government centrally, but this case study of facial recognition shows pressure can be exerted via litigation. There may be more opportunities in influencing more localized structures of governance, such as the devolved administrations in Scotland, Wales, and Northern Ireland, where there may be more prospect of impact. Currently, these devolved administrations are governed by political parties which are not the Conversative party in power in the U.K. Parliament, and there may be a desire to distinguish their policies from that of the U.K. government for political reasons (heightened in the Brexit and COVID-19 contexts), leading to fragmentation and differentiation in policy and governance.[84] Furthermore, there may be fewer attempts from global capital, especially Big Tech firms, to influence these administrations in ways favorable to their interests. Such conditions present possibilities for localized negotiation and resistance to AI and which have been realized to some degree in reining in facial recognition, and which can be juxtaposed with the laissez-faire 'pro-innovation' approach of the U.K. government to AI.

Conclusion

Practices and applications of AI and AI ethics are occurring right here, right now throughout the world at local and everyday levels, with members of the general public encountering the

83   Ossewaarde and Gulenc, 'National Varieties of Artificial Intelligence Discourses'.
84   Ian Elliott, Karin Bottom, Paul Carmichael, Joyce Liddle, Steve Martin, and Robert Pyper, 'The Fragmentation of Public Administration: Differentiated and Decentered Governance in the (dis)United Kingdom', *Public Administration* 100.1 (2022): 98–115.

technology in its myriad forms. These encounters—and negotiations and contestations—are rarely the focus, however, of AI ethics discussions and initiatives. Through the case study of facial recognition in the U.K., I have demonstrated how looking at the local is key to understanding how AI ethics plays out, is formed, and informed in practice, producing at times law and policy change with 'bite', which serve individuals and communities rather than state power and capital, a 'bite' the ethics-washed higher-level AI ethics initiatives often lack. Accordingly, we need to engage more with social movements and everyday law and policy in localities seeking to build, form, and inform better AI. This is where real change, which does not necessarily serve political and economic power, can happen, now.

Acknowledgements

I would like to thank Xaroula Kerasidou, reviewers Jake Goldenfein and Nancy Salem, and editor Thao Phan for comments on an earlier version of this paper.

Funding disclosure

No specific funding source funded this research, it was conducted during my salaried employment and outside of those hours. During writing this paper I hold and have held grants funded by UKRI but they did not support this paper.

References

Ada Lovelace Institute. 'Beyond Face Value: Public Attitudes to Facial Recognition technology', 2019, https://www.adalovelaceinstitute.org/report/beyond-face-value-public-attitudes-to-facial-recognition-technology/.

Akbari, Azadeh. 'The Threat of Automating Control: Surveillance of Women's Clothing in Iran', in Aleš Završnik and Vasja Badalič (eds) *Automating Crime Prevention, Surveillance, and Military Operations*, Cham: Springer, 2021, pp. 183–99.

Beraldo, Davide and Milan, Stefania. 'From Data Politics to the Contentious Politics of Data', *Big Data & Society* 6.2 (2019).

Bietti, Elettra. 'From Ethics Washing to Ethics Bashing: A View on Tech Ethics from Within Moral Philosophy', Proceedings of ACM FAT* Conference, 2020, https://ssrn.com/abstract=3513182.

Big Brother Watch. 'Face Off: The Lawless Growth of Facial Recognition in UK Policing', 2018, http://bigbrotherwatch.org.uk/wp-content/uploads/2018/05/Face-Off-final-digital-1.

Bradford, Anu. *The Brussels Effect: How the European Union Rules the World*. Oxford: Oxford University Press, 2020.

Buolamwini, Joy and Gebru Timnit. 'Gender Shades: Intersectional Accuracy Disparities in Commercial Gender Classification' in Proceedings of the 1st Conference on Fairness, Accountability and Transparency, PMLR 81, 2018, 77–91.

Burgess, Jean, Mitchell, Peta, and Highfield, Tim. 'Automating the Digital Everyday: An Introduction', *Media International Australia*, 166.1 (2018): 6–10.

Chubb, Jennifer and Reed, Mark. 'The Politics of Research Impact: Academic Perceptions of the Implications for Research Funding, Motivation and Quality', *British Politics* 13 (2018): 295–311.

Daly, Angela. 'Algorithmic Oppression with Chinese Characteristics: AI Against Xinjiang's Uyghurs' in *Artificial Intelligence: Human Rights, Social Justice and Development: Global Information Society Watch 2019 Report,* 2019, pp. 108–112.

Daly, Angela, Devitt, S. Kate and Mann, Monique. 'AI Ethics Needs Good Data' in Pieter Verdegem (ed) *AI for Everyone? Critical Perspectives,* London: University of Westminster Press, 2021, pp. 103–22.

Daly, Angela, Hagendorff, Thilo, Hui, Li, Mann, Monique, Marda, Vidushi, Wagner, Ben, and Wang, Wayne Wei. 'AI, Governance and Ethics: Global Perspectives' in Hans Micklitz, Oreste Pollicino, Amnon Reichman, Andrea Simoncini, Giovanni Sartor and Giovanni De Gregorio (eds) *Constitutional Challenges in the Algorithmic Society,* Cambridge: Cambridge University Press, 2022, pp. 182–201.

Daly, Angela. 'Neo-Liberal Business-As-Usual or Post-Surveillance Capitalism with European Characteristics? The EU's General Data Protection Regulation in a Multi-Polar Internet' in Rolien Hoyng and Gladys Pak Lei Chong (eds), *Critiquing Communication Innovation: New Media in a Multipolar World,* East Lansing: Michigan State University Press, 2022 (forthcoming).

Davies, Pascale. 'UK Schools Suspend Use of Controversial Facial Recognition Technology', *Euronews,* 25 October 2021, https://www.euronews.com/next/2021/10/18/schools-in-scotland-start-using-facial-recognition-on-children-paying-for-lunch.

Dearden, Lizzie. 'Police Stop People for Covering Their Faces From Facial Recognition Camera then Fine Man £90 After he Protested', *The Independent,* 31 January 2019, https://www.independent.co.uk/news/uk/crime/facial-recognition-cameras-technology-london-trial-met-police-face-cover-man-fined-a8756936.html.

Edwards, Rosalind. 'Why Do Academics Do Unfunded Research? Resistance, Compliance and Identity in the UK Neo-liberal University', *Studies in Higher Education* 47.4 (2022): 904–14.

Elliott, Ian, Bottom, Karin, Carmichael, Paul, Liddle, Joyce, Martin, Steve, and Pyper, Robert. 'The Fragmentation of Public Administration: Differentiated and Decentered Governance in the (dis) United Kingdom', *Public Administration* 100.1 (2022): 98–115.

Ewick, Patricia and Silbey, Susan. *The Common Place of Law: Stories from Everyday Life,* Chicago: University of Chicago Press, 1998.

Feathers, Todd. 'Facial Recognition Is Racist. Why Aren't More Cities Banning It?', *Vice,* 25 May 2021, https://www.vice.com/en/article/4avx3m/facial-recognition-is-racist-why-arent-more-cities-banning-it.

Finn, Mike. *British Universities in the Brexit Moment: Political, Economic and Cultural Implications.* Bingley: Emerald Publishing, 2018.

Gleeson, Sean. 'How Smart are Hong Kong's Lampposts?', *AFP Fact Check,* 4 September 2019, https://factcheck.afp.com/how-smart-are-hong-kongs-lampposts.

Hagendorff, Thilo. 'The Ethics of AI Ethics: An Evaluation of Guidelines', *Minds & Machines* 30 (2021): 99–120.

Hagendorff, Thilo. 'Blind Spots in AI ethics', *AI Ethics* (2021).

Hamed, Assiah. 'Co-op Defends Facial Recognition Cameras in Bristol Stores Amid Claims of 'Orwellian' Surveillance', *Bristol Post,* 9 December 2021, https://www.bristolpost.co.uk/whats-on/shopping/co-op-defends-facial-recognition-6302476 (accessed 1 February 2022).

Hamilton-Smith, Niall, McBride, Maureen, and Atkinson, Colin. 'Lights, Camera, Provocation? Exploring Experiences of Surveillance in the Policing of Scottish Football', *Policing and Society* 31.2 (2021): 179–94.

Heikkilä, Melissa. 'The Walls are Closing in on Clearview AI', *MIT Technology Review*, 24 May 2022, https://www.technologyreview.com/2022/05/24/1052653/clearview-ai-data-privacy-uk/.

Hunton Andrews Kurth. 'UK Court of Appeal Finds Automated Facial Recognition Technology Unlawful in Bridges v South Wales Police', 12 August 2020, https://www.huntonprivacyblog.com/2020/08/12/uk-court-of-appeal-finds-automated-facial-recognition-technology-unlawful-in-bridges-v-south-wales-police/.

Jobin, Anna, Ienca, Marcello, and Vayena, Effy. 'The Global Landscape of AI Ethics Guidelines', *Nature Machine Intelligence* 1 (2019): 389–99.

Kaun, Anne. 'Suing the Algorithm: the Mundanization of Automated Decision-making in Public Services Through Litigation', *Information, Communication & Society* (2021).

Kazansky, Becky, Torres, Guillen, van der Velden, Lonneke, Wissenbach, Kersti, and Milan, Stefania. 'Data for the Social Good: Towards a Data-Activist Research Agenda' in Angela Daly, S. Kate Devitt and Monique Mann (eds) *Good Data*, Amsterdam: Institute of Network Cultures, 2019, pp. 244–59.

Kazansky, Becky. '"It Depends on Your Threat Model": The Anticipatory Dimensions of Resistance to Data-driven Surveillance', *Big Data & Society* 8.1 (2021).

Kazim, Emre, Almeida, Denise, Kingsman, Nigel, Kerrigan, Charles, Koshiyama, Adriano, Lomas, Elizabeth and Hilliard, Airlie. 'Innovation and opportunity: review of the UK's national AI strategy', *Discover Artificial Intelligence* 1.14 (2021): 1–10.

Kewalramani, Manoj and Seth, Rohan. 'Networked Protests & State Responses: The Case of Hong Kong 2019-2020', Takshashila Discussion Document 2020-03, 2020, https://ssrn.com/abstract=3580591.

Lee, Dave. 'San Francisco is First US City to Ban Facial Recognition', *BBC,* 15 May 2019, https://www.bbc.co.uk/news/technology-48276660.

Leung, Kevin and Lee, H.Y. 'Implementing the Smart City: Who Has a Say? Some Insights from Hong Kong', *International Journal of Urban Sciences*(2021): 1–25.

Long, Lisa and Joseph-Salisbury, Remi. 'Black Mixed-race Men's Perceptions and Experiences of the Police', *Ethnic and Racial Studies* 42.2 (2019): 198–215.

Lu, Alex Jiahong. 'Toward Everyday Negotiation and Resistance Under Data-Driven Surveillance', *Interactions* 29.2 (2022): 34–8.

Lynch, Euan. 'The Use of Live Facial Recognition Technology in Scotland: A New North-South Divide?', *UK Human Rights Blog*, 25 February 2020, https://ukhumanrightsblog.com/2020/02/25/the-use-of-live-facial-recognition-technology-in-scotland-a-new-north-south-divide/.

Mann, Monique. 'Social (In)security and Social (In)justice: Automation in the Australian Welfare System' in *Artificial intelligence: Human rights, social justice and development: Global Information Society Watch 2019 Report,* 2019, pp. 68–72.

McCann, Michael. 'Law and Social Movements: Contemporary Perspectives', *Annual Review of Law and Social Science* 2.1 (2006): 17–38.

McGowran, Leigh. 'The Issues with the EU's Draft Regulation on Facial Recognition AI', *Silicon Republic*, 17 May 2022, https://www.siliconrepublic.com/enterprise/the-issues-with-the-eus-draft-regulation-on-facial-recognition-ai.

Mega, Marcello. 'Cops Fear Gangsters are Evading Law as Glasgow's Facial Recognition Cameras Remain Mothballed', *Daily Record*, 11 August 2020, https://www.dailyrecord.co.uk/news/scottish news/scots-cops-fear-gangsters-evading-22499468.

Moule, Richard, Burruss, George, Gifford, Faith, Parry, Megan, and Fox, Bryanna. 'Legal Socialization and Subcultural Norms: Examining Linkages Between Perceptions of Procedural Justice, Legal Cynicism, and the Code of the Street', *Journal of Criminal Justice* 61(2019): 26–39.

Nijjar, Jasbinder. 'Police–school Partnerships and the War on Black Youth', *Critical Social Policy*, 41.3 (2021): 491–501.

ÓhÉigeartaigh, Seán, Whittlestone, Jess, Liu, Yang, Zeng, Yi, and Liu, Zhe. 'Overcoming Barriers to Cross-cultural Cooperation in AI Ethics and Governance', *Philosophy and Technology* 33 (2020): 571–93.

Ossewaarde, Marinus and Gulenc, Erdener. 'National Varieties of Artificial Intelligence Discourses: Myth, Utopianism, and Solutionism in West European Policy Expectations', *Computer* 53.11 (2020): 53–61.

Parida, Tulsi and Ashok, Aparna. 'Consolidating Power in the Name of Progress: Techno-solutionism and Farmer Protests in India' in Frederike Kaltheuner (ed), *Fake AI,* Manchester: Meatspace Press, 2021, pp. 161–9.

Phan, Thao, Goldenfein, Jake, Mann, Monique, and Kuch, Declan. 'Economies of Virtue: The Circulation of "Ethics" in Big Tech', *Science as Culture*, 31.1 (2022): 121–35.

Pink, Sarah, Ruckenstein, Minna, Berg, Martin and Lupton, Deborah. 'Everyday Automation: Setting a Research Agenda' in Pink, Sarah, Berg, Martin, Lupton, Deborah, and Ruckenstein, Minna (eds) *Everyday Automation: Experiencing and Anticipating Emerging Technologies*, London: Routledge, 2022, pp. 1–20.

Rezende, Isadora Neroni. 'Facial Recognition in Police Hands: Assessing the 'Clearview Case' From a European Perspective', *New Journal of European Criminal Law* 11.3 (2020): 375–89.

Ruthven, Graham. 'The Criminalization of Scottish Soccer Fans', *Vice*, 23 February 2016, https://www.vice.com/en/article/9apyad/the-criminalization-of-scottish-soccer-fans.

Ryder, Matthew. 'Independent Legal Review of the Governance of Biometric Data in England and Wales ('The Ryder Review')', Ada Lovelace Institute (2022), https://www.adalovelaceinstitute.org/wp-content/uploads/2022/06/The-Ryder-Review-Independent-legal-review-of-the-governance-of-biometric-data-in-England-and-Wales-Ada-Lovelace-Institute-June-2022.pdf.

Sarat, Austin and Kearns, Thomas (eds) *Law in Everyday Life*, Ann Arbor: University of Michigan Press, 1995.

Scottish Parliament Justice Sub-Committee on Policing. 'Facial Recognition: How Policing in Scotland Makes Use of This Technology', SP Paper 678, 1st Report (Session 5), 2020, https://sp-bpr-en-prod-cdnep.azureedge.net/published/JSP/2020/2/11/Facial-recognition--how-policing-in-Scotland-makes-use-of-this-technology/JSPS0520R01.pdf.

Shahi, Afshin and Abdoh-Tabrizi, Ehsan. 'Iran's 2019-2020 Demonstrations: The Changing Dynamics of Political Protests in Iran', *Asian Affairs* 51.1 (2020): 1–41.

Sharma, Suneet. 'Case Law: R (Bridges) v Chief Constable of South Wales Police: The Use of Facial Recognition Software by the Police is Lawful', *Inforrm blog*, 6 September 2019, https://inforrm.org/2019/09/06/case-law-r-bridges-v-chief-constable-of-south-wales-police-the-use-of-facial-recognition-software-by-the-police-is-lawful-suneet-sharma/.

U.K. Government. 'National AI Strategy', 21 September 2021, https://www.gov.uk/government/publications/national-ai-strategy.

U.K. Government. 'Establishing a Pro-innovation Approach to Regulating AI', 20 July 2022, https://www.gov.uk/government/publications/establishing-a-pro-innovation-approach-to-regulating-ai.

UKRI Economic and Social Research Council. 'Defining Impact', https://www.ukri.org/councils/esrc/impact-toolkit-for-economic-and-social-sciences/defining-impact/.

UNESCO. 'UNESCO Member States Adopt the First Ever Global Agreement on the Ethics of Artificial Intelligence', 25 November 2021, https://en.unesco.org/news/unesco-member-states-adopt-first-ever-global-agreement-ethics-artificial-intelligence.

Urquhart, Lachlan and Miranda, Diana. 'Policing faces: the present and future of intelligent facial surveillance', *Information & Communications Technology Law*, 31:2 (2022): 194-219.

Veale, Michael and Zuiderveen Borgesius, Frederik. 'Demystifying the Draft EU Artificial Intelligence Act—Analysing the Good, the Bad, and the Unclear Elements of the Proposed Approach', *Computer Law Review International* 22.4 (2021): 97–112.

Wagner, Ben. 'Ethics as an Escape from Regulation: From 'Ethics-Washing' to Ethics-Shopping?' in Bayamlioglu, Emre, Baraliuc, Irina, Janssens, Liisa, and Hildebrandt, Mireille (eds) *Being Profiled: Cogitas Ergo Sum: 10 Years of Profiling the European Citizen*, Amsterdam: Amsterdam University Press, 2018, pp. 84–9.

Weale, Sally. 'ICO to Step in After Schools Use Facial Recognition to Speed Up Lunch Queue', *Guardian*, 18 October 2021, https://www.theguardian.com/education/2021/oct/18/privacy-fears-as-schools-use-facial-recognition-to-speed-up-lunch-queue-ayrshire-technology-payments-uk.

Weitzberg, Keren. 'A Very British Problem: The Evolution of Britain's Militarised Policing Industrial Complex', Report for Campaign Against the Arms Trade and Netpol, 2022, https://caat.org.uk/app/uploads/2022/08/A-Very-British-Problem-WEB.pdf.

White, Nadine. 'Met Police Faces Legal Action Over 'Racist' Gangs Matrix Database', *Independent*, 1 February 2022, https://www.independent.co.uk/news/uk/home-news/met-police-gangs-matrix-database-b2004293.html.

Willim, Robert. 'Imperfect Imaginaries: Digitisation, Mundanisation, and the Ungraspable' in Gertraud Koch (ed) *Digitisation: Theories and Concepts for Empirical Cultural Research*, Abingdon: Routledge, 2017, pp. 53–77.

Wong, Janis. 'Protests Decentralised: How Technology Enabled Civil Disobedience by Hong Kong Anti-extradition Bill Protesters', *LawArXiv*, 2020, https://osf.io/preprints/lawarxiv/efvwn/.

Wong, Pak-Hang. 'Cultural Differences as Excuses? Human Rights and Cultural Values in Global Ethics and Governance of AI', *Philosophy and Technology* 33 (2020): 705–15.

Zalnieriute, Monika. 'Burning Bridges: The Automated Facial Recognition Technology and Public Space Surveillance in the Modern State', *Science and Technology Law Review*, 22.2 (2021): 284–307.

DINING OUT ON DATA: ETHICS, VALUE, AND THE CALCULATION OF RISK APPETITES

TSVETELINA HRISTOVA AND LIAM MAGEE

Data ethics and AI ethics constitute an increasingly contested terrain where scholars, activists, state institutions, and industry actors compete to define principles for ethical practice. While mechanisms like state-sanctioned ethical frameworks, activist- and scholar-led initiatives like the FAIR data principles,[1] and industry projects like Microsoft's Aether Committee have been widely discussed, international standards, as one of the governmental technologies that influence how data ethics is understood and practiced, remain largely out of the focus of researchers. In this chapter, we examine the role of a series of interconnected standards on risk management that have grown to play a significant role in shaping a particular understanding of data ethics.

We begin with an introduction to several of these global standards, whose connections to each other and to precedent national standards can be difficult to untangle. Based on the Australian and New Zealand standard for risk management AS/NZS 4360-2004, which serves as the foundation for the international standard for risk management ISO 31000, these standards codify a specific relationship between risk and value. This relationship foregrounds how states and industry actors imagine the social dimensions of data use as well as their own role in the global digital economy. The Australian standard AS/NZS 4360-2004 and ISO 31000 introduce a new framework of risk management, where risk is conceptualized as ambivalent: positive in some cases and negative in others. The ambivalence of risk leads to an approach to risk management based on the 'risk appetite' of organizations and institutions — i.e. their readiness to take risks informed by expected gains. This framework of risk management is incorporated in the work of the new ISO subcommittee ISO/IEC JTC 1/SC 42, which develops standards for artificial intelligence. ISO/IEC JTC 1/SC 42 is part of a larger initiative for the development of standards for AI led by a special sub-committee of the joint technical committee for standardization in the field of information and communication technologies, JTC 1. JTC 1 formed in 1987 to combine standardization efforts of two major international standard bodies, the International Standards Organisation (ISO) and the International Electrotechnical Commission (IEC). The ISO/IEC JTC 1/SC 42 sub-committee, formed more recently in 2018, has been tasked with the role of developing standards in the field of artificial intelligence. The significance of such a project cannot be underestimated — IEC and, in particular, ISO have established what scholars have termed a 'global governance by consensus',[2] and their respective global standards impact most industries through the need of compliance in a multitude of ways. As part of the series of standards developed by the subcommittee, the group is also working on a standard of risk management in AI, ISO/IEC

---

1   M. Wilkinson, M. Dumontier, I. Aalbersberg, et al., 'The FAIR Guiding Principles for Scientific Data Management and Stewardship', *Sci Data* 3, 160018, (2016).

2   C.N. Murphy, and J. Yates, *The International Organization for Standardization (ISO): Global Governance through Voluntary Consensus*. Milton Park: Routledge, 2009.

DIS 23894, which is explicitly based on ISO 31000 as stated in its introduction:

> This document is intended to be used in connection with ISO 31000:2018. Whenever this document extends the guidance given in ISO 31000:2018, an appropriate reference to the clauses of ISO 31000:2018 is made followed by AI-specific guidance, if applicable. To make the relationship between this document and ISO 31000:2018 more explicit, the clause structure of ISO 31000:2018 is mirrored in this document and amended by sub-clauses if needed.[3]

Beyond the mere replicability of standards, the case of ISO 31000 suggests an emerging socio-technical configuration where risk becomes conducive to how ethics and governance are imagined and enacted in relation to data subjects. Users and companies alike are imbued with inherent 'risk appetite' that allows for varying degrees of contingency to be permissible in the context of big data and AI and charts the boundaries of expected and allowed data practices. Data subjects also become implicated in the complex interplay between technological standards and the geopolitical ambitions of nation states; an interplay in which the purpose of local data and AI regulation is to serve as a testbed for global frameworks of governance.

Standards occupy a complex position with regards to this political and economic space. Keller Easterling[4] uses specifically the example of ISO to propose the concept of 'extrastatecraft': a characterization of technological and economic mechanisms for the rearrangement of relations of power, control, and production that are not guided exclusively by nation state governments and that can reshape the political structure and the spatial dimensions of power within and across states, cities, or continents. Andrew Barry[5] makes a similar argument, suggesting the notion of technological zones which are defined not by the traditional political power of state governments but by complex technological infrastructures and relations. For both scholars, the play of forces within networks of extrastatecraft and technological zones is shaped by the interconnectedness of technical infrastructures, protocols, and economic and political power. Standards occupy this extrastatecraft space of regulation outside of the norms of political governance by forging alliances between companies and state institutions, and by introducing the principles of consensus-making and technical constraints as modes of exercising control and shaping a space that enables certain economic flows and relations while restricting others.

While their explicit entanglement with ethics is comparatively recent, technical standards have long formed a key part of the socio-technical assemblages[6] within which data is defined and put to use in different calculations and statistical operations. They have historically played

---

3   ISO/IEC, 'Draft international standard ISO/IEC DIS 23894', Information technology—Artificial intelligence—Risk management, 2022.

4   Keller Easterling, K. *Extrastatecraft: The Power of Infrastructure Space*. London: Verso Books, 2014.

5   Andrew Barry, 'Technological Zones', *European Journal of Social Theory*, 9(2), (2006): 239–53.

6   C. Aradau and T. Blanke, 'The (Big) Data-security assemblage: Knowledge and critique', *Big Data & Society*, 2(2) (2015): 1–12; R. Kitchin, 'Thinking Critically About and Researching Algorithms', *Information, Communication & Society*, 20(1), (2017): 14–29.

an important role in how data infrastructures and networks are governed,[7] how different digital file formats are defined[8] and how the key principle of interoperability, which allows for the circulation of data across different systems, is conceived and enacted.[9] Standards have been instrumental in generating the conditions for big data collection, exchange, and analysis. And as we have noted, alongside their role in defining data formats and network infrastructures, in a more general sense standards occupy an ambiguous space where they shape political and economic processes through what are essentially 'extrastatecraft'[10] methods of consensus-building and technocracy. We see standards like ISO 31000 as part of the complex and shifting socio-technical assemblages of data and algorithms through which the relation of data to risk is determined. While data has been extensively studied as part of the instrumentarium of risk management in algorithms for preemptive control and policing),[11] ISO 31000, through the new AI standard ISO/IEC DIS 23894, positions data and AI themselves as objects of risk evaluation and mitigation.

These standards are instrumental in articulating a relationship between risk and value which, as part of the socio-technical regime of control that standards establish, becomes increasingly important for how data use and ethics are imagined, and for how institutions and states see their role in the governance of big data and AI. As we discuss below, one interesting aspect to the control extended from the technical to the imaginary is the standardisation of a 'risk' vocabulary. For example, a significant role in this process is afforded to the construed notion of 'risk appetite', and to related terms, which together forge an alternative institutional imaginary, one that already devotes to data a distinctive moral as well as economic agency.

The new ways in which risk features in the calculation of how to govern and benefit from a digital economy have consequences for how it is understood and operationalised across different domains and by different geopolitical actors. This is especially notable in the technologies of 'governing through consensus', such as standards and guidelines, which allow room for negotiation and translation of practices across the domains of private business, national agendas, and international collaboration and influence. The case we focus on here, the risk management standard ISO 31000, is a prominent example in this sense, not only because it reaffirms the language of risk-taking and risk appetite as essential for successful governance but also because the life of this standard reveals the stakes and hopes that underpin the formulation of guidelines for ethics and risk in AI.

---

7   Alexander Galloway. *Protocol: How control exists after decentralization*. MIT Press. 2004.
8   I. Hoelzl and R. Marie, *Softimage: Towards a New Theory of the Digital Image*, Bristol, UK: Intellect Books, 2015.
9   T. Hristova, *Data Infrastructures and Digital Labour: The Case of Teleradiology*, PhD diss., Western Sydney University, Sydney, 2020.
10   Easterling, *Extrastatescraft*.
11   L. Amoore, 'Data Derivatives: On the Emergence of a Security Risk Calculus for our Times', *Theory, Culture & Society*, 28(6), (2011):24–43; Amoore, 'Security and the Incalculable', *Security Dialogue*, 45(5), (2014): 423–39; Amoore, *Cloud Ethics*. Durham: Duke University Press, 2020; C. Aradau and T. Blanke, 'The (Big) Data-security assemblage: Knowledge and critique', *Big Data & Society*, issue 2(2) (2015): 1–12; V. Eubanks, *Automating Inequality: How High-Tech Tools Profile, Police, and Punish the Poor*, New York: St. Martin's Press, 2018, among many.

As an international standard, ISO 31000 becomes a signifier for a new way of carving out influence and leadership in data-intensive industries, through the development and lobbying for standards and ethical norms by different national or local actors. It suggests that risk, along with its changing meaning and functions, exercises transformative effects not just through the adoption of the principles of risk appetite, but also through the specific geopolitical and geoeconomic ambitions that lie at the heart of initiatives for standard-making. Contrary to a colloquial understanding of technical standards as ones grounded in the objectivity of measurements, science, and rationality, standards do play an important role in shaping and articulating geopolitical and geoeconomic ambitions and borders. Even when standards are developed by non-governmental bodies, the geographical origin of the standard and the composition of the organisation behind it are seen as representing specific national interests. As we show elsewhere about cases where technological standards have been utilised in geopolitical and geoeconomic struggles,[12] political state power and technological zones are often entangled in shaping and reshaping the reach of a standard. The perception that certain countries gain influence by the international adoption of standards supported by them is very much part of how these entanglements are enacted.

Standardizing Risk in the New Data Economy

Risk has traditionally been conceptualized in a range of ways, according to the scale and site of its application. One well-accepted definition comes from disaster management: a combination of *hazard, exposure,* and *vulnerability.*[13] Organizational risk is often defined in similar terms: as a combination of *likelihood* (comparable to hazard) and *severity* (combining exposure and vulnerability). But risk is seen to have a much more profound role in social and political life. For example, Georg Simmel in *The Philosophy on Money* connects risk to an essential relation between abstract economic value and a social register of trust. He argues[14] that in economies of currency and credit, where there is an underlying element of uncertainty (or social risk), trust becomes an integral part of how value is produced by constructing the necessary context of an ethics of sociality that can accommodate and offset the dangers of risk-taking. Reflective of the ways risk was later to become itself the explicit object of organizational attention, Ulrich Beck[15]argues risk management has developed as a defining feature of governance in the postmodern age. Risk positions, he argues, supplant class positions as the key to contemporary existence and the production, management, and containment of risk have come to replace earlier governmental concerns with value and value distribution.

12   Hristova, *Data Infrastructures and Digital Labour*; T. Hristova, B. Neilson, and N. Rossiter, 'Digital Infrastructure, Liminality, and World-Making Via Asia On the Block Train: Rethinking Block Technologies on the YuXinOu Express', *International Journal of Communication* 15 (2021).
13   IPCC, '2—Determinants of Risk: Exposure and Vulnerability—IPCC', https://www.ipcc.ch/pdf/special-reports/srex/SREX-Chap2_FINAL.pdf.
14   G. Simmel, *The Philosophy of Money*, Milton Park: Routledge, 2004, 177–8.
15   U. Beck, *Risk Society: Towards a New Modernity*, trans. Ritter, M., Newbury Park, CA: SAGE Publications, 1992.

In the past two decades, in managerial discourse and in the family of standards related to ISO 31000, risk now appears as an ambivalent rather than purely negative presence. ISO 31000 establishes a terminology where risk is defined as an 'effect of uncertainty on objectives' and further explained as being 'a deviation from the expected [... that] can be positive, negative or both, and can address, create or result in opportunities and threats'.[16] This interpretation, widely adopted thanks to the significant clout of the International Standards Organisation, casts risk as a field of uncertainty that can be productive of gains and value for companies and institutions. The allure of risk reaffirms the core objectives that the standard sets for the principles of risk management: value creation and protection.

If risks create opportunities, then there is an imperative to pursue risk-taking. The accompanying ISO Guide 73:2009 formulates this imperative through the concept of 'risk appetite'—'the amount and type of risk that an organization is willing to pursue or retain'.[17] In the subsequent interpretation of risk appetite by the global consultancy firm Deloitte[18] the metaphor of consumption is taken even further, and becomes integrated into a framework of different levels of risk that leave a company either hungry, satiated or overfed with the amount of risk it takes on. However strained, the digestive metaphor reminds us of the historical figurations of the economic organization *as a body*: a corporation that is also corporeal, that lives and breathes, that warrants its own legal protections, and that consumes even as it produces. Even the language of university risk management statements can illustrate how closely its governance resembles a comparable decision-making framework to gambling consumption: calculating odds, then placing bets on low or high-risk outcomes depending upon an organizational appetite.

The adoption of these concepts of risk appetite and risk tolerance in the global ISO 31000 standard becomes a replicable model in all other standards related to risk management, including the standard for information technology security management ISO/IEC 27001 and the abovementioned standard for risk management in AI. The notion of risk and the parameters of risk management in the context of national, corporate and international governance have been significantly transformed by this standard, which introduces new understanding of how risk should be handled. The concept of acceptable risks and risk appetite also becomes influential in the way public institutions think of their duties with regards to state-collected data. For instance, the 2017 *Data availability and use* report published by the Royal Productivity Commission in Australia largely encourages the sharing of data between public and private entities and, specifically, the sharing of public datasets for the purposes of encouraging the economic growth and innovation in the local digital industry. Notably, it builds its argument for a more liberal approach to data sharing around the notion of risk appetite and the increased tolerance of risks related to the sharing of personal data in society. The report argues that as societal standards of privacy have

---

16   (ISO 31000: 2018), 3.1.
17   (ISO Guide 73:2009), 3.7.1.2.
18   Deloitte, 'Risk Appetite Frameworks: How to Spot the Genuine Article', available at https://www2.
      deloitte.com/content/dam/Deloitte/au/Documents/risk/deloitte-au-risk-appetite-frameworks-financial-
      services-0614.pdf, 2014.

shifted—due in no small part to the role of social media companies in normalising new practices of data sharing—so federal agencies should also adopt greater organisational risk in the sharing of data.

The emergence of AI risk management standards related to ISO 31000 suggests an intensification of attention to data and its value. Yet the economisation of data—by which we mean here the production of value, measured either through direct financial gain or through indirect reputational, HR or political benefit—is by no means novel. We situate our discussion here with the emergence of AI in the 2010s from its so-called 'winter' in prior decades. According to LeCun,[19] Chief Scientist at Facebook and a pioneer of AI, this emergence was the product of an alignment between hardware (specifically, the adaptation of GPUs to parallel data processing), software (open source libraries like Facebook's *PyTorch* and Google's *TensorFlow*), research refinements (in particular, the use of neural networks, stochastic gradient descent and back propagation) and the accumulation of large text, image and other media data sets. For technology companies like Facebook, Google, Baidu, and Alibaba—leaders in AI research as well as, by far, the largest monetizers of online advertising—the connections between data and value materialize both through the efficiencies of delivering relevant ads to consumers, and through the range of AI-driven services, from search results to content moderation, they offer to those consumers. Less conspicuous in terms of value is the ability to secure prominent data scientists, like LeCun and Geoffrey Hinton (Google), on the promise of being able to work with massive data sets to solve social and computational problems and produce 'state-of-the-art' AI research. In a period where the algorithmic paradigm appears to be shifting from large code bases to smaller code models training on plentiful data, the prevalence of data not only serves to produce economies of scale and differentiate organisations to advertisers and consumers, but also functions as a key HR attractor.

For the new titans of capitalism, and indeed for other private and public institutions, the governance of data is core business. Its very presence also produces risk to the value it creates. Data can be stolen, revealed, misused, corrupted, ignored, and skewed. Though far from the only subject for risk management, the centrality of data to organisational operations has meant that it is no less critical to the progressive formalization of risk through procedures, reviews, and standards in the twentieth and twenty-first century.[20] And varied data crises, from famous security breaches to the mobilisation of social network graphs for targeted political messaging,[21] also have inadvertently produced an avowedly ethical organisational subject, committed through terms, conditions, principles, charters, pledges, policies, and standards to protecting data within its orbit of control. As we argue here, at the same time as this subject places its ethics on display as one among so many paraded virtues, it also prepares for it to be placed at risk in the production of

19   Y. LeCun, 'Deep Learning Hardware: Past, Present, and Future', *IEEE International Solid-State Circuits Conference-(ISSCC)* 2019: 12–19.
20   M. Power, 'The Risk Management of Everything', *The Journal of Risk Finance*, 5(3), (2004): 58–65.
21   L. Munn, T. Hristova, and L. Magee, 'Clouded Data: Privacy and the Promise of Encryption', *Big Data & Society*, 6(1), (2019): 1–16.

value. Thus, the growing number of initiatives for the development of ethical frameworks of AI are not necessarily indicative of an attempt to minimise the risk of data harms. On the contrary, they can similarly speak of a turn towards embracing and socialising these risks.

This changing landscape of how risk is operationalized in the data economy and in the regulation of AI means that we are faced with a different constellation, in which notions of ethics are established and enacted. In this new context, data, automation, and artificial intelligence are not just reinforcing a mode of governance devoid of doubt and uncertainty.[22] They are also deployed in economies of risk where risk is acceptable within certain levels and is even sought after because of the crevice of uncertainty and ambiguity it opens and the possibilities for economic gain and other forms of value to be realised from it. This characterization resonates with early theorizations of the relationship between risk and entrepreneurship, innovation and capital, as argued, for example, by Brouwer,[23] who discusses the varied characterizations of the risk-taking entrepreneur by Weber, Schumpeter and Knight. But whereas these theorists, and despite their differences, each imagined early-stage capitalist risk eventually giving way to the rationalistic and monopolistic late-capitalist organization, in the present data economy it is possible to see risk as being deliberately reinjected by those organizations themselves, as a sort of energizing device to lift flagging rates of profit. In other words, risk is a feature of established and highly rationalist market incumbents as much as of disruptive entrepreneurs.

With the adoption of risk appetite by economic actors, ethics becomes key for negotiating the boundaries of extractivism and profit-making with regards to a highly socialized resource like data. This is done not only through an obvious contention with ethics codified into law and governance (see below, where we discuss Floridi's distinction between hard and soft ethics), exemplified in the numerous cases of law-skirting and infringement by Facebook, Google, and other actors. It is also evident in the corporate territorialization of the ethical field itself: developing AI ethics groups, making interventions in scholarly and activist debates (e.g. Facebook's FAIR group, or Microsoft's Aether committee), and developing the very standards by which AI and data use is judged and governed.

As we have argued, attempts to define what ethics of artificial intelligence entails are indicative of the role that ethics acquires in the international competition for AI leadership. The example of ISO 31000 and its provenance from a local Australian standard to a global standard whose model is replicated and referenced is a case in point: it not only shows the geopolitical stakes of exerting influence over the framing of key concepts related to risk and ethics, but also demonstrates that infrastructures like standards can operate alternately as extrastatecraft and as advancing the interests of specific nation states.

---

22   Amoore, 'Doubt and the Algorithm: On the Partial Accounts of Machine Learning', *Theory, Culture & Society*, 36(6), (2019): 147–69.
23   M.T. Brouwer, 'Weber, Schumpeter and Knight on Entrepreneurship and Economic Development', *Journal of Evolutionary Economics*, 12(1), (2002): 83–105.

Risk Infrastructures and the Geopolitics of AI Ethics

The case of ISO 31000 feeds into a particular national imaginary and geopolitical ambitions in Australia. Since the notion of risk outlined in the Australian standard for risk management AS/NZS 4360:2004 has been adopted in ISO 31000, it forms the basis of subsequent interpretations of risk in the text of documents regulating the use of artificial intelligence and, specifically, the risk management standard ISO/IEC 23894 and the standards for trustworthiness of AI.[24] This connection serves as a sort of claim of the Australian state of its involvement in shaping the global regulatory frameworks of artificial intelligence and provides a paradigmatic model for how to reproduce and assert this type of influence again. Standards Australia itself is part of the working group of ISO/IEC JTC 1/SC 42 and has, in addition, established a local Mirror Committee IT-043 that replicates the work on the international one and introduces the finished standards to Australia. The composition of the local chapter and the statements of Standards Australia can lead us to assume that acquiring a distinctive profile in shaping the ethics of AI is one of the key objectives of Australia in the international committees. It is indicative of these ambitions that the chair of the Mirror Committee, Aurelie Jacquet, is heavily involved in work on ethics and trustworthiness of AI. As she explains, ethics and the establishment of ethical norms and regulations form a central part of the tasks of her group.[25]

This novel extension of standards into the domain of the ethical may be welcomed, as an acknowledgement of the work by many critical scholars and activists to foreground ethical considerations in AI. But the case of ISO 31000 and the ambitions around it reveal how the extrastatecraft space of technological zones can be imbued with local national aspirations. Through these entanglements, risk is operationalised and incorporated within new geopolitical constellations and economic objectives with respect to AI and its emerging ethical frameworks. In some of its latest documents, the Australian standard-setting organisation—Standards Australia (SA)—outlines a very specific path for the country to claim leadership in the AI innovation space. In its 2020 report *An Artificial Intelligence Standards Roadmap: Making Australia's Voice Heard,* SA argues that Australia can take a different path to ensuring a leading position in the emerging economy through leading the development and implementation of standards, especially ones concerned with risk and ethics. The document discusses this possibility through the language of international markets, outlining the fact that Australia is not in a position to export AI technology, which is the more obvious path to gaining clout and prestige in the global AI race. Musing on this perceived deficiency of the national AI industry, SA sees the export of standards and guidelines as an alternative economic and political strategy. It specifically sees the example of ISO 31000 as a case that can be replicated in the future—a homegrown standard that is exported and becomes an influential global standard. The reference to the ISO 31000 model suggests that, in the development of AI strategies and standards, risk is operationalised not only as a concept but also through already

24   C. Naden, 'It's All About Trust', 2019, https://www.iso.org/news/ref2452.html.
25   Silverpond, 'The Role of Ethics in AI Development, Implementation and Governance', 2021, https://
     silverpond.com.au/ai-community/australian-ai-ecosystem-survey/aurelie-jacquet-2020-2021-
     australian-ai-ecosystem-survey/.

existing models of capitalising on frameworks of risk management. The standard for risk management is seen as a model that should be replicated—as a case of exportability and, importantly, as a case of rethinking the role and function of the nation state in international politics of standard-making.

This last point is a key part of the deliberations of SA. The idea of exporting a standard is articulated through the possibility of construing Australia as a test bed for the development of new standards:

> International Standards continue to provide the optimal channel for the design, development, deployment and evaluation of AI in a consistent manner. However, given the significant activity being undertaken within academia, consulting and some businesses on proposing, developing and trialling approaches to risk management and auditing of AI systems, there is an opportunity to codify some of these learnings, producing documents that can attest to Australian expertise, experience and workable solutions. This might subsequently form the basis for an International Standard. There is precedent for this, with Australian stakeholders having played a significant role in the development of AS/NZS 4360 (Risk Management), which was subsequently refined and adopted as an International Standard (ISO 31000:2009, Risk management – Principles and guidelines). A dedicated hub within Standards Australia, which brings disparate expertise together, would be the best way to achieve this. It could provide a test-bed, of the kind alluded to in the NIST Roadmap, where specific propositions, which could form the basis of content for Standards, could be tested with industry and other stakeholders.[26]

By entertaining the possibility of framing Australia as a test bed or an experimental hub for the development of global AI standards in areas like ethics and risk management, SA suggests a model that itself operationalises risk at multiple levels. The very idea of treating the country as a test bed is ridden with the contentious relationship between experiment and risk. Melinda Cooper[27] in her work on clinical trials and experimental labor argues that post-Fordist capitalism embraces a new political economy of risk that, especially in the IT and biomedical sectors, reframes risk as a source of value. This new approach to risk ties together experiment, innovation and the surpluses unlocked by the risks that workers and experimental subjects are expected to undertake. Cooper's conclusions may appear less relevant in a comparatively highly regulated nation like Australia, with respect to the fields of health and medicine. However, in nascent economic domains like data extraction, the country's combination of relatively poor protection and high digital uptake make it an ideal site

---

26   Standards Australia, *An Artificial Intelligence Standards Roadmap: Making Australia's Voice Heard. Final Report*, 2020, 35–36, https://www.standards.org.au/getmedia/ede81912-55a2-4d8e-849f-9844993c3b9d 1515-An-Artificial-Intelligence-Standards-Roadmap12-02-2020.pdf.aspxhttps://www.standards.org.au/getmedia/ede81912-55a2-4d8e-849f-9844993c3b9d/1515-An-Artificial-Intelligence-Standards-Roadmap12-02-2020.pdf.aspx.

27   M. Cooper, 'Experimental Labour—Offshoring Clinical Trials to China', *East Asian Science, Technology and Society: An International Journal*, 2(1), (2008): 73–92; Cooper, M.E. *Life as Surplus: Biotechnology and Capitalism in the Neoliberal Era*. Seattle: University of Washington Press, 2011.

for experimentation. We can easily see how the ambition to establish Australia as a test bed for standard development and the notion of risk appetite introduced by SA in 2004 are both consistent with this new economy of risk and experiment in late capitalism—an economy characterized by distinct geopolitical contours that enable capital to exploit specific ideal meeting points of regulatory environment, data accumulation, and declared 'risk appetite'.

The proposition of SA does, however, also introduce a new understanding of how the state relates to its subjects through a reconceptualization of risk as a technology of governance. Namely, this reframing happens through the notion of a test bed for innovation—an idea that has long found wide acceptance in the IT industry through various forms of launchpads, innovation hubs, and other experimental zones supported by state governments. The state as an experimental space carries the legacy of the entanglement of risk and containment that is at the heart of the very foundation of Australia as a settler colonial state and a penal colony,[28] and echoes other 'radical' policy experiments in the 2000s and 2010s with border control and mandatory detention, disastrously exported to Europe and other zones where human travel has become increasingly surveilled and militarized. Indeed, the standardization of risk management produces a generalizable model of political and economic calculation that can traverse institutional types (state, corporate, supranational, or otherwise 'extrastate') as well as objects of calculation (both human subjects and human-related electronic data about them). What is significant here at a geopolitical level is the role of middle-power countries that seek to embed themselves into the dynamics of AI superpower rivalry by performing specific critical functions, such as the elaboration of technical standards, that also can be framed within these high-risk manoeuvres as benign and politically neutral.

In this context ethics acquires a specific role as part of a complex tripartite market device that relates it to risk and value. In policy documents and standards-setting efforts the need to regulate AI and impose some level of ethical oversight through concepts like trustworthiness and ethics is tightly linked to the ambition of claiming leadership in the global space of AI economy. In 2019, the National Institute for Standards and Technology at the US Department of Commerce claims that 'United States global leadership in AI depends upon the Federal government playing an active and purpose-driven role in AI standards development'.[29] This entanglement of standard-building and leadership in AI is echoed in a 2020 report of Standards Australia where the notion that standards can help shape national leadership in the field of artificial intelligence is reinforced in the title: 'An Artificial Intelligence Standards Roadmap: Making Australia's Voice Heard'. A similar ambition is expressed in the Digital Strategy of the European Union where the proposed legal framework on AI is seen as a means to 'position Europe to play a leading role

---

28   L. Veracini, 'Understanding Colonialism and Settler Colonialism as Distinct Formations', *Interventions*, 16(5), (2014): 615–33.
29   National Institute for Standards and Technology, 'U.S. Leadership in AI: A Plan for Federal Engagement in Developing Technical Standards and Related Tools Prepared in Response to Executive Order 13859', 9 August 2019.

globally'.[30] Albeit not directly articulated in the same terms, the Chinese Ethical Norms for New Generation Artificial Intelligence (The National New Generation Artificial Intelligence Governance Specialist Committee 2021) are also largely interpreted in Western analysis as a sign of leadership ambition in the field of machine learning and artificial intelligence on the side of the government of China.[31]

These documents articulate national and regional ambitions for leadership in innovation in a global territoriality mapped across the still-emerging contours of machine learning and automation. At the same time, through definition, standardisation and operationalisation these frameworks also act to construct implied universal parameters of AI ethics that define and serve to hedge the risks that crystallise along these frontiers of innovation. Less a contradiction, these two purposes organise a specific relationship between ethics and risk. Moreover they help to explain why middle powers like Australia can occasionally receive such prominence in standard-setting arrangements: comparatively out of sight, they act as testing grounds or laboratories where successes can be scaled up through negotiations with countries with major technology interests, like China, the US, and the EU. Countries sponsoring such experimentation benefit through direct 'breakthrough' technologies (like WiFi in the case of Australia) and temporary elevation from periphery status in cycles of technological innovation.

Nonetheless, standard-setting arrangements for ethical AI, and AI for the most part unfold close to centres of research and development. This link between a leading position in the economy of data and the construction of specific parameters of what ethical AI is does not act to inhibit, for the most part, corporate profiteering through the mining of data and training of machine learning models. Rather they articulate a set of coordinates through which corporate actors especially are expected to navigate. Nor do nation states simply imprint standards; as the otherwise widely diverse circumstances of Chinese and US government oversight and interrogation of technology firms like Alibaba, Tencent, Facebook, Google, Apple, and Microsoft show, such coordinates are capable of being multiplied, repositioned or re-emphasised, as the calculations of what we identify as the tripartite risk-ethics-value equation between regulatory and corporate actors are seen to diverge.

Roxana Radu[32] notes that '[t]he countries hosting technology industry giants have taken the lead, with the ambition to dominate AI development at the global level in the next decade.' The ambition to claim leadership in the AI market through regulation is paradoxical and conflicting, and reveals the uneasy interdependencies between national government and multinational tech giants. It is not always clear what local initiatives with

---

30   European Commission, 'Regulatory Framework Proposal on Artificial Intelligence', 2022, https://
      digital-strategy.ec.europa.eu/en/policies/regulatory-framework-ai#:~:text=The%20proposed%20
      AI%20regulation%20ensures,address%20to%20avoid%20undesirable%20outcomes.
31   H. Roberts, J., Cowls, J. Morley, J. et al. 'The Chinese Approach to Artificial Intelligence: An Analysis of
      Policy, Ethics, and Regulation', AI & Soc 36, (2021): 59–77.
32   R. Radu, 'Steering the Governance of Artificial Intelligence: National Strategies in Perspective', Policy
      and Society 40(2), (2021): 182.

global ambitions, especially in the field of developing trustworthy, fair, responsible, or ethical AI, aim to achieve: market regulation, government oversight, or geoeconomic dominance through technocratic means. Nor can domestic agitation, including criticisms of technology overreach, which in the US has been voiced on both left and right side of politics, be ignored, even when the results of such agitation may appear to constrain nationalistic ambitions. A further paradox of calls to regulation has been the guarded support of those corporations most likely to be affected. CEO of Facebook, Mark Zuckerberg, has for example endorsed greater government oversight of his company's operations, no doubt aware that the costs of regulatory compliance are much easier borne by market incumbents and can be controlled both through investment in standards bodies and political lobbying. The roundabout logic of this endorsement inverts the public–private logic of the early Internet described by Birnhack and Elkin-Koren,[33] where states mobilized private firms registered within their jurisdictions for regulation and governance of the then-emerging cyberspace. Facebook's call for regulation asks for a reciprocal form of protection, in a situation where risks of non-compliance (such as fines) are relatively easily borne, and can be offset by an assumed greater public trust, once appropriate legislation is enacted. As scholars have argued, the support of Big Tech for ethics guidelines and norms suggests that ethics had become instrumentalized as a means to avoid—or just as likely, to steer—government oversight and regulation.[34]

The European Union General Data Protection Regulation (GDPR) has already proved the cross-border impact of legislative instruments and standardisation attempts that are focused on data and digital technologies.[35] GDPR's repercussions for companies around the world is enabled through the specific scope of the EU legislation—it applies to data of EU citizens— and the difficulties, especially for smaller organizations, to enforce differential rules for each individual user of platforms and web services that are global in their reach and use. The GDPR model has shown that local initiatives for the regulation of digital technologies and innovation can shape the global geopolitical and geoeconomic landscape for the data industries, establishing a national or supranational state actor as a leader—not just in a symbolic sense but also by having real impact on the digital economy. As Metzinger argues[36] from 'inside the tent' of AI ethics guideline development, the ambivalence of single nation-states like the US and China – regulating but also complicit in backing corporations with strong national affiliations – actually mean it is incumbent upon supranational or federated groups to build such guidelines for the rest of the world to follow.

---

33   M. Birnhack and N. Elkin-Koren, 'The Invisible Handshake: The Reemergence of the State in the Digital Environment', *SSRN Electronic Journal* 8(6), 2003: 1–57
34   T. Metzinger, 'Ethics Washing Made in Europe', *Der Tagspiegel*, 8 April 2019, https://www.tagesspiegel.de/politik/eu-guidelines-ethics-washing-made-in-europe/24195496.html; B. Wagner, 'Ethics as an Escape from Regulation. From "Ethics-washing" to Ethics-shopping?' in (eds) Bayamlioglu, E., Baraliuc, I., Janssens, L.A.W., Hildebrandt, M., Amsterdam (eds) *Being Profiled*, Amsterdam University Press, 2018, 84–9.
35   M. Goddard, 'The EU General Data Protection Regulation (GDPR): European Regulation that has a Global Impact', *International Journal of Market Research*, 59(6),(2017): 703–5; C. Niebel, 'The Impact of the General Data Protection Regulation on Innovation and the Global Political Economy', *Computer Law & Security Review*, 40, (2021): p.105523.
36   Metzinger, 'Ethics Washing Made in Europe'.

At the same time, the example of GDPR and its effect on digital innovation complicates the notion of what geopolitics is in the current environment. The EU legislation has had some contradictory consequences in terms of reconfiguring political and economic power. On one hand, it is largely seen as establishing the influence of the EU and what is termed 'European values' on the future development of data-based innovation.[37] On the other hand, and as a concrete case of the paradoxical effects of regulation we note above, GDPR has had the unanticipated consequence of consolidating corporate power and monopolies in the digital space by forcing some of the small actors out of competition, due to the added weight of monitoring for privacy compliance.[38] Johnson, Shiver, and Goldberg note that the introduction of GDPR, shortly after its adoption, led to a drop in the number of web partners of tech giants like Google and Facebook and to an increase of the market share of these big corporations.[39] This example of (perhaps) unintended market consolidation caused by the GDPR underscores the complexities of a multitude of actors involved in the development of data regulation and impacted by national, regional and transnational initiatives.

There is a comparable ambiguity in the role of geopolitical actors in the case of China. Chinese initiatives for regulating artificial intelligence and the ethics of data use and machine learning are often interpreted through the notion of a monolithic one-party state. However, the constellation of actors is more varied. The Chinese strategy for AI development entails coordination between central and local government, as well as select 'national champion' companies like Alibaba, Baidu, and Huawei.[40] Notably, the *Ethical Norms for the New Generation Artificial Intelligence* published by the Chinese government in late 2021[41] incorporate the rules of market competition as part of the ethical production and supply of AI—rules that can be interpreted in various ways but indicating regardless mixed political and economic agendas that underpin the understanding of what ethics is.While the effects of this and other Chinese state actions has led to a withering away of the market capitalization of firms like Alibaba,[42] they seem directed as much to the alignment of corporate with state interests—in for example the 'self-sufficiency' of China's

---

37 A. Daly, 'Neo-liberal Business-as-Usual or Post-Surveillance Capitalism with European Characteristics? The EU's General Data Protection Regulation in a Multi-Polar Internet', in *Communication Innovation and Infrastructure: A Critique of the New in a Multipolar World*, East Lansing: Michigan State University Press, (forthcoming, 2021) pp.66–95; O.J. Gstrein. and A.J. Zwitter, 'Extraterritorial Application of the GDPR: Promoting European Values or Power?', *Internet Policy Review* [online] 10(3) (2021), available at: https://policyreview.info/articles/analysis/extraterritorial-application-gdpr-promoting-european-values-or-power.

38 G. Johnson, G., S. Shriver, and S. Goldberg, 'Privacy & Market Concentration: Intended & Unintended Consequences of the GDPR', 2021. *3477686*.

39 Johnson, Shriver, and Goldberg, 'Privacy & Market Concentration: Intended & Unintended Consequences of the GDPR', 15.

40 H. Roberts, J., Cowls, J. Morley, J. et al., 'The Chinese Approach to Artificial Intelligence: An Analysis of Policy, Ethics, and Regulation'.

41 International Research Center for AI Ethics and Governance, 2021.

42 From its highpoint of $304.69 USD on October 1 2020, Alibaba's US-listed holding company has declined by 69 percent at time of writing (June 4) (Yahoo Finance. Alibaba Group Holding Limited (BABA), 2022, https://finance.yahoo.com/quote/BABA/).

semiconductor supply, an area in which Alibaba has made recent surprising in-roads[43]—
as to the establishment of greater competition or the pursuit of 'common prosperity.'[44]

The varied cases of regulation seek to enshrine equally varied ideas of ethical data governance. Indeed, Luciano Floridi[45] suggests that we need two notions of ethics when analyzing data and AI ethics: hard (or normative) ethics and soft (or post-compliance) ethics. Soft ethics operates within the parameters of existing legislation and the feasibility of adhering to legal and moral norms of action. It entails calculation and compromise, and is openly motivated and constrained by existing political and economic realities. While Floridi links soft ethics to an evolutionary development of governance systems and places EU at the helm of political entities where soft ethics can be applied without compromising human rights, his distinction between ethics as moral philosophy and ethics in the context of legislative and technocratic norms of compliance and regulation reveals one important aspect of data ethics and AI ethics that we draw upon. Ethics in the field of digital technology and AI is increasingly reshaped and defined by initiatives for regulation and self-regulation of the industry. This development points to the contested political terrain within which a notion of the ethical is constructed; one that has also shaped the normative concepts of western moral philosophy that are often seen as universal and remain unquestioned. Indeed, Floridi's high regard for GDPR can be seen to further the perception of a deceptively universalist morality at the expense of a disregard for the emergence of locally informed and politically grounded principles of data ethics such as Indigenous data sovereignty. The Eurocentricity of moral philosophy has been criticised from multiple standpoints with authors like Rosi Braidotti, Nikita Dhawan and Homi Bhabha[46] questioning the assumptions of universal applicability from the perspective of feminist, posthumanist, and postcolonial studies. Paradoxically, the emergence of industry-led notion of data ethics serves as yet another reminder of the inherently political work of establishing a field of ethical practice and the categories that define it. In the case of ISO 31000, we see a notion of ethics construed in relation to two other key concepts of political and economic governance: risk and value.

Conclusion

The operationalization of risk and ethics in the socio-technical infrastructures of standard-making and legislative documents suggests that states, companies and supranational organisations navigate and construct a new geopolitical framework of what ethics, risks and

43   Dashveenjit Kaur, 'China's most advanced chip may soon come from Alibaba', *Techwire Asia*, 21 October 2021. https://techwireasia.com/2021/10/the-new-chip-by-alibaba-may-be-one-of-the-most-advanced-in-china/.
44   Brian Liu and Raquel Leslie, 'China's Tech Crackdown: A Year-In-Review', *Lawfare*, 7 January 2022. https://web.archive.org/web/20220506205610/https://www.lawfareblog.com/chinas-tech-crackdown-year-review.
45   L. Floridi, 'Soft Ethics and the Governance of the Digital', *Philosophy & Technology*, 31(1), (2018): 1–8.
46   R. Braidotti, *Transpositions: On Nomadic Ethics*. Cambridge: Polity, 2006; N. Dhawan, 'Can Non-Europeans Philosophize? Transnational Literacy and Planetary Ethics in a Global Age', *Hypatia*, 32(3), (2017): 488–505; H. Bhabha, 'Culture's In-between', in S. Hall, and P. du Gay (eds) *Questions of Cultural Identity*, London: SAGE, 1996, pp. 53–60.

their mediation, through devices of control and management, entail. We argue that value stands in a kind of paradoxical relationship to these other terms. On the one hand, it works to destabilise any geopolitical sureties underpinned by standards, producing new vectors of risk operation and putting into question the possibility of universal ethical principles. On the other, value in its various determinations—economic for corporations, geopolitical for states, and, at least within a literature devoted to the benefits of AI, epistemic for those whose data might, in the hands of medical, legal, or consumer institutions, be wrangled into more accurate predictions—also prepares the ground upon which risks can be taken and ethical principles prepared. Together, these three concepts and their shifting configurations help organize the marketplace of data exchange and algorithmic production.

In the context of AI regulation, this interrelationship operates through two distinct conceptualizations of risk. First, in algorithms and tools of risk management, preemptive control, and profiling, AI is articulated as a technology to eliminate risks.[47] Second, through the notion of 'risk appetite', AI enters into ambiguous relations of tolerable levels of risks to individuals, communities, and nation-states, which are justified as part of the striving for leadership and innovation in the field of machine learning and AI. As productive agents in this new economy, risks of harms generated by data-supported decisions and systems motivate the capitalization of risk itself, a move that, though different in practice, is consistent with the operationalization of risk in finance.[48] This operationalization appears to be part of the framework of financial and social behaviour of organisations in handling big data, and to that extent, every case of data breach or data harm helps to make new markets for that operationalization. Strategies for dealing with contingency are increasingly modelled through 'risk appetite' statements[49] which in the context of data economies prioritize sharing and interoperability in order to unlock the value potential of datasets, but also factor in the costs inherent in managing risk.

The complex composition of the value of big data reiterates the dependency described by Simmel between trust and risk in the social relations of the new economy. Rather than functioning as an abstract moral category or code that sits outside and presides over such relations, ethics here supplies the frameworks of sociality and trust within which the value of big data can be produced and circulated. The case of Standards Australia and their global ambitions for AI leadership through standardization show that the socialization of risk is becoming a central part of the data economy, not just in the sphere of production and use, but also in the domain of regulation. This leads to a paradoxical relationship between risk and ethics: the development of AI and data ethics regulations provides the framework within which data-produced risks can be contained, even while ethics itself becomes a vehicle for

---

47   L. Amoore, 'Data Derivatives: On the Emergence of a Security Risk Calculus for our Times'; Amoore, 'Security and the Incalculable'; Amoore, *Cloud Ethics*; 2020, Aradau and Blanke, 'The (Big) Data-security assemblage: Knowledge and critique' Eubanks, *Automating Inequality: How High-Tech Tools Profile, Police, and Punish the Poor*, among many.

48   Cooper, 'Experimental Labour—Offshoring Clinical Trials to China', A. Akhigbe, A.D. Martin, and A.M. Whyte, 'Dodd–Frank and Risk in the Financial Services Industry', *Review of Quantitative Finance and Accounting*, 47(2) (2016): 395–415.

49   Productivity Commission, 2017; PricewaterhouseCoopers, 2012.

the socialization of new forms of risk through experimental hubs and laboratory practices that can be scaled up to the level of a whole nation-state. This claim does not diminish the importance of social pressure and reputational stakes in the push for adopting ethical practices for exploiting big data,[50] but rather accentuates it, stressing that managing trust and ethics are now integral to the extraction of economic value from highly socialized resources such as the mass aggregates of social data we now collectively produce.

Funding disclosure

Work on this article was conducted as part of the project The Geopolitics of Automation (ID: GA64648) funded under the Discovery funding scheme of the Australian Research Council.

References

Akhigbe, A., Martin, A.D., and Whyte, A.M. 'Dodd–Frank and Risk in the Financial Services Industry', *Review of Quantitative Finance and Accounting*, 47(2) (2016): 395–415.

Amoore, L. 'Data Derivatives: On the Emergence of a Security Risk Calculus for our Times', *Theory, Culture & Society*, 28(6), (2011): 24–43.

——. 'Security and the Incalculable', *Security Dialogue*, 45(5), (2014): 423–39.

——. 'Doubt and the Algorithm: On the Partial Accounts of Machine Learning', *Theory, Culture & Society*, 36(6), (2019): 147–69.

——. *Cloud Ethics*. Durham: Duke University Press, 2020.

Aradau, C. and Blanke, T. 'The (Big) Data-security assemblage: Knowledge and critique', *Big Data & Society*, issue 2(2) (2015): 1–12.

——. 'Politics of Prediction: Security and the Time/Space of Governmentality in the Age of Big Data', *European Journal of Social Theory*, 20(3), (2017): 373–91.

Barry, A. 'Technological Zones', *European Journal of Social Theory*, 9(2), (2006): 239–53.

Beck, U. *Risk Society: Towards a New Modernity*, trans. Ritter, M., Newbury Park, CA: SAGE Publications, 1992.

Bhabha, H.K. 'Culture's In-between', in Hall, S. & du Gay, P. (eds) *Questions of Cultural Identity*, [CA: SAGE Publications], 1996, pp. 53–60.

Birnhack, M. and Elkin-Koren, N. 'The Invisible Handshake: The Reemergence of the State in the Digital Environment', *SSRN Electronic Journal* 8(6), (2003): 1-57.

Brouwer, M.T. 'Weber, Schumpeter and Knight on Entrepreneurship and Economic Development', *Journal of Evolutionary Economics*, 12(1), (2002): 83–105.

Braidotti, R. *Transpositions: On Nomadic Ethics*. Cambridge: Polity, 2006.

Clarke, R. 'Big Data, Big Risks', *Information Systems Journal*, 26(1), (2016): 77–90.

Cooper, M. 'Experimental Labour—Offshoring Clinical Trials to China', *East Asian Science, Technology and Society: An International Journal*, 2(1), (2008): 73–92.

---

50 W.A. Günther, M.H.R. Mehrizi, M. Huysman, and F. Feldberg, 'Debating Big Data: A Literature Review on Realizing Value from Big Data', *The Journal of Strategic Information Systems*, 26(3), (2017): 191–209; R. Clarke, 'Big Data, Big Risks', *Information Systems Journal*, 26(1), (2016): 77–90.

Cooper, M.E. *Life as Surplus: Biotechnology and Capitalism in the Neoliberal Era*. Seattle: University of Washington Press, 2011.

Daly, A. 'Neo-liberal Business-as-Usual or Post-Surveillance Capitalism with European Characteristics? The EU's General Data Protection Regulation in a Multi-Polar Internet', in Hoyng, R. & Pak Lei Chong, G. (eds), *Critiquing Communication Innovation New Media in a Multipolar World. US–China Relations in the Age of Globalization*, Michigan State University Press, 2022, pp. 29–54.

Deloitte. 'Risk Appetite Frameworks: How to Spot the Genuine Article', available at https://www2. deloitte.com/content/dam/Deloitte/au/Documents/risk/deloitte-au-risk-appetite-frameworks-financial-services-0614.pdf, 2014.

Dhawan, N. 'Can Non-Europeans Philosophize? Transnational Literacy and Planetary Ethics in a Global Age', *Hypatia*, 32(3), (2017): 488–505.

Easterling, K. *Extrastatecraft: The Power of Infrastructure Space*. London: Verso Books, 2014.

The National New Generation Artificial Intelligence Governance Specialist Committee. 'Ethical Norms for New Generation Artificial Intelligence', 2021, English translation available at: https://cset. georgetown.edu/wp-content/uploads/t0400_AI_ethical_norms_EN.pdf.

Eubanks, V. *Automating Inequality: How High-Tech Tools Profile, Police, and Punish the Poor*, New York: St. Martin's Press, 2018.

European Commission. 'Regulatory Framework Proposal on Artificial Intelligence',2022, available at: https://digital-strategy.ec.europa.eu/en/policies/regulatory-framework-ai#:~:text=The%20 proposed%20AI%20regulation%20ensures,address%20to%20avoid%20undesirable%20outcomes.

Galloway, A. *Protocol: How Control Exists after Decentralization*, Cambridge, Massachusetts: MIT Press, 2004.

Goddard, M. 'The EU General Data Protection Regulation (GDPR): European Regulation that has a Global Impact', *International Journal of Market Research* 59 (6, 2017): 703–5.

Gstrein, O.J. and Zwitter, A.J. 'Extraterritorial Application of the GDPR: Promoting European Values or Power?', *Internet Policy Review* [online] 10(3) (2021), available at: https://policyreview.info/articles/analysis/extraterritorial-application-gdpr-promoting-european-values-or-power.

Günther, W.A., Mehrizi, M.H.R., Huysman, M. and Feldberg, F. 'Debating Big Data: A Literature Review on Realizing Value from Big Data', *The Journal of Strategic Information Systems*, 26(3), (2017): 191–209.

Floridi, L. 'Soft Ethics and the Governance of the Digital', *Philosophy & Technology*, 31(1), (2018): 1–8.

Foucault, M. *Security, Territory, Population: Lectures at the Collège De France 1977–1978*, trans. G. Burchell. New York: Picador, 2007.

Hoelzl, I. and Marie, R. *Softimage: Towards a New Theory of the Digital Image*, Bristol, UK: Intellect Books, 2015.

Hristova, T. *Data Infrastructures and Digital Labour: The Case of Teleradiology*, PhD diss., Western Sydney University, Sydney, 2020.

Hristova, T., Neilson, B. and Rossiter, N. 'Digital Infrastructure, Liminality, and World-Making Via Asial On the Block Train: Rethinking Block Technologies on the YuXinOu Express', *International Journal of Communication* 15 (2021): 2613–2630.

International Research Center for AI Ethics and Governance. *The Ethical Norms for the New Generation Artificial Intelligence, China*, 2021, available at: https://ai-ethics-and-governance. institute/2021/09/27/the-ethical-norms-for-the-new-generation-artificial-intelligence-china/.

ISO/IEC. 2022. International standard ISO/IEC DIS 23894. Information technology—Artificial intelligence—Risk management. International Organization for Standardization/International Electrotechnical Commission, (draft), Available at: https://www.iso.org/standard/77304.html.

ISO/IEC 27001. Information security management. International Organization for Standardization/International Electrotechnical Commission, 2013, https://www.iso.org/standard/54534.html.

ISO Guide 73:2009. Risk management—Vocabulary, International Organization for Standardization, 2009, https://www.iso.org/obp/ui/#iso:std:iso:guide:73:ed-1:v1:en.

ISO 31000: 2018 Risk management—Guidelines, International Organization for Standardization, 2018, https://www.iso.org/obp/ui/#iso:std:iso:31000:ed-2:v1:en.

Johnson, G., Shriver, S. and Goldberg, S. 'Privacy & Market Concentration: Intended & Unintended Consequences of the GDPR', 2021, https://dx.doi.org/10.2139/ssrn.3477686.

Kitchin, R. 'Thinking Critically About and Researching Algorithms', *Information, Communication & Society*, 20(1), (2017): 14–29.

LeCun, Y. 'Deep Learning Hardware: Past, Present, and Future', *IEEE International Solid-State Circuits Conference-(ISSCC)* 2019: 12–19.

Metzinger, T. 'Ethics Washing Made in Europe', *Der Tagspiegel*, 8 April 2019, https://www.tagesspiegel.de/politik/eu-guidelines-ethics-washing-made-in-europe/24195496.html.

Munn, L., Hristova, T., & Magee, L. 'Clouded Data: Privacy and the Promise of Encryption', *Big Data & Society*, 6(1), (2019): 1–16.

Murphy, C.N. and Yates, J. *The International Organization for Standardization (ISO): Global Governance through Voluntary Consensus*. Milton Park: Routledge, 2009.

Naden, C. 'It's All About Trust', 2019, https://www.iso.org/news/ref2452.html.

National Institute for Standards and Technology. 'U.S. Leadership in AI: A Plan for Federal Engagement in Developing Technical Standards and Related Tools Prepared in Response to Executive Order 13859', 9 August 2019, https://www.nist.gov/system/files/documents/2019/08/10/ai_standards_fedengagement_plan_9aug2019.pdf.

Niebel, C. 'The Impact of the General Data Protection Regulation on Innovation and the Global Political Economy', *Computer Law & Security Review*, 40, (2021) 105523: p. 1–15.

Power, M. 'The Risk Management of Everything', *The Journal of Risk Finance*, 5(3), (2004): 58–65.

Productivity Commission. 'Data Availability and Use: Productivity Commission Inquiry Report', 2017. Available at: https://www.pc.gov.au/inquiries/completed/data-access/report/data-access.pdf.

Radu, R. 'Steering the Governance of Artificial Intelligence: National Strategies in Perspective', *Policy and Society* 40(2), (2021): 178–93.

Roberts, H., Cowls, J., Morley, J. et al. 'The Chinese Approach to Artificial Intelligence: An Analysis of Policy, Ethics, and Regulation', *AI & Soc* 36, (2021): 59–77.

Silverpond. 'The Role of Ethics in AI Development, Implementation and Governance', 2021, https://silverpond.com.au/ai-community/australian-ai-ecosystem-survey/aurelie-jacquet-2020-2021-australian-ai-ecosystem-survey/.

Simmel, G. *The Philosophy of Money*, Milton Park: Routledge, 2004.

Standards Australia. *An Artificial Intelligence Standards Roadmap: Making Australia's Voice Heard. Final Report*, 2020, https://www.standards.org.au/getmedia/ede81912-55a2-4d8e-849f-9844993c3b9d/1515-An-Artificial-Intelligence-Standards-Roadmap12-02-2020.pdf.aspx.

Veracini, L. 'Understanding Colonialism and Settler Colonialism as Distinct Formations', *Interventions*, 16(5), (2014): 615–33.

Wagner, B. 'Ethics as an Escape from Regulation. From "Ethics-washing" to Ethics-shopping?' in Bayamlioglu, E., Baraliuc, I., Janssens, L.A.W., Hildebrandt, M. (eds) *Being Profiled*, Amsterdam: Amsterdam University Press, 2018, 84–9.

Wilkinson, M., Dumontier, M., Aalbersberg, I. et al. 'The FAIR Guiding Principles for Scientific Data Management and Stewardship', *Sci Data* 3, 160018, (2016): 1–9.

Yahoo Finance. Alibaba Group Holding Limited (BABA), 2022, https://finance.yahoo.com/quote/BABA/.

MILITARY VIRTUES AND THE LIMITS OF 'ETHICS' IN AI RESEARCH

MICHAEL RICHARDSON

War trades on virtue. The virtue of warriors, of just causes, of doing what must be done in the face of adversity to sustain nation or religion. War's virtue extends to antiquity, at least in the West, but its modern articulation bears distinct characteristics. Virtuous war is now technological war, war applied with precision, information, rationality, and proportionality bequeathed by technological revolutions of logistics, science, and computation. In the shift currently underway to autonomous weapons systems (AWS) and the incorporation of artificial intelligence (AI) more generally into warfare, virtue functions to sell publics and institutions on the necessity of ever more complex, more codified, and more inscrutable emergent technologies. Virtue does not simply flow from AWS and military AI, but is imbued in them by the incorporation of laws and ethics within the systems themselves. Or so the story goes. Just as the virtues of virtuality contributed to the obscuring of the violence of America's forever wars in the aftermath of 9/11, so too do the embrace and promotion of the virtues of autonomous systems risk occluding the reproduction and intensification of existing injuries and injustices, as well as the creation of new forms of violence and oppression.

While Big Tech's forays into U.S. military contracts tend to attract controversy—think Google and the outrage over its work to apply TensorFlow algorithms to drone image processing as part of the Department of Defense's (DoD) Project Maven initiative—interdependencies between militaries and private and civil institutions are equally pernicious in the thriving ecologies of start-ups, research translation hubs, defence funding programs, government initiatives, cash-strapped universities, and grant-hungry academics that can be found across the globe. In these economies of virtue, 'ethics' serve not only to facilitate mutually beneficial collaborations by cloaking military violence but also as potential commodities, able to be coded into the very technologies at hand.[1] Defence researchers and companies can not only *be* virtuous, but also can *make* war virtuous too. In this chapter, I examine the emerging military technology industry in Australia and its relation to academia to argue that military economies of virtue operate in ways that are similar to and different from those at work at the wider nexus of the tech sector and AI research in the academy.

Militaries are well behind the private sector in AI and big data development and expertise. This reality is accelerating collaborative, industry-led processes that mimic aspects of the Silicon Valley model of agile development, as the head of Pentagon's Algorithmic Warfare Cross-Functional Warfare Team (AWCFT) admitted on its formation in 2017.[2] This move-fast-and-

---

1   Thao Phan et al., "Economies of Virtue: The Circulation of 'Ethics' in Big Tech," *Science as Culture* 31.1 (2021): 121–35.

2   Department of Defence, 'Memorandum for the Establishment of an Algorithmic Warfare Cross-Functional Team (Project Maven),' 26 April 2017, https://www.govexec.com/media/gbc/docs/pdfs_edit/establishment_of_the_awcft_project_maven.pdf.

break-things approach could have serious repercussions given the life and death situations in which military technology is often applied. But militaries are not only valuable clients for Big Tech, but also increasingly important sources of funding for academic research. In the context of military AI, 'ethics' possesses an economic function that frames, facilitates, and feeds engagements between industry, academia, and military institutions. Military technologies and especially weapons systems are often framed by distinct ethics discourses, which emerge from a melange of the laws of armed conflict, international humanitarian law, specific and predefined rules of engagement, and—more nebulously—a warrior ethos. Militaries, including the Australian Defence Force (ADF), tend to see ethics as instrumental and principally related to conduct on and off the battlefield by individual soldiers, rather than enmeshed with larger questions of justice or societal obligation. Ethics are typically posed as both values to hold and problems to solve. When this approach encounters military AI, the limits of 'ethics' as a framework for reducing harm become clear: ethics are already subordinated to martial violence in that they are always concerned with enabling its infliction.

Military Virtues

According to international relations scholar James Der Derian, the growing centrality of computation to warfare that began in the Cold War and accelerated dramatically in its aftermath signals the emergence of a new mode of armed conflict led by the United States. 'At the heart of virtuous war,' writes Der Derian, 'is the technical capability and ethical imperative to threaten and, if necessary, actualise violence from a distance—*with no or minimal casualties*.'[3] Of course, virtuous war has not eliminated killing, nor the killing of civilians, as the use of drones and autonomous systems by the United States and Israel readily attests. Nor does virtuous war stop at violence itself: war in Der Derian's conception is also virtual, in the sense that it depends more and more upon information and abstraction. While the attempt to capture both 'virtue' and 'virtual' in his coining of a new form of warfare is somewhat murky, his analysis nonetheless points to the close relation between emergent forms of warfare dependent on simulation, modelling, computation, automation, and autonomy and the discursive refiguring of warfare that legitimises its centrality. As Der Derian points out, virtuous war is produced by and in turn sustains an amorphous array of agencies, actors, and institutions that he calls the military-industrial-media-entertainment network, or MIME-NET.[4] Hovering close at hand is the university and its researchers.

Tight ties between militaries and academia are far from new, both in the U.S. and elsewhere. During the Cold War, the Department of Defense (DoD), Central Intelligence Agency (CIA), and the Defence Advanced Research Projects Agency (DARPA) began directly funding research in the U.S. and around the world across a host of disciplines, from nuclear physics to psychology to medicine to anthropology. DARPA also funded the Strategic Computing Initiative, which pumped over USD\$1bn into advanced computation and artificial intelligence from 1983 to 1993. But military funding was also critical to the very emergence of computation and

---

3   James Der Derian, *Virtuous War: Mapping the Military-Industrial-Media-Entertainment Network*, 2nd edn., New York: Routledge, 2009, p. xxxi.
4   Der Derian, *Virtuous War*, p. 83.

cybernetics, which laid the conceptual and mathematical foundation for contemporary techniques of machine learning that are often packaged and promoted as 'Artificial Intelligence,'[5] even if they largely depend on human labour.[6] Whether applied to military or civilian contexts, contemporary techniques of machine learning depend on compute power that often far exceeds the capacity of university labs, even when resources are pooled between institutions. This has contributed to what Meredith Whittaker calls the 'capture' of AI research by Big Tech, in which researchers become dependent on access to platforms run by Amazon, Google, and Microsoft, and so tend to undertake research that fits within AI paradigms that reproduce the existing infrastructures as beneficial and necessary.[7] This dependence operates in the shadow of recurring controversies surrounding the social, cultural, and political impacts of Big Tech (and particularly Facebook, Google, and Amazon).

These controversies in turn intensify the need for 'economies of virtue' in which 'virtue and ethics are the primary objects that are produced and circulated by groups inside Big Tech— through the establishment of, for example, ethics boards and working groups—and also outside, from universities, research institutes, consultancies, and other allied industries.'[8] As the editors of this volume point out in their recent provocation on the subject, this economy arises in a context of a growing crisis in public funding of Western universities and of research in particular, which has intensified dependencies such as that of AI research on Big Tech dollars. Examination of these relations in a commercial setting is critical, but military, national security, and intelligence entanglements cannot be excised from the equation or treated as a minor case study. While the critical scholarship on the incorporation of AI into war and national security continues to grow, the institutional role of universities and funding mechanisms in that process demands more attention.[9]

Universities, as Alison Howell persuasively argues, have not been recently 'militarised' but have always been institutions produced by martial politics and in service of martial ends.[10] As noted above, the internet more generally and AI itself owed and continue to owe much to military funding and objectives, both in direct and indirect ways. Today in the United States, one of the leading proponents of military AI development and a cheerleader for an

5   Orit Halpern, *Beautiful Data: A History of Vision and Reason since 1945*, Durham: Duke University Press, 2015.
6   Jathan Sadowski, 'Potemkin AI,' *Real Life*, 6 August 2018, https://reallifemag.com/potemkin-ai/.
7   Meredith Whittaker, 'The Steep Cost of Capture,' *Interactions* 28.6 (2021): 50–55.
8   Phan et al., 'Economies of Virtue,' p. 2.
9   See, for example, Louise Amoore, 'Algorithmic War: Everyday Geographies of the War on Terror,' *Antipode* 41, no. 1 (2009): 49–69; Louise Amoore, *Cloud Ethics: Algorithms and the Attributes of Ourselves and Others* Durham: Duke University Press, 2020; Rocco Bellanova, Katja Lindskov Jacobsen, and Linda Monsees, 'Taking the Trouble: Science, Technology and Security Studies', *Critical Studies on Security* 8.2 (2020): 87–100; Jeremy Packer and Joshua Reeves, *Killer Apps: War, Media, Machine*, Durham: Duke University Press, 2020; Lucy Suchman, 'Algorithmic Warfare and the Reinvention of Accuracy,' *Critical Studies on Security* 8.2 (2020): 1–13; Lucy Suchman, Karolina Follis, and Jutta Weber, 'Tracking and Targeting: Sociotechnologies of (In)Security', *Science, Technology, & Human Values* 42.6 (2017): 983–1002.
10 Alison Howell, 'Forget "Militarization": Race, Disability and the "Martial Politics" of the Police and of the University', *International Feminist Journal of Politics* 20.2 (2018): 117–36.

international AI arms race is former Google CEO Eric Schmidt, now the head of Defence Technology Innovation Board. For Schmidt and his fellow travellers, military AI applications are always already virtuous precisely because they secure the state against threat and strengthen its standing in the global arena. All this could be understood as an attempt to securitize AI itself, such that much of the work that happens in this sphere enters into a domain outside ordinary politics and, in doing so, operates in the exceptional space of security.[11] The task, then, is to examine *how* militaries participate in economies of virtue in AI research, because the way they conceive and commodify ethics is often different from civilian actors.

This chapter takes up this question of how militaries participate in economies of virtue by examining the Australian context, rather than the American. This examination is instructive because Australia is in the early days of a deliberate strategic effort to accelerate its military industries, both to provide homegrown technology and to produce a new export sector. In military spending terms, Australia is a moderate player, committing $44.619 bn in 2021–22, or 2.09 percent of GDP and 1.4 percent of total global defence spending (compared to 39 percent by the US and 13 percent by China), but with those figures set to grow under commitments made by the Morrison government, including at least $70bn for nuclear powered submarines under the new tripartite AUKUS arrangement.[12] In export terms, Australia's defence industry is barely a player at all, with just $5.5bn in exports in 2019–20. But that figure is up from $1.5bn in 2017–18, the direct result of a range of government initiatives, targeted investment strategies, academic research funding programs, and knowledge transfer hubs. Together, these aim to hothouse military technology start-ups by echoing the public–private partnerships so beloved by neoliberal infrastructure builders.

To show how military ethics functions within economies of virtue, this essay argues that three critical dynamics around 'ethics' are shaping the emerging military technology industry in Australia and its relation to academia. I begin by examining how ethics function as a martial commodity in military technology start-ups, using the case study of Cyborg Dynamics Engineering and its Athena AI platform. Next, I turn to the discursive function that ethics serves in the growing defence industries in Australia by examining the role of new Defence Collaborative Research Centre (DCRC) initiatives, with a focus on the Trusted Autonomous Systems DCRC in Brisbane, Queensland. Third, I make the deliberately provocative proposal that 'ethics' facilitates engagement with universities, with research funding as a central factor, materialised through centres, networks, symposiums, and workshops. In this context, ethics

---

11   Barry Buzan, Ole Wæver, and Jaap de Wilde, *Security: A New Framework for Analysis*, Boulder: Lynne Reiner Publishers, 1998.

12   Science Department of Industry, 'Growth opportunities,' Text, Department of Industry, Science, Energy and Resources, Department of Industry, Science, Energy and Resources, 30 March 2021, https://www.industry.gov.au/data-and-publications/defence-national-manufacturing-priority-road-map/growth-opportunities; Ministers for the Department of Industry, Science, Energy and Resources, 'Action Plan to Supercharge Research Commercialisation,' 2 February 2 2022, https://www.minister.industry.gov.au/ministers/taylor/media-releases/action-plan-supercharge-research-commercialisation; Tory Shepherd, 'Australia's Aukus Nuclear Submarines Could Cost as Much as $171bn, Report Finds,' *Guardian*, 13 December 2021, sec. World news, https://www.theguardian.com/world/2021/dec/14/australias-aukus-nuclear-submarines-estimated-to-cost-at-least-70bn.

serves as a keyword of the defence-academia-industrial complex. In closing, I argue that martial conceptions of ethics and virtue are a distinct yet critical component of economies of virtue that require further research and sustained critical attention.

Military Ethics as Code and Commodity

Ethics, laws, and codes abound in military context, from the Laws of Armed Conflict (LOAC) to Codes of Conduct to more amorphous yet morally forceful concepts such as the warrior ethos. States themselves are constrained—in theory, if not always in practice—by international laws, which determine both the instances in which war may be deemed just and which protect the rights of civilians within conflict. When soldiers go to war, 'they are bound by a series of ethical principles that proscribe particular actions and forbid others.'[13] Virtuous conduct might not be set out in such principles, but instead be culturally produced and maintained within particularly armed services or units. We might think of virtue as more closely tied with morality—with good character—whereas ethics concerns behaviour and the limits of what is allowable in certain circumstances. Both military ethics and virtue are not immutable but rather have developed substantially over time, often in association with the rise of new forms of warfare such as the proliferation of airpower in the twentieth century. Conflated with codes and laws governing conduct, ethics tend to be narrowly conceived in military contexts, whereas soldiers can feel a more complex and intense relation to the warrior ethos.

With the emergence of technologies for finding, selecting, targeting, and killing, the potential to code ethics into computational systems has proven alluring to military leaders. As Christian Enemark has observed, the rise of drone warfare changes the ethical calculus of war for states, as the lack of exposure of soldiers to risk and the arguable reduction in civilian casualties promises to produce more ethical warfare through technological advancement.[14] Autonomous weapons systems promise to further remove the fallible and flawed human decision-making from the equation, transforming the codes of law, ethics, and conduct into computational decision-trees that can be applied in measured, flexible, and reliable fashion by autonomous systems, whether 'intelligent' or not. Here, questions of ethics often turn on the relation of a human operator to the kill decision—in-the-loop, on the loop, or off-the-loop—or, more fundamentally, on a moral insistence that killing in war should always be a human decision.[15] If contemporary developments in AWS and the failure of the 2021 Convention on Conventional Weapons (CCW) to regulate their use is an indication, the stance that views automated killing as morally reprehensible is in grave trouble. There are huge philosophical and practical implications of the increasing

---

13   Matthew Beard, 'Beyond Tallinn: The Code of the Cyberwarrior?' in *Binary Bullets: The Ethics of Cyberwarfare*, Fritz Allhoff, Adam Henschke, and Bradley Jay Strawser (eds), New York: Oxford University Press, 2016, p. 139.

14   Christian Enemark, *Armed Drones and the Ethics of War: Military Virtue in a Post-Heroic Age*, London: Routledge, 2014.

15   Elke Schwarz, *Death Machines: The Ethics of Violent Technologies*, Manchester: Manchester University Press, 2018; Noel Sharkey, 'Automating Warfare: Lessons Learned from the Drones', *Journal of Law, Information and Science* 21.2 (2011): 140–54.

autonomy of warfare, whether in terms of the material operation of AWS or in relation to the algorithmic processes and thinking that underpin them, which threaten to overwhelm the very possibility of law containing martial violence that preempts and outpaces human capacities to think and decide.[16]

But while scholars, activists, and publics around the world remain apprehensive about the dangers of 'killer robots,' the question of whether machines will decide on lethal actions has largely been decided in practice. Here the distinct nature of military ethics actually facilitates the emergence of ever-more autonomous technologies. Even if they are embedded in a detailed social, institutional, historical, and philosophical context (see, for example, the Australian Defence Force 2021 Military Ethics doctrine), military ethics still need to be operationalized for the battlefield so that soldiers can make swift life and death decisions. Understood as codes, ethics becomes codable—capable of being translated into computational form, taught to intelligent systems, and applied in specific contexts. As Elke Schwartz observes, this 'logic of an ethics module is reliant on a conception of ethics as codifiable, as ascertainable, and as producing clear, secure and, ideally, certain outcomes.'[17] Coded ethics becomes a commodity, central to the sales pitch of start-ups and all too appealing to the officers tasked with overseeing the development and procurement of algorithmic and autonomous technologies.[18]

The Australian start-up Cyborg Dynamics Engineering offers a telling case study. Its flagship product is the Athena AI, a platform for weapons targeting and battlefield analytics. As the company website states, 'Athena AI is one of the only vision-based AI systems on the market that combines AI computer vision, AI enabled decision support and display of the AI information in a user interface.' While not itself an autonomous weapons system, Athena AI is designed to augment human targeting and, crucially, to provide object recognition and ethical and legal evaluation tools. In public presentations and on the company website, Cyborg Dynamics touts these ethical capabilities as critical distinctions. In a short reflective academic article by the founder of Cyborg Dynamics and collaborators at or affiliated with the Trusted Autonomous Systems Defence Collaborative Research Centre describe the technology as aiming to 'augment human ethical and legal decision-making on the battlefield by reducing the "fog of war," and improving abidance with international humanitarian law.'[19] While that article demonstrates the iterative and responsive approach to ethics undertaken in the development of Athena AI, an extended quote from the company website reveals how ethics becomes a value-add in marketing rhetoric:

> Athena AI is one of the only trusted AI products, having worked with International Weapons Review, military legal officers and military ethicists to help define a suitable

---

16   See, for example, Max Liljefors, Gregor Noll, and Daniel Steuer (eds), *War and Algorithm*,(London; New York: Rowman & Littlefield International, 2019.

17   Schwartz, *Death Machines*, p. 16.

18   Elke Schwarz, 'Silicon Valley Goes to War: Artificial Intelligence, Weapons Systems, and Moral Agency', *Philosophy Today* 65.3 (2021): 549–69.

19   Tara Roberson et al., 'A Method for Ethical AI in Defence: A Case Study on Developing Trustworthy Autonomous Systems', *Journal of Responsible Technology* 11 (2022): 1.

data assurance and test methodology for AI vision and decision support certification. Our inbuilt decision support tools have legal and rules of engagement considerations where applicable.

Positioned first in a list of advantages for the system, this encoding of ethics through the tying of LOAC, rules of engagement, and other such codes to specific combat instances positions Athena AI as an improvement upon the status quo. Familiar components of an economy of virtue are evident too, through the participation of the boutique legal consultancy International Weapons Review (IWR). As with the tech-critical entities caught up in the economies of virtue described by this volume's editors, organisations like IWR are not 'the problem' per se—in IWR's case, the firm is run by experienced military lawyers with strong scholarly standing—but are nonetheless part of the varied, evolving terrain of military ethics economies.[20] What goes unsaid in Cyborg Dynamics' rhetoric is that the various detection and classification functions of the platform—enabled, according to the company website, by multi-staged neural networks—are implicitly legitimated and amplified by the legal architecture that the system claims to provide. From a political standpoint, 'ethics' here serves to lower the intensity of political engagement by transforming concerns over military technologies into the technocratic domain where computation meets law. But in industry, ethics functions to boost the commodity value of the system: the system itself is virtuous because it is already encoded with ethics and thus it promises to make the armed services that deploy it more rigorous in their adherence to ethical codes.

Ethics and the Infrastructures of Research Translation

Companies like Cyborg Dynamics are part of a burgeoning ecology of small and medium enterprises (SMEs) within the Australian defence industries. Under the conservative leadership of former prime minister Malcolm Turnbull, defence industry growth was deemed a crucial national priority, both to reduce dependencies on foreign imports and to generate jobs. However, the Australian Defence Forces are not large enough purchasers to sustain a viable domestic defence industry. As the Australian Department of Defence's Defence Export Strategy states, '[n]ew markets and opportunities to diversify are required to help unlock the full potential of the Australian defence industry to grow, innovate and support Defence's future needs.'[21] Via the 2020 Defence Strategic Update, then prime minister Scott Morrison committed AUD$270bn over the next decade to defence spending, aimed at increasing and updating Australia's military capacity and with significant opportunities for industry and workers, with various skill training programs designed to support naval shipbuilding and other defence priorities.

Within this push, AI and other high-tech systems play an important role in positioning the Australian defence industry as innovative, forward-looking, and poised to contribute to the priorities of its allies. The flagship project in this regard is the Boeing Airpower Teaming System (ATS), described by the American defence giant on its website as a 'smart, uncrewed force

20   Phan et al., 'Economies of Virtue', p. 10.
21   Australian Department of Defence, *Defence Export Strategy*, Commonwealth of Australia, 2018.

multiplier.' Developed in collaboration with a number of Australian SMEs, the project—nicknamed 'Loyal Wingman'—aims to develop a fast, attacking drone aircraft capable of operating in support of human pilots engaged in dangerous missions, allowing pilots to remain at a safe distance from high intensity conflict zones or providing additional firepower in the event of an aerial dogfight. As such, the ATS must operate with significant autonomy for navigation, guidance, and targeting, which in turn demands considerable expertise and opens up major ethical questions about the use of force.

Situations like this are where research translation institutions such as the Trusted Autonomous Systems Defence Cooperative Research Centre (TAS) play a critical role, both in facilitating the involvement of Australian enterprises and in foregrounding ethics in the design and promotion of autonomous systems in defence. In operation since 1990, Cooperative Research Centres (CRCs) are an Australian government initiative designed to connect academic research with 'industry-led' projects, with funding typically awarded in the tens of millions and over several years to a partnership involving at least one industry and one university partner. A number of CRCs have some crossover with national security, such as the Data to Decisions (D2D) and Cyber Security CRCs, but are more oriented to civilian concerns or, if securitized, more likely to be concerned with defence-adjacent activities like law enforcement and signals intelligence. The Defence Cooperative Research Centre is a more recent subset, funded by the Next Generation Technologies Fund which has been allocated $730 million from 2016–17 to 2025–26 to invest 'in forward-looking game-changing capabilities aligned with Defence priorities,' according to a Department of Industry, Innovation and Science fact sheet. As the first Defence Cooperative Research Centre, TAS has received considerable resourcing and funding from the Australian government as well as the Queensland state government, which is also the only state to have a drone industry strategy. While the Boeing ATS project has garnered by far the most media attention, the bread and butter of TAS is smaller projects with SMEs, many based in Queensland. But the CRC is also engaged in its own initiatives to develop assurance and ethical frameworks for autonomous systems in defence.

A core component of this is their 'Ethics and Law of Trusted Autonomous Systems' program, conducted in conjunction with University of Queensland's Future of War and Law Research Group. As the TAS website states, their 'Ethics Uplift Program engages diverse stakeholders to provide evidence-based and practical risk management for ethical and deployable AI in Defence.' As in the economies of virtue that surround Big Tech, the purpose of this program is not to question or critique the foundational grounds of defence industries but to 'produce ethics, legal, safety and accountability frameworks for use of the electromagnetic spectrum, robotics, autonomous systems and artificial intelligence deployed within human-machine (HUM-T).' Led by TAS Chief Scientist Dr Kate Devitt, an ethicist by training with a track record of robust critical scholarship on data and ethics, it can certainly be argued that such initiatives should be understood in favourable terms as doing crucial work to ensure that ethics are built into defence industry projects and products from the beginning. An absence of such frameworks would not stall initiatives, such an interpretation would argue, but only mean that they go ahead with ethics less central to their conception. There is merit in such claims, and TAS has also been able to leverage its close relationship with the

ADF to co-author 'A Method for Ethical AI in Defence,' a technical report of the Defence Science & Technology Group (DSTG), a military entity that funds, facilitates, and prototypes new technology initiatives.

In the context of TAS, we need to understand 'ethics' as operating in at least two modalities. The first is that outlined above, in which TAS plays an infrastructural role in ensuring that ethical considerations are foundational to military technologies developed in Australia. The second modality sees these ethics initiatives as functioning discursively to legitimate defence industries within academia and with wider publics. In this sense, the Trusted Autonomous Systems Defence Cooperative Research Centre can be understood as a kind of ethics clearing house, connecting legal, philosophical and other humanities research with military institutions, practitioners, and industry, with a particular emphasis on start-ups. Doing so enables 'ethics' to be 'built in' to AI and autonomous systems, with difficult questions around the ethics of such technologies in the martial context pursued in conjunction with or adjacent to their development. As the extensive list of TAS-supported academic publications attests, TAS and its affiliated researchers take theoretical and practical questions of ethics seriously.[22] Nor is TAS funded to generate large scale critique of military operations or military spending as such, but rather to develop home-grown defence industries that conform to Defence values and ethics. As is often the case in innovation contexts, the presence of social scientists and ethicists constitutes a kind of care work, which here becomes care for the virtues of the nation and its Defence endeavours.[23] As such, TAS can be understood as a vital cog in Australia's economies of military virtue. This is not to dismiss out of hand recent initiatives to deploy AI to identify cultural assets for Western Yalanji peoples, help preserve Cape York languages, or develop an autonomous marine vessel code of practice, but rather to recognise that all such endeavours are bound up with the production and commodification of virtue.

Virtue, Academia, and 'Ethics' in Research Funding

Within the Australian academy, research funding has been placed under increasing pressure over the last two decades, and particularly under the conservative government in power since 2013. In 2014, competitive grant funding by the Australian Research Council (ARC) stood at $886m; eight years later in 2022, it was $815m. As a researcher fortunate enough to receive ARC funding, I can attest to the luck involved in having such

---

22   See, for example, S. Kate Devitt, 'Normative Epistemology for Lethal Autonomous Weapons Systems' in Galliott, Jai, MacIntosh, Duncan and Ohlin, Jens David (eds) *Lethal Autonomous Weapons: Re-Examining the Law and Ethics of Robotic Warfare*, Oxford: Oxford University Press, 2021, pp. 237– 58; S. Kate Devitt et al., 'Developing a Trusted Human-AI Network for Humanitarian Benefit,' (preprint); Jai Galliott, Duncan MacIntosh, and Jens David Ohlin (eds), *Lethal Autonomous Weapons: Re-Examining the Law and Ethics of Robotic Warfare*, Ethics, National Security, and the Rule of Law, Oxford; New York: Oxford University Press, 2021; Eve Massingham, 'Automation of the Spectrum, Automation and the Spectrum: Legal Challenges When Optimising Spectrum Use for Military Operations', *Law, Technology and Humans* 3. 2 (2021): 91–106; Tara Roberson et al., 'A Method for Ethical AI in Defence: A Case Study on Developing Trustworthy Autonomous Systems'.

23   Ana Viseu, 'Caring for Nanotechnology? Being an Integrated Social Scientist,' *Social Studies of Science* 45.5 (2015): 642–64.

grants awarded—especially in the humanities. A growing government emphasis on impact, engagement with industry, and especially research commercialisation has pushed funding more towards applied and away from basic research. In 2022, the Morrison Government announced a $2.2bn fund dubbed 'Australia's Economic Accelerator, of which $1.6bn was earmarked for research that can be 'commercialised' in alignment with National Manufactory Priorities, which include 'defence and space'. Within this context, 'ethics' functions as a keyword for the role of humanities and social science (HASS) research, particularly in the military sphere, as it enables claims of value within research spaces otherwise focused on technological development. With defence and national security framed as virtuous endeavours, ethics also provides a common language with computer science, engineering, psychology, and other disciplines more closely aligned historically to defence research. Humanities research into communication, for example, can help do information warfare the right way or assist in the development of 'ethical' autonomous battlefield systems.

Measuring the full extent of the impact of military funding on Australian academic research is exceedingly difficult, even in general terms. At the most prosaic level, there is the problem of classifying so-called 'dual use' research, such as when the US Department of Defence funds medical research. But there are also other challenges. How do you define and delimit defence vs national security vs intelligence funding? Can initiatives funded by the office of the prime minister, by cabinet, or even by premiers be identified when explicit budgets are not available? What about top secret initiatives? Or disparities between budgeted amounts and actual expenditure? While Australian government spending does entail certain degrees of transparency and accountability, defence funding can be much more difficult to trace due to the scale, secrecy, complexity, and overall opacity of the national security elements of the state. That said, in Australia much of the more overt—and substantive—defence funding flows from the Defence Science & Technology Group (DSTG), an entity within Defence that seeks to coordinate research priorities and provide an interface for both academia and industry. Collaborative initiatives such as the Operations Research Network (ORNet) directly address defence operations (command and control, force design, operational planning, etc), while the Science Partnerships (DSP) program provides a common framework for working with defence and counts every public university in the country as a member. At the state level, organisations such as the Defence Innovation Network (in NSW and the ACT) or the Defence Science Institute (VIC) work closely with DTSG to link up university researchers with SMEs around priority problems. Academia thus engages with defence via an evolving institutional infrastructure, which works to couch defence priorities in the language of science and provide fora through which Defence personnel can engage directly with researchers across a range of fields.

Virtue and ethics easily become the discursive and affective enablers of increasingly militarised academic research. To take one example, the influential Australian Strategic Policy Institute (ASPI) has publicly advocated for much closer ties between academia and defence with a strong focus on the virtues of national security. While ASPI is constituted as a nonpartisan think tank, its agenda is firmly in line with an expansive national security state and, beyond Australia's borders, with allied nations through the Five Eyes intelligence partnership with the U.S., U.K., Canada, and New Zealand. In a series of blogs, opinion pieces, and reports, ASPI chief executive Peter Jennings and former chief defence scientist Robert Clark have called for a 'Five Eyes friendly' university sector and the creation of an Australian DARPA, the Pentagon's famous Defence Advanced Research Projects Agency, responsible for innovations ranging from the early internet to retrofitting Hellfire missiles to Predator drones after 9/11.[24]

Universities are often eager hosts for new defence initiatives. My own institution, which runs the Australian Defence Force Academy in Canberra, has the UNSW Defence Research Institute, the webpage of which consists of gritty war-tech images and very little actual information, including none at all about who is involved with the institute. More often, though, defence initiatives are highly touted and full of information. Our Trusted Autonomy research group and Institute for Cyber Security, for example, are widely touted and active entities within the university, and UNSW is well represented in the Cyber Security CRC launched in 2018 with $50m in government funding. Some of the scholars involved in such initiatives are colleagues that I know and respect; so again, my point is not to cast stones. After all, even if my own research is not defence-funded, my university receives significant income from the ADF and, like almost all Australian universities, relies on state funding for both teaching and research. What's important is that on-the-ground infrastructure such as this is critical to meet the kinds of cross-disciplinary problems posed by contemporary defence challenges, as articulated most clearly in the Australian context by the DSTG (Defence Science, Technology and Research Group) STaR shots which include topics such as Agile Command and Control, Disruptive Weapons Effects, and Information Warfare. This last is one area in which HASS researchers on automation and AI are particularly appealing, as attested to by the invitations for involvement in bids that I've received from my own faculty. Despite being a humanities researcher critical of military technology and militarization more generally, I often find myself in strange circumstances—workshops, symposiums, and discussion groups with defence-funded researchers or even defence personnel. For me, these are valuable opportunities to see inside the system, and understand its motivations and logics. My engagements with the Trusted Autonomous Systems CRC, for example, have been deeply informative, not least for the degree of insight they offer into the nuanced and even critical work going on adjacent to and inside militaries.

The risk, however, is that in such contexts, 'ethics' becomes something that HASS researchers can contribute to grant bids, while virtue operates in the framing of such research as a national necessity that can save lives and secure prosperous and safe futures. The slippery nature of 'ethics' within these economies of virtues means that it can simultaneously signify both the codable rules developed by computer scientists and the processes, procedures, and fora produced by legal scholars, philosophers, and

---

24   Robert Clark and Peter Jennings, 'An Australian DARPA to Turbocharge Universities' National Security Research: Securely Managed Defence-Funded Research Partnerships in Five-Eyes Universities,' *Australian Strategic Policy Institute blog*, 14 July 2021, https://www.aspi.org.au/report/australian-darpa-turbocharge-universities-national-security-research-securely-managed.

communications researchers, to name a few. Researchers who might otherwise be squeamish about doing 'defence work' can thus allow 'ethics' to insulate them from the kinetic operations and lethal violence that are the animating ethos of militaries around the world, Australia included. This in turn serves the interests of industry and defence, as it produces buffers of virtue that cloud the brutality at hand. 'Ethics' can thus be understood as a kind of floating signifier, a malleable referent that attaches itself to a host of situations and can readily be marshalled for martial ends.

Conclusion

This nexus between the academy, defence, and industry should come as no surprise: universities have always been martial institutions, bent to martial ends and imbued with a martial politics. Universities are, after all, institutions of empire and colony even more than they are sites of learning, knowledge-making, and dissent. Yet the forms that this martial nature takes change with the times, with technology, and with ideological and economic sensibilities. In this chapter, I have argued that in the convergence of the military, the university, and industry on AI and autonomous technologies, a distinct form of economy can be detected, in which 'ethics' functions as commodity and currency dependent on context and 'virtue' draws heavily on military and statist values. In the sketch I have attempted here of an evolving Australian industry centred on new military technologies, 'ethics' greases the wheels of collaboration, cloaks the violent purposes of defence, and yet is always reducible in practice to a narrow and codable set of prescriptions, drawn from a predefined body of laws and conventions regarding armed conflict, weapons, and human rights. A shallow 'ethics' is nothing new, of course, but the crucial role it plays in the Australian context matters. Mapping and analysing this confluence of AI research, industry and application is a critical task because it operates according to a different logic and economy of funding than is the norm within tech support for academic research on AI and big data. This military formation of 'ethics' has the potential to metastasize into other contexts, particularly as cash-starved universities look to one of the only remaining well-funded institutions in Australian public life.

To ask the famous question: what is to be done? The growing enmeshment of Big Tech in the American military establishment is hardly surprising, given the history of technology translation between Silicon Valley and DoD, but it has not been smooth. The 2018 Google Walkouts, sparked in part by the company's involvement in Project Maven, indicates one potential fault line. High-skilled tech workers are more mobile than most, with high demand for their skills and so possess more leverage than individuals in most industries. But despite the high profile of the Walkouts and Google's very public backdown on Project Maven, the fundamental relationship between tech and militarism has not changed substantially. When TAS was announced as an initiative at QUT, students launched a #booksnotbombs campaign (Figure 1) that focused on the inclusion of military giants BAE and Thales within the CRC funding model. While the campaign didn't succeed, it and the Walkouts do suggest the necessity of collective responses within academia and tech to the growing influence of military dollars in both domains. For critical academics working in this space, one vital step is to follow the money—not by accessing military funding, but by mapping its movement through the university and para-academic system. Conducting such a forensic exercise would no doubt demand collective labour, as well as the formation of new networks of knowledge. Undertaking that project would not, of course, undo or even slow the operation of this particular economy of virtue. But it would expose the scale of the problem and move from the mix of general claims and specific instances articulated here into a more robust critique of how virtue operates at the nexus of militaries, academic, and AI research.

Fig 1: Banner from the Disarm QUT campaign. Image credit: Monique Mann.

Acknowledgments

In addition to the editors and reviewers who provided astute guidance on this piece, I am deeply grateful to Dr Kate Devitt, who offered detailed, unflinching, and constructive feedback on an earlier version. Kate's willingness to engage with an essay critical of TAS is testament to her own ethical rigour and generosity of thought but should not be read as an endorsement of its arguments. All errors that remain are my own.

Funding Disclosure

This research was funded by ARC DECRA DE190100486, an Australian government initiative. It was also supported by the University of New South Wales, which is a member of the Defence Science Program and institutional home of the Australian Defence Force Academy.

References

Amoore, Louise. 'Algorithmic War: Everyday Geographies of the War on Terror', *Antipode* 41.1 (2009): 49–69.

Amoore, Louise. *Cloud Ethics: Algorithms and the Attributes of Ourselves and Others*. Durham: Duke University Press, 2020.

Australian Defence Force. *ADF Philosophical Doctrine—Military Ethics. Australian Defence Force*, 2021, https://theforge.defence.gov.au/adf-philosophical-doctrine-military-ethics.

Australian Department of Defence, *Defence Export Strategy*, Commonwealth of Australia, 2018.

Beard, Matthew. 'Beyond Tallinn: The Code of the Cyberwarrior?' in Allhoff F, Henschke A, and Strawser BJ (eds) *Binary Bullets: The Ethics of Cyberwarfare*, New York: Oxford University Press, 2016, pp. 139–56.

Bellanova Rocco, Jacobsen, Katja Lindskov, and Monsees, Linda. 'Taking the trouble: science, technology and security studies', *Critical Studies on Security* 8.2 (2020): 87–100.

Boeing. 'Airpower Teaming System', https://www.boeing.com/defense/airpower-teaming-system/index. page.

Buzan, Barry, Wæver, Ole and de Wilde Jaap. *Security: A New Framework for Analysis*. Boulder: Lynne Reiner Publishers, 1998.

Clark, Robert and Jennings, Peter. 'An Australian DARPA to Turbocharge Universities' National Security Research: Securely Managed Defence-funded Research Partnerships in Five-Eyes Universities', ASPI, 2021.

Department of Defence. 'Memorandum for the Establishment of an Algorithmic Warfare Cross-Functional Team (Project Maven)', 2017, https://www.govexec.com/media/gbc/docs/pdfs_edit/establishment_of_the_awcft_project_maven.pdf.

Department of Industry. 'Growth opportunities. Department of Industry, Science, Energy and Resources', 2021, https://www.industry.gov.au/data-and-publications/defence-national-manufacturing-priority-road-map/growth-opportunities.

Der Derian, James. *Virtuous War: Mapping the Military-Industrial-Media-Entertainment Network*, 2nd edition, New York: Routledge, 2009.

Devitt, S. Kate. 'Normative Epistemology for Lethal Autonomous Weapons Systems' in Galliott, Jai, MacIntosh, Duncan and Ohlin, Jens David (eds) *Lethal Autonomous Weapons: Re-Examining the Law and Ethics of Robotic Warfare*, Oxford: Oxford University Press, 2021, pp. 237–58.

Devitt, S. Kate, Scholz, Jason, Schless, Timo and Lewis, Larry (preprint). 'Developing a Trusted Human-AI Network for Humanitarian Benefit', *Journal of Digital War* 'My War' special issue, 2022.

Enemark, Christian. *Armed Drones and the Ethics of War: Military Virtue in a Post-Heroic Age*, New York: Routledge, 2014.

Galliott, Jai, MacIntosh, Duncan and Ohlin, Jens David (eds). *Lethal Autonomous Weapons: Re-Examining the Law and Ethics of Robotic Warfare*, Oxford, New York: Oxford University Press, 2021.

Halpern, Orit. *Beautiful Data: A History of Vision and Reason since 1945*, Durham: Duke University Press, 2015.

Howell, Alison. 'Forget "Militarization": Race, Disability and the "Martial Politics" of the Police and of the University', *International Feminist Journal of Politics* 20.2 (2018): 117–36.

Liljefors, Max, Gregor Noll, and Daniel Steuer (eds). *War and Algorithm*, London; New York: Rowman & Littlefield International, 2019.

Massingham, Eve. 'Automation of the Spectrum, Automation and the Spectrum: Legal Challenges When Optimising Spectrum Use for Military Operations', *Law, Technology and Humans* 3.2 (2021): 91–106.

Ministers for the Department of Industry, Science, Energy and Resources. 'Action Plan to supercharge research commercialisation', 2022, https://www.minister.industry.gov.au/ministers/taylor/media-releases/action-plan-supercharge-research-commercialisation.

Packer, Jeremy and Joshua Reeves. *Killer Apps: War, Media, Machine*, Durham: Duke University Press, 2020.

Phan, Thao, Jake Goldenfein, Monique Mann, and Declan Kuch. 'Economies of Virtue: The Circulation of 'Ethics' in Big Tech', *Science as Culture* 31.1 (2021): 1–15.

Roberson, Tara, Stephen Bornstein, Rain Liivoja, Simon Ng, Jason Scholz, and Kate Devitt. 'A Method for Ethical AI in Defence: A Case Study on Developing Trustworthy Autonomous Systems', *Journal of Responsible Technology* 11 (2022).

Sadowski, Jathan. 'Potemkin AI.' *Real Life*, 6 August 2018, https://reallifemag.com/potemkin-ai/.

Schwarz, Elke. *Death Machines: The Ethics of Violent Technologies*, Manchester: Manchester University Press, 2018.

———. 'Silicon Valley Goes to War: Artificial Intelligence, Weapons Systems, and Moral Agency', *Philosophy Today* 65.3, (2021): 549–69.

Sharkey, Noel. 'Automating Warfare: Lessons Learned from the Drones.' *Journal of Law, Information and Science* 21.2 (2011): 140–54.

Shepherd, Tory. 'Australia's Aukus Nuclear Submarines Could Cost as Much as $171bn, Report Finds' *Guardian*, 13 December 2021, sec. World news, https://www.theguardian.com/world/2021/dec/14/australias-aukus-nuclear-submarines-estimated-to-cost-at-least-70bn.

Suchman, Lucy. 'Algorithmic Warfare and the Reinvention of Accuracy', *Critical Studies on Security* 8.2 (2020): 1–13.

Suchman, Lucy, Karolina Follis, and Jutta Weber. 'Tracking and Targeting: Sociotechnologies of (In) Security', *Science, Technology, & Human Values* 42.6 (2017): 983–1002.

Viseu, Ana. 'Caring for Nanotechnology? Being an Integrated Social Scientist', *Social Studies of Science* 45.5 (2015): 642–64.

Whittaker, Meredith. 'The Steep Cost of Capture', *Interactions* 28.6 (2021): 50–5.

SECTION III:

ACTION

'OPEN SECRETS': AN INTERVIEW WITH MEREDITH WHITTAKER

INTERVIEWED BY JATHAN SADOWSKI AND THAO PHAN

Jathan Sadowski (JS): Let's start with your background. How did you come to work in this area, starting with Google and then co-founding AI Now?[1]

Meredith Whittaker (MW): I'm someone who fell into it. To me, Google was just a job and not a calling. I think this lens helped to ground my perspective: looking at tech issues in terms of labour, looking at academia as an industry. I went to Berkeley and graduated undergrad in 2006. I was broke and Google was a local company that was hiring. At the time, Google was expanding rapidly. 'Up and to the right'[2] seemed like it would go on forever and you would hear people like Sheryl Sandberg say in grave seriousness that Google had 'unlocked' the secret to a forever growing capitalism that is also good for the world. It felt gross, but deeply fascinating. And it was very hard to explain to my friends. It was definitely not in line with my Food Not Bombs[3] comrades. But at the same time there was no counter narrative in sight. The sense that tech had figured it out was hegemonic. And I was plopped into that environment as a contractor doing customer support for Writely, a Google acquisition that later became Google Docs.

When I started, I made $45K a year—more than my parents had ever made. It was very exciting, but it wasn't my identity, and I didn't reflexively try to love it. I wasn't predisposed to love a job. I approached waged work as a type of scam. I don't come from a class where your identity is your job. Your job is something you hate and you do because you have to (the less the better) and then life is everything that happens afterwards.

JS: In 2006 Google was very much still the rising giant. I can only imagine with that kind of money, that kind of prestige, that early after graduating, a lot of people would have happily been like, 'Where's the Kool-Aid? I'm drinking up.'

MW: Yes, it was a wild place. They had free juice. They had those TOTO bidet toilets, that are like $1000 each, in every bathroom. Something was definitely working for some folks. And this is part of what was so fascinating at that time. I was just trying to work it all out, asking naive questions like, what exactly is making all this money? Where is this coming from? Ordering information... what the hell does that actually mean?

One of the reasons I was able to rise and thrive at Google, for a time, was that my background didn't prepare me at all for the environment. I was unversed in the civility politics of the

---

1   This interview was conducted before Meredith began her positions as a Senior Advisor on AI at the U.S. Federal Trade Commission and then as President of Signal.
2   'Up and to the right' is a Silicon Valley expression to describe a strong growth curve.
3   Food Not Bombs is an anti-capitalist, global social movement who protests forms of manufactured waste and scarcity. The movement focuses specifically on food waste, collecting discarded food items and turning them into meals for the community.

professional elite. I didn't realize that Google's blank cheque wasn't actually written for me. I was chasing perks like 20 percent time,[4] and still believed in these corporate narratives about flat hierarchy, meritocracy, the idea that the best ideas win wherever they come from. I put those around me in the awkward position of either taking me aside and explaining how implicit inequality in the workplace functions or giving me a pass. So I was guilelessly riding around campus on Google's Gbikes meeting people in other buildings proposing 20 percent projects and generally wide-eyed trying to cash that blank cheque. There was a lot of free space at Google in 2006, and I didn't know I wasn't supposed to take it, so I did.

And this worked! I was eventually brought on to a new team in engineering to work on document standards, and I began running a group, which was actually extremely spicy and gave me a front-row view into how corporations were working through standards bodies and volunteer organisations to shape technical standards in ways that benefitted them, all while maintaining the veneer of a collective, expert consensus. The rising tech industry was parasitizing and co-opting these older forms in ways that, to an outside observer, weren't obvious. From there, I went on to help found and run M-Lab, Google's Open Research Group, AI Now, and so on.

Thao Phan (TP): Can you say how many years in total you were at Google?

MW: I started July 2006 and my last day was July 2019. So, 13 years.

TP: Do you think there was a particular moment that really changed your view of what was going on or were there specific events? Was it always alienating or was there a particular moment where you said, 'Actually it's beyond alienating now. Now it's unethical. Now it goes against my personal ethics'?

MW: There are a number of inflection points. I had an English Literature and Rhetoric degree, which I was drawn to because that's where the cool kids were at Berkeley. I didn't understand everything I was exposed to there, but there was an affective draw—like, the weirdos are over there, and I love them. I'll read this shit that doesn't make sense because I'm doing it in a community with people who seem kind and strange and cool. This is the early 2000s. Post-structuralism is coursing through the veins of academia, they're still taking psychoanalysis seriously, and I'm thrown in with barely a map, reading Lacan and wondering if I even know how to read anymore. I'm so confused. I'm like a child.

So I had a lot of exposure to ways of thinking structurally about power, but these approaches had no tangible referent in my daily life at that time. I think it was actually those ideas that later became tools for grappling with what I was experiencing at Google. It was there that I started returning to Foucault, to Marxist theory, to early anarchist thinkers (who weren't taught in college but who I was familiar with) and suddenly feeling it light up in me as I began to recognize the way power was operating.

---

4   An employee benefit scheme championed by Google that guarantees employees can spend 20 percent of their time on self-directed side projects.

Developing an analysis I felt comfortable with about Google and tech was a long, agonistic process. And it's ongoing. But I think I was assisted in this task because I already had a critical inclination and also because I didn't go through the traditional CS degree training. I wasn't the right gender, I didn't come from the right class, I'm not familiar with the ceremonies that take place in corporate workplaces that mark someone's belonging, so I'm persistently struggling with feelings of alienation, and I'm necessarily asking questions about things that others take as received wisdom. This helped place a prophylactic layer between me and the Kool-Aid.

I didn't know what a server was when I started. I knew nothing about computational tech, and, as I did with the promises made by the company as a whole, I took a lot of things at face value. Like the claim that Google 'Organised all the world's information'. OK, cool, everyone is nodding along; that must be a thing Google does! But then in trying to understand what I figured everyone else knew, I would ask a really stupid question, like what's information? And then, as often as not, a gaping hole would appear as I processed the fact that information meant content formatted in HTML and accessible to a web crawler. I would spin out on those questions and revelations. They were like worry beads. But there wasn't an intellectual community that I could do that with, so it was isolated and halting, and to handle it I read a lot. When I learned that a thing called 'science and technology studies' existed I genuinely almost cried. I had been looking for people to talk to for so long!

JS: You said something earlier that I think is a really great point and also deceptively powerful when you were talking about how this was just a job. Like you clock in, you clock out, you fucking hate your work, and then life is what happens after that and before that, not during that time period. But I think that is actually a lowkey radical thing to believe right now, especially in our space and especially in what Max Weber calls vocations. These kinds of professions that are seen as 'callings.' I think the tech sector and academia both raise themselves up like these are not jobs, these are callings and you need to love what you do and you need to be devoted to what you do.

Then the flipside that nobody ever says is like, 'Yeah, well, it doesn't love you back and it's not devoted to you back.' But I think that idea of it being a vocation, as not being a job, also prevents a lot of people from being that internal critic of their profession or asking those kinds of questions. I wonder if you could just speak a little bit more about the radicality of recognising this as a job, but also the kind of absence of that consciousness in the professions we work in?

MW: I think about this a lot, because obviously my life arc at Google concluded with a devotion to labour organising and an interrogation of the question of who is a tech worker? What is tech work? What the fuck are we doing? And I think this question points to the need for more interrogation of the way that these institutions are able to hijack or shape our sense of self, our sense of belonging, and our space for community and sociality, and channel those into demands for almost familial loyalty.

What is at stake for people if they don't view a fancy professional title as a calling or identity? What do they lose if they treat it like a job, the way I treated my dishwashing or retail gigs? What do they lose? This is true in academia and tech. When I talk to academics, which is the milieu I'm now in, the profession-based self-regard is very, very similar to tech.

To me, what is so radical and genuinely enjoyable about organising is the process of breaking down these emotional connections to the employer, to the job, and redirecting this affection, this loyalty, to the people around you. This is the process of making solidarity, and solidarity exists when you identify yourself more with who you love and your bonds together than with your place in an institutional hierarchy. This identity built within community and solidarity can displace the identity built by job ladders and performance reviews. It doesn't happen overnight. It's a reflexive practice that requires breaking down your sense of self and its dependence on your standing within these institutions and working to redefine yourself in relation to each other and the bonds of friendship and love that connect you as humans to your colleagues.

I think this process needs to start with recognising that these are jobs. If they pay you, they ultimately get to tell you what to do, however many layers of obfuscation that power relationship may be shrouded in. No one actually forgets who pays them, ever. And getting a prize in your job—whether it's an NSF grant, or a promotion, or tenure—doesn't mean you're a better person. It means you're pleasing those with power over you. Putting it this way cuts at the knees of getting As for a living.

JS: It is wild how many academics I have actually and seriously heard say that the source of funding or support for their work doesn't influence their work. Like, they really do see themselves as these Randian Übermensches who are totally void of any external influence, who rise above the power struggles and they just do their own thing. People just fund their work because they love what they're already doing.

MW: Yeah, and here again we can ask, what are the stakes of them believing otherwise? I can say personally, never in my life for a second have I forgotten who pays me because I don't get to live if I'm not paid. You don't forget that. And I've felt conflicted as Faculty Director of AI Now when, for example, I'm writing something that I know that it's going to hit a deep nerve. It's going to piss off a lot of people and open things up in a way that the tech companies on whom the university is dependent for funding are going to hate. And I have to balance this with my duties of care to AI Now's postdocs, to the people who need to enter the job market out of AI Now. What happens to the institute's funding, prestige, and ability to support its people if I, or AI Now, make the wrong donors or university trustees uncomfortable?

TP: It must be an interesting moment as a labour organiser when you find yourself in that position of power. When you're able to make jobs for others, give job security to others. It's an incredible amount of responsibility. But do you think it can become an alibi? A justification to oneself for accepting morally compromised funding (e.g. military funding or industry funding that comes from mining). I know that many academics feel their main responsibility is to create jobs for others. That in this precarious and ethically compromised funding landscape, the best we can do is just to make jobs and redistribute funds.

MW: Another way to put it is that you're a boss. And in the context of the university, in my context, also a middle manager whose job is to make the university administration happy by bringing in money and increasing the university's prestige in a way that doesn't trouble donors. And you actually don't have that much power within these universities. There are layers and layers of well-paid administrators: Provosts and Vice Provosts, Deans and Vice Deans. There isn't a direct boss like in industry, or structures that enforce a labour relationship in a transparent way, so the worker discipline happens in indirect ways and is largely enforced through internalized self-discipline that seems to come more easily to people trained at doing well on tests and getting good grades. They're very good at predicting what will please those giving the grades. This may look like independence at a very shallow level (e.g., no one is physically leaning over my shoulder while I write) but it's anything but. And I think the personal sense of independence and agency—the assumption that academics work out of pure devotion to knowledge untouched by the concerns of bare life—undermines our ability to see how fiercely these structures do work on us, and ultimately makes it extremely hard to organize and develop labour consciousness.

JS: There's a weird psychology and sociology happening in academia. I've long said too many academics are aspirational middle managers. Their goal is to have a little bit of power over a small fiefdom within a larger organisation. I think that also shows in the proliferation of middle management positions within universities. It does a lot to obscure the political economy at work there as well, where nobody is a worker, everybody is a manager.

MW: And it's built on the backs of the precarity economy, the adjunct workforce that does most of the actual teaching at universities. That is what the university is now. You have a couple of hold-out positions—tenure-track jobs with security and health insurance and some prestige—and the chance at getting one of these scarcer-and-scarcer jobs helps enforce compliance among the thousands of people competing for what could be literally two or three jobs in their field. And if they don't get a job that year? Too bad, into the adjunct pool you go. This is why I don't think there's a solution to the problems that plague the university that doesn't centre labour organising because what's happening is a raw contest of power. They're not going to give us more power and agency and security because we've come up with a better theorem.

JS: I do want to talk about AI Now and your transition from being this internal critic within Google to an external critic of the larger industry. There's a term, which is taken from the military, called red teaming. Big organisations love to have red teams. They're like friendly critics who act like the opposing side in a war or in the marketplace or whatever so that then we can better understand their strategies and how to counter those strategies. But at the end of the day an internal critic or a red team still has to be part of the group. They still have to be dedicated to the organisation.

MW: I love the red team analogy. It's a containment strategy that I see used by these companies in which they give someone like me a platform but no power over decision-making. Microsoft Research serves a similar purpose in my view. This allows the company to claim that they consulted critics and synthesised our views, giving a patina of legitimacy to whatever they were going to do anyway. I will say it took me a while to realise this.

I co-founded AI Now much before I left Google. So I was, in a sense, an embodied example of some of these conflicts, although I would argue that I was also subverting them in certain ways, or at least testing their outer limits by funnelling significant Google money to critical work housed outside of the company, and in turn funnelling some of that to others doing radical work. But the ability to up and found a university institute while employed as a tech worker deserves attention here and shows the extent of the structural porosity between the university and the tech industry. The university, particularly computer science and engineering disciplines are dependent on tech company funding and infrastructure. And this meant that no one batted an eye when the idea of AI Now was raised.

To get a sense of how this happened, how it got to the point it's at now, we can look at the recent history of 'AI' and machine learning. Go back only 15 years, and the field of 'AI' was a backwater. There were a handful of stalwarts researching machine learning and related disciplines. They would meet up at small conferences in mid-tier hotels in San Diego or whatever. They didn't have their own labs, they're not running flashy centres, mainly because these fields weren't considered very important or profitable. Then, around 2010 you had this consolidation of the winners of the tech economy, the companies whose surveillance advertising business model made them rich and increasingly central to tech.

The Facebooks, the Googles, etc. were already structured such that they had massive infrastructure for processing and collecting data, massive market reach which gave them access to continually refreshed flows of data. This kind of reach and access is not something you can just snap your hands and buy. So they had these ingredients: centralized infrastructure, data, and access to markets that make them new data constantly. And the big a-ha moment was the revelation that when you expose these older machine learning techniques to the quantity of labelled data and to the massive computing infrastructure, you could make them do things that they didn't do before. Which is empirically performing better on one or another benchmark. But the 'AI' techniques weren't what was new; what was new was the concentration of data, infrastructure, and reach.

This was a wakeup call for these tech companies. There was a recognition that hey, we have data, we have compute, and now, in the form of decades-old ML techniques, we have a kind of magic sauce we can pour over these things that we can use to create 'intelligent' products and services that can justify our incursion into a vast array of markets.

Now these companies had the ability to claim that they were building general purpose or smart, intelligent, superhuman etc. technologies that would augment or replace decision-making across myriad domains, while of course entrenching their power.

So what does this have to do with the extensive entanglement between academia and the tech industry? Because there weren't that many 'AI' dudes, and most of them were in some dusty lab at some university minding their business. Then the early-to-mid 2010s come and suddenly there was this hiring boom where these guys were being offered football player salaries. All of the companies were suddenly competing to recruit 'AI' researchers because they realised that 'AI' was super profitable. And the rush to hire 'AI' researchers was also a rush to fund 'AI' research—research that required serious computational infrastructure and access to large amounts of labelled data that could be put to use in ways that were considered cutting edge. So systems of dual affiliation became popular, in which a researcher would retain their university position and title while working for a tech company. And importantly, the turn toward 'AI' meant that universities were scrambling for data and infrastructure—things that the tech industry controlled—if they wanted to remain competitive in the CS and STEM rankings. I wrote more about this captured relationship in The Steep Cost of Capture,[5] which maps this out and provides some analysis of why this entanglement is so dangerous to academic independence and critical work.

JS: Could you talk about Project Maven,[6] the walkouts at Google, and all the other stuff happening around that time period?

MW: Maven was a secretive contract that Google signed with the Pentagon to build machine vision 'AI' for drone targeting and surveillance. It was a small contract, but it was designed as an on-ramp to prepare Google to have a better chance of bidding for the JEDI contract, which was a massive initiative to provide all the computational infrastructure and 'AI' for the military from battlefield to command station.

Google was strategic. They brought in Diane Greene, who was the former VMware CEO who brought in a large number of people from her government relations team. I learned about the Maven contract in late 2017 when my job at the time was to say, 'Watch out for AI, it's fake and weird', and hope people listened.

Then I'm looking at Maven and I'm like, I'm being played. We're all being played. This is fucking egregious. How could I not put my body on the line for this given that I am making my money and my name on supposedly criticizing it? I mean, we're talking about Google, a company that has figurative dossiers of our most sensitive information, our friends, our purchases, our location? And now Google wants to build machine vision systems, trained on god knows what shitty data, to equip the illegal US drone war with more automated surveillance and targeting systems? Google, a multinational company with more workers outside the US than within it, wants to work for the US military, a relationship of dependency that could give the US state increasing ability to pressure Google and leverage those ties? No.

This was where I turned to labour organising, along with a small group of others. It was clear that we weren't going to convince them with ideas. They knew those ideas, they'd heard me and others lay out our tight and well-crafted arguments. We were right. That wasn't

5   Meredith Whittaker, 'The Steep Cost of Capture', *ACM Interactions* 28. 6 (2021): 51–55.
6   For further discussion on Project maven, see Richardson in this collection.

the issue. So we needed to build a force capable of actually taking on their power. And I had no idea if it was possible. At that point it was an experiment with a handful of us. But we tried. I wrote an open letter, the 'Cancel Maven' letter, which garnered thousands of signatures. This was early 2018, and it hit a nerve. Because at least at that time there were a lot of people in the company who really believed that they were serving the public good and thought Google should not be in 'the business of war,' as the letter put it. The company didn't see it coming, and we had the advantage of being well out ahead of them for at least the first three or so months.

We just pushed it as far as we could go, even as Google leadership was continually trying to engage and contain, which did at times backfire for them. So, for example, they hosted a town hall that was broadcast across the world where they flew me out to Mountain View to be on the stage and do three sessions of debate, the first starting at 8am, the last starting at 8pm, to get global coverage. And what astounded me was that none of the executives prepared. I had only 48 hours' notice and still I had pages and pages of notes, had rehearsed, had all my numbers and stats on flashcards. And they walked out and hadn't prepared. So there were a lot of ways that we benefited from their hubris and unforced errors. And happily at that point I had enough capital via my work and my reputation to be taken seriously.

We were able to cancel that contract and also able, I think, to inflame a desire for organising among people who then began to contribute and lay the groundwork for building longer term power. By the end of Maven, I knew I was fucked in terms of my ability to stay at Google. I knew they'd wait a little, not go in all at once. But they were going to come for me because I was no longer a dissenting voice. I'd actually cost them something, and they no longer found that cute. So I figured that the only thing I could do was push the gas as hard as I could and keep organizing and see what happened while keeping meticulous notes and not letting my guard down

Maven was the first wave of visible elite tech worker organising targeting the tech industry as it exists now. It flushed the tech nervous system with the idea that organizing was a legitimate and useful means of checking these powerful companies and enacting some of the 'ethical' outcomes that otherwise sit on shelves as position papers never implemented. The walkout was the most visible manifestation of this newly accepted form of resistance. It was so lovely. It came together quickly and was organized by mainly femmes and people in operational roles whose job is to organise shit all day anyway—very much the glue that keeps the company together. And suddenly there are hundreds of hyper competent, mainly femmes, turning their daily wage work skills against the company, using all this talent differently.

In about three days a whole apparatus came together with ground teams that were passing out flyers of the talking points to every location across the globe, with regional leads who checked in with the core organizers, with distribution networks to ensure everyone had the latest protocol, with a team of people who were iterating and taking feedback on the demands. Just a whole polished infrastructure from scratch. I feel so inspired just talking about it. It really demonstrates the possibilities for collective action, and how much we can do if we redirect our labour. It also transformed people. People were happy! Suddenly we had a clear example of the difference between a world where we direct our energy and social relationships into making Google money, and one where we direct this toward creating a world we want. And I saw people start to ask, 'What else can we do?' These moments where the possibilities of reclaiming our labour are made explicit are so powerful. And it's no accident that it was right after the walkout[7] that Google got serious about cracking down.

TP: I wonder if we could just shift the conversation now to hard and soft power in the institution. You saw all these problems when you were working in industry and then you have this pivot into academia but then you also see the same exercise of power through funding, through other forms of influence. Could you take us through the kinds of influence that you see Big Tech exercising on academics?

MW: While I was in Google it was common practice to fund friendly academics. It was common practice on the policy team to, say, shape a white paper or an academic paper alongside friendly researchers, whom you were also likely funding. And then when the friendly paper with the graph you wanted showing YouTube is good for musicians, or whatever, made you more money was published (i.e. entered the canon as a fact) you got a pat on the back because you were able to, say, plant that little fact in Eric Schmidt's speech in front of the European Commission, or similar. These things weren't hidden. They were common practice and a key component of policy, comms, and lobbying strategy.

I'm an academic now, but I have never had been treated better by a university than when I was a tech worker with money. And once I was at NYU full time, I began to see the other side. To see how the political economy at the university works, and how essential grants and funding are for success, and how contingent they are on doing a certain type of not-too-radical work. While I was at Google, I'd known they were courting academics to influence them, but I hadn't realized exactly how much power that influence wielded. What a stranglehold these companies had, particularly in light of the neoliberal university's search for big donors, and the pervasive unwillingness to piss off those donors.

This hit me and AI Now hard. We were warned by the NYU engineering school (where we were situated) to align our views with the views of other engineering centres, which were generally positivist and technocratic. In early 2021, we were told that we didn't align with the strategy of the school and that we needed to find another home. Then, in late 2021, NYU informed us that they were going to take all of our gift money, leaving us with the choice of litigating, which is expensive and which AI Now, as a part of NYU, can't pay for, or of walking and trying to make up the over four million dollars that was effectively stolen by the university.

---

7   The Google 'Walkout for Real Change' was a series of synchronised walkout events organised by Google employees in protest of claims of sexual misconduct, gender inequality, and systemic racism. The demonstrations took place in November 2018 and included over 20,000 employees worldwide.

We are still dealing with the fallout of this, and the future isn't certain. And again, there wasn't a way to succeed ourselves out of this situation. This all happened while AI Now was, by any given measure, one of the most impactful university centres doing critical tech research in the world. We've shaped a field along with a handful of others. We are meeting all the benchmarks and exceeding them by orders of magnitude in ways that universities ostensibly care about. We get all the press, yada yada yada. But when push comes to shove, these don't animate the neoliberal university. At the end of the day, the only interpretation left to me is that the engineering school knows it's not rising in the rankings if they don't get an Amazon-sponsored machine learning centre, if they don't get infrastructure grants from Meta, etc. These are fundamental requirements for 'cutting edge' CS research, and AI Now was in the way. And I don't think the threat to critical work can be made any clearer. For these universities there is no contest between the $250K Ford Foundation grant we can secure to hire a couple of postdocs and the $15 million that Eric Schmidt just gave to Yale for some new AI center. They know that. We don't have much leverage.

Amy Westervelt has this really good podcast called *Drilled* where she looks at the history of climate denialism. She looks at the time where Exxon was funding and catalyzing rigorous climate research in pursuit of potentially changing its business model to provision non-carbon sources of energy. Why not if you can make money either way? Then at some point they decided that they weren't actually interested in exploring those non-carbon sources. Around this time, they decided to push the climate scientists out, and eventually to fund and platform climate denial and fringe research that could backstop it. This shifted the field of climate research, and created an environment where vocal critics were targeted, where they faced threats to their careers. I see tech being at a similar inflection point. For a moment, they thought they could absorb and recuperate criticism. That moment has passed, and critical work is in a very precarious position right now. We need much more space to discuss and strategize given this, and I worry that the polite rooms assembled by funders aren't providing this.

TP: I'd like to come back to the question of labour. How does the political economy of funding affect the nature of labour today in the institution? Many academics now feel like they have to operate as brands in order to attract funding and other opportunities. This is not meant as an insult, but you are also a kind of microcelebrity in the field. But I guess, even your example with AI Now—exceeding all the KPIs yet still under threat from your home institution—shows that reputation amongst peers is not enough. You must also have the right kind of brand and partnerships.

MW: Yep. I mean, I'm definitely a public personality, something that felt like it just happened to me. The whole being a brand thing is tricky and unpleasant. It makes it harder to meet new people and relate to them because there's a different you, the you as a regular person with feelings, than what they know or assume from Twitter and soundbites. Anyway, I think this is part of the relentless and exhausting competition for attention and recognition that we hope results in even scraps of funding, which we are relying on to create some stability that can support the work. And microcelebrity is one tactic. All of this is what happens when you withdraw the social wage and implement a system of precarious labour that represents most academic work at this point.

I see this leading to a culture of sedimenting accomplishments and acclaim, trying to out-succeed the forces of precarity and insecurity. And it's pernicious and has a lot in common with the 'model minority myth' and the myth of the meritocracy, insofar as it reads accomplishments and success as reliable metrics, and tries to accumulate them in pursuit of status and standing that have more to do with class and white supremacy than with 'merit.' And this impulse—to get all As so you can get health insurance—is the enemy of organizing. Organizing requires a workers' consciousness, and it requires that we get real with ourselves and each other as people and say this fucking tower of accomplishment culture is not good for any of us. It makes us into competitors not comrades—and oh yes, it's not keeping us safe. The people with power are not microcelebrities, they aren't known, they get the benefit of privacy and security. They don't have to go out there and dance just to get a quarter thrown at them from some foundation in return for a promise to complete a bunch of deliverables. And I should mention that this model is not true on the right. The Kochs, the Mercers, the money flowing in from tech is sizable, and it's secure, and it's not asking people to dance for yearly funding. It's funding them richly and letting them do their thing, which happens to be convenient for those in power.

The whole thing is also set up also to create these burnout cycles where you're never quite secure enough to plant a taproot and sit down and do work that is quiet and critical and takes a long time to foment. Instead, we're all chasing the latest buzzwords and hoping to shove a round peg into a square hole so we can keep our people employed. This produces work that doesn't match the moment, to be diplomatic about it. We saw this over the last five or so years with everyone jumping on the 'AI' bandwagon, and justifiably so, because that's where there's a smidgen of money that could hopefully keep the roof over the humanities and social sciences.

TP: I'm so glad you said that. I think so many people would be so shocked to hear that AI Now is struggling within its own institution. Especially here in Australia because, as you say, AI is so hot right now and ethics is so hot right now and one of the few places in the humanities where you can get a job. Both Jathan and I, are employed in one of these 'AI for social good' type centres.

We're coming to terms with the fact that if we didn't position ourselves in this way there would be no work for us, and I think so many humanities institutions and humanities scholars are desperately running towards AI ethics as a means of survival in a really hostile landscape. And so to hear even the most successful of us—AI Now—is struggling I think would be really shocking for a lot of people.

MW: It's shocking and emotionally very difficult. I think it's actually not uncommon to see the people who may have been the strong dissenters fall away or be pushed out of a movement or space once the targets of such dissent get a handle on how to manage it. And in AI Now's case, we were very strong critics. I brought everything I knew from a decade plus inside tech into that work, knowledge that isn't easy to get in academia. And especially in the last year or so, we did not pull punches. We're directly criticising Eric Schmidt in ways that go right for the money. I know why they don't like us because we've been effective at flipping some of these scripts in ways that are inconvenient for people with a huge amount of capital, a huge amount of power. NYU is not going to take on Schmidt with me and a couple of foundations, who by the way were extremely supportive of us throughout. But they can cozy up to Schmidt by taking me out and silencing this work.

JS: I feel like much of what we've discussed in this interview can be seen as something of a collection of open secrets in academia and industry. I think people working in these spaces see this capture and influence in action and we see its effects, direct and indirect, on the work we do and the organisations we work within. But even acknowledging that there's a growing number of critical voices calling out these dynamics, it's still much more common to not say anything at all. And I think that's for a number of reasons. Perhaps we benefit from these relations or hope to one day. Or perhaps we don't see anything wrong with the current arrangements or don't see how things could be any different. Or perhaps we think it would just be professionally rude and personally uncomfortable to say something. Or, and I think rightfully so, we fear the career consequences of speaking out, as you've been talking about Meredith.

But considering all that then, how do we go about doing what needs to be done, and doing what you actually are doing in your work, which is confronting that dynamic of capture, co-optation, and compromise? How do we go about doing that in a way that is both head-on and immediate?

MW: There's a flip answer that is, in part, you do it by doing it. You say it by saying it and then you go to the bathroom and throw up. You just do it. But I think there is also... I felt that I had some kind of obligation to name this stuff because I had happened, through wild luck and the contingency of circumstance, to have been inside Google seeing it from one side and then in the type of elite academia that was encrusted with tech money. I was very well positioned to know how these flows of capital worked, and I had a front row seat

So I felt a duty to contribute what I knew, which is privileged information that is not visible from within academia for the most part, back into the hopper of knowledge. And if I didn't do that, that's not solidarity and it's not actually using what I know and what my analysis has gained through these experiences to further any future I would want to be part of. If we don't name the extent of the capture, if we don't take seriously the task of mapping it, I think we're in a really dangerous spot. It's not like silence is going to keep us safe—the pyramid scheme is crumbling, and logging onto the academic gig work platform to low-bid against your colleagues for an adjunct teaching assignment is the future unless we change it. It's the present already for too many. Acknowledging these dynamics is where organising can start. And it's where we can begin to privilege comradery relationships over professional networking.

Of course, this is hard and vulnerable. Especially so for adults who love to get A's, for people who have built their sense of security and self-worth around their ability to collect accolades from people in positions of power.

We also have to stand face to face with the stakes. Waged work is totalizing. People die for lack of a wage. People's loved ones die. This is not exaggerating. Some people won't be able to take the risk of putting themselves out there, nor should they—people with chronic health problems who need insurance, people on visas whose ability to work could be taken away, etc. We have to identify the solidarities we need, and the way academic struggles are interconnected with others. A robust social wage would really help with a lot of these problems. We wouldn't be trying to like tweak funding disclosure paragraphs on fucking conference papers if we had secure work. We wouldn't be gagging for funding at all, in the same way. So parts of our movement, of our organizing, needs to focus attention on these fundamentals, on making sure people can organize and take risks more safely. We want a world where people don't face a choice between naming what is true and being able to afford insulin.

'DROPOUTS': AN INTERVIEW WITH LILLY IRANI, ALEX HANNA, KHADIJAH ABDURAHMAN

INTERVIEWED BY JAKE GOLDENFEIN

The participants in this interview connected through their collective decision to withdraw from the 'Power and Accountability in Tech' conference, hosted by UCLA's Institute for Technology, Law & Policy in November 2021. Here, they reflect on the politics of 'dropping out,' connecting it to central themes of the edited volume. Recalling that the analytical work of Economies of Virtue is to untangle the complex dilemmas and paradoxes facing researchers in their interactions with industrial capital, dropping out responds to another dimension of the politics of industry money. Whereas many scholars seek out interaction with industry through direct recruitment, funding support, or presentation platforms, dropping out demonstrates a commitment to delegitimizing the co-option of scholarly forums for building industrial interests' intellectual and reputational capital. While industry-supported events often amplify congenial ideas, the participation of critical scholars still provides intellectual legitimacy. Critical voices may cloak problematic ideas in scholarly livery, helping to construct a framing of even-handed analysis, participant diversity, and intellectual rigour. The labour of critical scholars thus becomes a tool for industrial interests to leverage academic authority into policy that supports their agenda. Of course, the politics of the forum are critical, and not all industrial money is equal. So when is it appropriate to engage, to call-out, or to drop out?

Jake Goldenfein (JG): Let's start with introductions.

Lilly Irani (LI): My name is Lilly Irani. I'm an Associate Professor at UC San Diego, and I've been organizing with Amazon Mechanical Turk workers for a few years, trying to improve their work conditions. For a long time before, I ran a software system with Six Silberman for workers on the Amazon Mechanical Turk platform. I also organize a Tech Workers' Coalition. Before I went into academia, in my twenties, I worked at Google in the Church of Make the World a Better Place, in what I didn't really realize then was the tentacles of a digital infrastructural empire. If Tech Workers' Coalition had existed, maybe I would have stayed and organized, but organizing was not at all part of my self-understanding or social knowledge in my 20s.

Alex Hanna (AH): I'm Alex Hanna, and I'm a Research Scientist on the Ethical AI Team at Google.[1] I mostly study how data and machine learning exacerbate racial, gender, and class inequalities. I don't quite have an organizing home right now, but in the past, I've done labour organizing, organizing for trans healthcare, and campaign-based things in the 'tech ethics' space.

J. Khadijah Abdurahman (KA): I'm Khadijah Abdurahman. Who am I professionally? I would say that I research predictive analytics in the child welfare system, which frankly, nobody

---

1   Alex Hanna has since left Google and is presently Director of Research at the Distributed AI Research Institute (DAIR).

cares about most of the time. I don't think people in tech think about child welfare or family policing whatsoever. I do a lot of organizing with academics, less on labour rights, and in certain ways, I'm trying to shift the discourse, I'm even trying to shift how people think about 'what is a discourse?'

JG: In the lead-up to the UCLA conference, Khadijah contacted me to point out that this specific UCLA Institute was funded to the tune of $4 million by the Charles Koch Foundation. A web search suggests that other philanthropies, like Brad Jones, the Troesh Family Foundation, and Anthony and Jeanne Pritzker Family Foundation also contributed, giving the institute a total endowment of something like $10 million. (Strangely, the grant documentation from the Charles Koch Foundation is no longer available online; it certainly was available at the time of the conference, but it was not available in more recent searches).

When Khadijah contacted me, I was somewhat unsure of how to proceed. I'm a relatively unknown scholar based on the other side of the world. Koch Foundation politics is not something that I innately understood. And so, I was worried my withdrawal would likely be meaningless. I wondered whether it would be better to use the time allocated to me in my panel to talk about Koch and industry funding. But once both Lilly and Alex had taken leadership on the issue, it made much more sense to withdraw as a gesture of solidarity to both of you.

Perhaps each of you could briefly explain how you came to initially be a participant in, and then ultimately a drop-out from, this event.

LI: I came to participate in the same way that I have been asked to participate in what seems like infinite workshops about fixing *something* with digital something over the last ten years. The Director of the Institute at UCLA reached out to me asking me to talk about tech worker activism. I said, 'Well, shouldn't you ask Meredith Whittaker, because she actually was at Google organizing against 'Project Maven'[2]—something I was involved with in solidarity as an academic doing a petition. And he said, 'Oh yes, I already asked Meredith, and she actually couldn't do it, which is why I'm asking you.' I said, 'Oh, that's great. We're on the same page.' Oh, how wrong I was. After I'd accepted, Khadijah reached out to me noting that this event had Koch funding. I ended up talking to Khadijah and Meredith, and Meredith said, 'Oh, I actually knew that, and I refused to participate on that basis,' which I didn't know.

For me, it was kind of a no-brainer to drop out, and in part. It was not only a function of my job security. It was also a function of having gone through a decade of what Meredith once called the 'critical AI industrial complex', where there's funding of all these events to talk about ethical issues, and tons of foundations, governmental organizations, universities wanting to put themselves on the map, get grants, and maybe influence the discourse. I've been to meeting after meeting like these over the last ten years on digital labour issues because of the work I was doing with Amazon Mechanical Turk workers. And I eventually reached the conclusion that those fora don't make a damned difference. In some ways, actually networking

2   See 'Open Secrets' in this collection.

with researchers and lawyers and policy people who work at these companies is a drain on energy that should actually be spent building solidarities and organizing with people who are most directly affected, and have the most to say about how these systems should change.

So one, these things can be a drain, and two, they can start to contain people who are hoping to change these platforms but don't have a plan. And so I thought the three hours that I was going to spend at this panel, and stressing out about what to say in this panel, could be better spent organizing with Turkers, or explaining to people about Koch funding, and joining and amplifying voices like Khadijah's.

Life is limited; we only have so many hours in a day, and I've decided to be way more selective about who I give my hours to, for what solidarities.

JG: Thank you for this hour; I appreciate it.

AH: I became involved with this workshop in the same kind of way. There was an invite. I had never heard of this centre. I asked somebody else at UCLA what the centre was about; they seemed to vouch for them. I don't necessarily want to call out who that person is. And then in the same way, I thought, 'Okay, might as well.' Khadijah then similarly reached out to me after the event was advertised on Twitter and alerted me to the Koch money. I was already kind of suspicious of the panel because it was framed around holding companies to account internally, and the people associated with it were from BSR [Business for Social Responsibility] and corporate social responsibility. That was not really a conversation that I was really interested in having because of its pretty clear limits.

Once Khadijah alerted me to that, I decided, 'Okay, yeah, I'm backing out of this,' and I stepped out of the event. I completely agree with Lilly that these things have their own economy—there's an 'economy of prestige' that is very much bound up in these same conversations around being *the* whistle-blower or being *the* person holding tech to account. But there are some pretty clear limits to doing that from a pedestal. And putting work into that without understanding the dynamic takes the air out of the room for people that have much deeper analyses based on being at the receiving end of harms—people who are organizing; people who are subject to disproportionate surveillance and carcerality.

KA: I wasn't invited to speak at this event. Also, I was thinking I often don't get invited to speak at different events. I don't think necessarily it's because of where I sit in the academic hierarchy, but because I spend a lot of time being like, 'What the fuck are you doing?' I was actually just laughing because Alex and I were supposed to be on another panel in the wake of Timnit Gebru[3] being fired, or 'resignated', or whatever the term is, that was also supposed to be on tech worker organizing. Initially they only told me Alex was going to be on the panel,

---

3   Timnit Gebru is a prominent computer scientist who was previously employed as the co-lead of the Google Research Ethical AI team. In December 2020, Google announced that she had resigned from her role, a claim that Gebru has denied, stating that she was fired following a dispute over an academic paper, in which she and other colleagues questioned the ethical risks of large language models.

and I thought, 'Yeah, sure. I'm down.' Then I learned that someone who not only wasn't a tech worker organizer, but an ardent white supremacist with a lot of prestige, was also going to be on the panel. So I said, 'Absolutely not. I will not participate in this, because it is a complete sham.' Since the event was at a public university, they're not allowed to publicly disinvite people. So they had to cancel the whole event, which was fine for me because why am I selling out for this? For me, I don't think that there's this place that you can arrive at where you're not morally implicated whatsoever. But to the degree I have agency, why should I be on this panel with a cartoon villain for no reason whatsoever? I do have a reputation for this, and it's pretty widely known, so that probably results in me not being invited to a lot of things.

With respect to the UCLA event, I had followed a piece that Kate Klonick published in The *New Yorker* about the Facebook Oversight Board, and I remember her being heavily criticized due to the length of time she spent embedded within Facebook. This was around the time that Jill Biden, the current President's wife, had been making a big deal of being called 'Dr Biden,' and people were making that analogy to say Kate Klonick is being unfairly targeted as a woman, i.e. this is misogyny, and she is being held to different standards. And I had thought, no, I'm pretty sure it's because she sold out to Facebook, and is peddling the corporate version of regime propaganda. Then I saw some tweets from David Golumbia, and I was able to figure out that Kate accepted a leadership position at Charles Koch Foundation Technology & Innovation. That to me was shocking, because again, we're all implicated into these filthy worlds of no morality and terrible money. But Koch is very specific. Koch is so systematic in discussions around Critical Race Theory, and pumping poison into the environment, and they have coined the process through which academic research is evacuated of any and all meaning. They systematically use funding in order to create a deregulated policy space in which capital can be further monopolized.[4] For Klonick to take the Koch money really stood out to me.

I then saw that Kate Klonick was scheduled to speak at the UCLA Law and Policy Institute's conferences on Platform Accountability and discovered that the event and institute are funded by Koch. I reached out to you guys. And I will say, I'm not going to name the specific people, but because we all operate on these networks of proximity (even for me, I'm affiliated with UCLA too), I knew people who said no—who refused to step down. And we [Khadijah and Jake] had a conversation about whether it is just virtue signalling to step down. And to me, I feel like that's a dangerous idea. I don't think every publicly made moral decision is a performance. I do think that what we do in the world matters. On the one hand, I might not feel the same way about somebody doing an event at Microsoft at this very moment. But I think that there are these moments when we have greater agency. For instance, when people were walking out at Google because of Project Maven, or the stuff around Timnit. Sometimes there's an opening for there to be a sea change.

AH: With the UCLA event, I was thinking, 'Yeah, there's a lot of friends of ours that do this stuff.' People we would actually consider allies or friends. There's a tension here, and you really have

4   For more on the Koch brothers and political laundering see Tim Dickenson, 'Inside the Koch Brothers Toxic Empire', *Rolling Stone,* 24 September 2014,https://www.rollingstone.com/politics/politics-news/inside-the-koch-brothers-toxic-empire-164403/.

to think about what the coalition looks like when people are taking money from certain places. I think Koch is a very piqued case, but I'm also thinking about the kind of conversations we were having after Google fired Timnit and we started asking people to stop taking Google money. Some people did, Queer in AI did, Black in AI did, I think Widening NLP (WiNLP) did. But then some people came back to me and said, 'Okay, we get this pittance from Google. That's going to put our programming at a disadvantage.'

I want to pull on this tension. There's no hard line here, but it is important to ask what does this tension do? I want to talk about these acts of refusal or pulling out, and what that does at particular moments. I think there's an analysis to be done there because it's not always clear to me when the impact of withdrawing or pulling out is going to be the most effective. I'd love to get your thoughts on that.

KA: I was thinking about how funding organizes community, and we haven't released this yet, but I did an interview with Safiya Noble and Meredith Whittaker about transformative justice when you're running centres of knowledge production.[5] One of the comments that Meredith made stuck with me: 'What is a community?' This is now a very Facebook-associated word, but a lot of times the community—this large umbrella of critical tech—is just whoever Aspen Institute, or whatever set of funders, have brought together. And one person in any group might not just be receiving Koch money, but might actually be supportive of Koch and libertarianism and all of that. Another person might centre incarcerated black women. A lot of what gets trafficked as community, or as friendships or proximity, is very artificially produced. That becomes even more mystifying during the pandemic when for the average person, the actual terms and conditions of these relationships that are presented in the form of an event, or a publication, or a 'discourse,' are not really visible. This is especially when discourses and disciplines are often created by institutions and are not necessarily accountable to us.

JG: In our [Jake and Khadijah's] conversation you made a very compelling point, which was that we have not reached normalisation of Koch foundation money in the tech policy / AI ethics space. It wasn't common yet, and it didn't have to be inevitable.

KA: In this specific case, it felt like there was an opening for a sea change around Koch money and academic accountability, especially because Koch's hegemony in this particular domain hasn't been cemented. On top of that, the contents of the event were a little bit questionable— somehow we're going to be holding platforms accountable through a panel?

So in this Alice in Wonderland rabbit hole, it did feel like this was a place where we could push, and it did feel uncomfortable, especially because I'm friends with some people that I was upset didn't step down. They're probably annoyed, like who am I, the academic nanny police shaming people for doing evil panels? But I do think we have to create some bright lines around what we will and will not do. It feels hard because a lot of how power operates is

5   'Holding to Account: Safiya Umoja Noble and Meredith Whittaker on Duties of Care and Resistance to Big Tech', *Logic: Beacons* 15 (2022), https://logicmag.io/beacons/holding-to-account-safiya-umoja-noble-and-meredith-whittaker/.

concealed, or is nebulous given our collective complicities. Additionally, we are in a pandemic, we're all stressed the fuck out; where do we compromise, and where do we push, and where do we demand that others also step up?

LI: There's this idea that there's too many funders, and it's overwhelming, and it's impossible. But it's not that when you draw one bright line, that's the bright line forever. Because to me personally, the bright line is capitalism. The question is whether saying no to Koch gets me closer to ending capitalism, to be honest. But each line drawing forces people to have the conversations about why this line is here, and what other lines may be needed in the future. It's not only about performing withdrawal, it's also about creating the conditions in which more people can build their education, build their analysis, get organized, and recognize the power we do have in withdrawing our labour or other forms of direct action.

I agree with Khadijah that Koch is pretty unique in all the ways that she brilliantly articulated, and I also feel the need to take that line to other places. But if we can't even agree on Koch, then we're not going to get to those other more subtle, more friendly, less well-researched kinds of places—bright lines that we'll need to draw in the future.

JG: Can we talk more about particular 'moments' or particular bright lines? Is Koch so egregious compared to everyone else that we're taking this money from?

KA: There's a tension! I really liked your paper on 'Economies of Virtue[6]', in part because it raised the issue of Minderoo. I'm very aware that I receive Minderoo funding, though somewhat indirectly through AI Now. I'd never heard of Minderoo because I didn't grow up in Australia. But the shit is super evil. It's based on Aboriginal land dispossession, Twiggy Forrest is a sixth-generation Australian colonizer, and specifically a champion of algorithmic allocation for welfare benefits, which overlaps with my work. Minderoo is not visible to Americans as an evil entity in the same way I'd imagine it is in Australia. I am aware that I am getting something that is evil, but I'm also operating in a situation of profound resource scarcity. We're in the Great Depression here, and I don't just say for myself personally, but I'm working with people who I'm constantly trying to funnel money to, who I don't want to ask to do things for free, and I feel responsible to find them money. That for me, is part of the tension.

In terms of flagging bright lines, one of them for me is around the police. I will sit here with you, Alex, and I might have a critique of Google, but if you were working for ICE [Immigration and Customs Enforcement], we wouldn't be on this Zoom call. And I'm sure vice versa. This is also more complex because we know that Google is entangled with the Department of Defence. I'm bringing this up specifically because Lilly and I were involved in this letter-writing to the FAccT[7] central committee (central committee is so Marxist–Leninist, but whatever it is called), asking them to come out and take a position about the police. 'Will you or will you

---

6   Thao Phan et al., 'Economies of Virtue: The Circulation of "Ethics" in Big Tech', *Science as Culture* 31 (2022): 121.
7   FAccT is the acronym for the Association for Computing Machinery Fairness Accountability and Transparency network, who host an annual conference titled ACM FAccT.

not support the police and police research?' And there was a refusal to draw this bright line, and that's something very clear for me.

JG: I remember the 2019 Privacy Law Scholars Conference (PLSC) and its relationship with Palantir. I recall there was an open letter requesting the conference remove Palantir as a sponsor, and the conference organizers responded by saying, 'Well, you know…we've got a sponsorship policy. It says they're not allowed to have any influence, so we'd rather have them at the table.' In the end, there was sufficient concerted academic pressure to dump them, but that happened *in spite of* the conference sponsorship policy, rather than because of it.

I think that response represents a broader problem of the depoliticization of these scholarly spaces. It's all become quite procedural, and you see it in conference sponsorship policies that are like, 'As long as the sponsor has no influence over the content or agenda of the event or the institute, then everything's fine.' And that evacuates the capacity to have bright lines that we won't cross, or even to think about them, because there's no space for taking an ethical position or developing your subjectivity as a researcher, according to whatever ethical stance you have in relation to that.

LI: When you mentioned the depoliticization of the university, Jake, the issue of academic freedom kept coming up in my head, because there are related things happening at my university right now.

One of the ways the Koch brothers defend what they do in universities is to call it 'academic freedom.' And academic freedom has now become about protecting the space for racist, misogynistic, fascist speech. I recall reading that in the 1930s and '40s in the United States, academic freedom was something that universities gave to faculty and graduate students, basically university workers that were unionizing under a socialist banner. Then I think the AAUP [American Association of University Professors] accepted a weak version of academic freedom and tenure in place of more substantive collective control over the university.[8] Academic freedom was thus held up as this ideal suggesting, 'You should be an individual. You should always have fidelity to what you think is your truth'. But any kind of sociological analysis around 'who is this community that's been constructed for you,' or 'what's the history of your discipline,' are then rendered as things that threaten individual scientific freedom. And I feel like the Koch Brothers traffic in that.

KA: Related to this point about moral evacuation and depoliticization is that an announcement of power is not unexaminable, but it is often forcefully concealed. In part, this is because of competing political projects that mediate the way funding happens. I wrote about one of these examples in a *Medium* blog post called 'Encoding Hindutva: Shalini Kantayya and Coded Bias'[9]

---

8   Referring to 1940 Statement of Principles on Academic Freedom and Tenure, https://www.aaup.org/
     report/1940-statement-principles-academic-freedom-and-tenure; Eli Meyerhff et al., 'Time and the
     University', *ACME: An International E-journal for Critical Geographies* 10(3) (2011): 483.

9   J. Khadijah Abdurahman, 'Encoding Hindutva: Shalini Kantayya and Coded Bias' *Medium blog*, 2 June
     2021, https://upfromthecracks.medium.com/encoding-hindutva-shalini-kantayya-and-coded-bias-

describing how the producer of Coded Bias had been the poster girl for the Hindu American Foundation, which has ties to the paramilitary organisation RSS, and Narendra Modi. The thing is, for 90 percent of the people in that movie, I don't think that they were like, 'Yay, Hindutva,' I think that they literally had no idea. They were asked to be in a movie that was generically against Big Tech, and they agreed. But once we begin to understand that 80 percent of H1B visas in the US go to India, and the majority of those go to Brahmins, we can see how that casteism is reproduced in Silicon Valley. Even one of the supervisors involved in Timnit's firing was Brahmin. And this is associated with a kind of anti-blackness. Various fascistic political projects are connected to this funding sphere. But we all can't know everything, and we don't all have the social context for everything. I know a little bit more about Hindutva, I know a little bit more about black American politics here compared to say, what's happening in Brazil with Bolsonaro. But this is some of what obfuscates the power dynamics of what's happening. A lot of these decisions happen in closed rooms, and understanding who ends up in those rooms is a very long historical project.

AH: I'm thinking about these comments on the depoliticization of academia alongside Khadijah's foreword to the Logic issue that mentions a letter that the Manhattan Project scientists sent to Truman pleading not to drop the atomic bomb.[10] AI scientists have found themselves in a sort of hapless political space. I listened to Geoff Hinton, who's one of the godfathers of machine learning or AI give a talk internally at Google. AI, or deep learning, had its resurgence because they happened to keep on jamming on this one type of technique since the '80s, and then they eventually had so much data that it actually worked. But then these people, the research scientists, all of a sudden had just immense amounts of power and were not sure what to do with it. Hinton recalled how they were getting huge offers after they won the ImageNet competition. He recounted how they were at NeurIPS one year, it was in a casino, and they were getting offers of millions and millions of dollars for the company that he had started with Alex Krizhevsky and Ilya Sutskever (who went on to co-found OpenAI).

These people didn't have a political analysis prior to that moment. And then they developed this thing that's the talk of the town, they're having millions, if not billions of dollars thrown at them, and this means they have less incentive to develop that kind of analysis.

But that's a weird idiosyncrasy of computer scientists. I'm a sociologist, but the way one is trained even in sociology, a discipline which ostensibly has something to do with analysing inequality, actually has very little to do with ameliorating inequality. At the big annual meetings of sociologists this perennial thing happens that's just so divorced from reality—the questioning of whether you should be engaged in some kind of politics. At worst, many people within the discipline are just outright right-wing white supremacists. But then, there's also a lot of these good liberals who are just really glad that Trump has gone, and now we just have to get back to doing what we were doing when Obama was in office.

721fe04f225f.

10   J. Khadijah Abdurahman, 'A Body of Work That Cannot be Ignored' Logic: Beacons 15 (2022) https://logicmag.io/beacons/a-body-of-work-that-cannot-be-ignored/.

So it's strange being in this space now, because these events are so entirely inconsequential. The process by which these people were simply good scientists, but then thrown into positions of power, means there's just more incentive to denude these things of any kind of political effect in the world.

KA: The Manhattan Project scientists, for all intents and purposes, didn't think of themselves as political actors. I think part of what I was getting at in that *Logic* editorial is my little joke about how techno-capitalism puts in charge of humanity people that didn't take the humanities. And so depoliticization is this excision of the humanities. At the same time, and Frank Pasquale makes this argument in the book about robots that's not about robots—'New Laws of Robotics'[11]—there's this idea that AI is displacing human expertise. The danger is that Zoom will collapse the middleman, we'll have no universities, etc. That means we need to rebuild our institutions, civic society, and the state, which have each been financialized, fragmented, and broken away as new money has concentrated into these new forms of capital.

But the reason that I specifically called in the black studies people [in that editorial], and tried to take a different orientation from calling out the morally evacuated people that drive me nuts, is because I know that they know more than me. The thing that black studies scholars particularly know more than me about is what it means to be human, and what the problems are with Enlightenment thinking. Because when I think about the moral bright lines, I think about Montesquieu saying, 'No more torture,' and, 'How are we going to organize these different polities?' But at the same time, that Enlightenment rationalism, the idea of 'just being a scientist' is predicated on colonialism and mass dispossession. It's predicated not just on IBM finetuning the transportation of Jews during the Holocaust, but also the Herero and Nama genocide that predated it.

So for me, the issue is this need to bring in social context; we need to bring in the humanities. But at the very same time, we're all *in a context*, and we're thinking with tools through which people have already been excluded from this category of human. Even our own imagination is foreclosed by that. And I don't feel like I have all the tools to figure that out, but I do know that it cannot just be individual. I think we're in trouble if we just go with the individual route. But I also don't know exactly what it means to be collective. I believe we need this labour organizing, I believe we need to be intentional, but we still operate in these institutions. I don't think the university is going away tomorrow. I also don't think Google is going away. So how do we operate on this structural level?

AH: This is very connected to questions of organization and manifestations of political leftism. Khadijah, I'm thinking about a thread you posted [on Twitter] maybe a few months ago that said something about some of your initial political homes being with the Revolutionary Communist Party. I have some sympathies for that; my first political home when I was 19 was 'News and Letters', which was a small Trotskyist sect run by Raya Dunayevskaya and C.L.R. James before they parted ways. They had this newspaper, which now you see young men with 'newsie caps'

---

11   Frank Pasquale, *New Laws of Robotics: Defending Human Expertise in the Age of AI*, Cambridge: Harvard University Press, 2020.

peddle on college campuses. But they did have these worker—thinkers really contributing to those magazines, and they were actually quite effective mediums for political organizing. It's part of a larger question about what political organizing looks like, and it's just such a fragmented sort of space right now. So much ink has been spilled on the state of the leftist organization. This idea of labour organization, or political organization, in this mass platformed era is not easy to crack.

In an essay by Dean Spade in *Social Text*,[12] he breaks down several activism strategies. The first is marching and overt activism, but then there's also these architectures of care which frame up a discussion of the importance of mutual aid. Much of his larger book[13] on mutual aid is about 'how to have a meeting,' and how to get people to commit to doing things; like, how to use sign-up sheets. I thought this was fantastic because it's a good prompt to revisit and think about what these networks look like if you start doing the 101.

JG: Alex, I think you've highlighted this real tension between some of the deeply individual imperatives that are a big part of what you earlier called an 'economy of prestige'—being the person that receives the kudos for calling out the bad corporate actor and getting the speaking engagements and academic kudos, etc.—and the collective imperatives of political organizing, which are not rewarded at all in the same way. And this inevitably has to do with how our institutional lives are organized.

LI: I don't know if by 'institutional' you mean the way the university is set up—is that what you're thinking about? I guess I have extreme ambivalence about the university, learned both from reading Moten and Harney about the Undercommons and Fugitive Planning[14] where they argue that the university is a site for making up governmental knowledge in some way; and also from the undocumented undergrads I teach who are coming to this space, and having a space away from where they grew up where they can encounter new people and new ideas, and become something that they want to become.

And so I guess I think of the university as my employer—do I try to reform my employer? Or do I try to organize to ultimately have some kind of substantive democratic ownership over my employer in the long term, and then the reforms that I bother fighting for are the ones that help us conceptualize what that would even be, as well as to build the skills and relationships that we need to get there?

Also, and I was thinking about this while Khadijah was talking about this question 'what is the human?', I totally understand the ways in which you mean that black studies can speak to that question, but at the end of the day I also don't cede that question to any academics. I feel informed by what black studies can teach us, and informed by what others can teach,

12   Dean Spade, 'Solidarity Not Charity: Mutual Aid for Mobilization and Survival', *Social Text* 142(38), (2020): 131.
13   Dean Spade, *Mutual Aid: Building Solidarity During This Crisis (and the Next)*, London: Verso, 2020.
14   Stefano Harney and Fred Moten, *The Undercommons: Fugitive Planning & Black Study*, London: Minor Compositions, 2013.

but we have to come up with the answer to that through our own organizing too. Maybe I'm idealistic about organizing, but I feel like it can be done in a way that draws out the best parts of the kinds of commitments that people can develop when they're challenged by having to figure out how to live together.

KA: I hear your ambivalence towards the academy. I think part of what I was trying to get at with the *Logic* editorial is that the Audre Lorde quote—this idea of you can't dismantle the master's house with the master's tools—is very layered. The academy does not own knowledge production. And so for me, when I'm thinking about black studies, I don't even necessarily mean this particular formatting through text that we disseminate in this almost liturgical way through academic lectures. It can exist in so many ways.

There's another tension around funding *through* universities. As someone who's permanently on the periphery, my relationship to the university is also informed by my duty to people. Because for me, some centralisation is required. Decentralization is very in vogue now, but there's this question of how am I getting resources to people? People who receive funding can become funnels, and they hopefully aspire to build this thing that they didn't have. When I wrote the 'Moral Collapse of AI Ethics,'[15] Safiya Noble joked, 'Do you have health insurance?' And I said, 'No, son, I'm poor, like actually poor.' And they hooked me up. I get funding from them, and you know what, they leave me alone. No one that I get funding from, Columbia, NYU, UCLA, ever asks me what the hell I'm doing, ever. No one checks in on me, I have no deadlines, I have no mandated meetings, I'm never on Zoom, ever. No one cares what I'm doing. The other aspect of this is that eventually I have to go get new funding for 2023. But I'm saying this is what people can create for other people through the university. And I feel like that's a real duty of care that Meredith and Safiya showed—and not only to me.

I also feel like I have academic freedom, to the degree I'd use that term. I feel like I can come up with a project and pitch it to people. For instance, I can critique Ben [Tarnoff] and Moira [Weigel], but they let me do whatever I wanted with *Logic*; they really didn't interfere. These opportunities exist. I think Minderoo funds the Incubator at UCLA, and I received a social impact grant, I think in total of $50,000. I was able to fund six projects globally, six people in Kashmir, one in Oromia, and I also asked nothing of them. I said, 'Do whatever you want with this,' and, 'If I can help you, I'll help you, but you don't have to report anything.' For the *Logic* issue, they normally pay people $250–$500 for an essay, but we gave people $2,000 to $4,000. My idea was to pump and infuse cash to all the people doing dope work but are broke all the time. $4,000 is not life-altering, but it gives people something. This is just to give you some concrete data points on what funding can look like. At the same time there's also evil things involved, but I don't know how to deal with that?

AH: There's a few things I want to pull on. When I was talking about the 'economy of prestige', and this idea that there are certain people that one must 'recruit' for talks, I'm not saying that these people are wrong for taking the speaking engagements. I've done plenty of that

15   J. Khadijah Abdurahman, 'On the Moral Collapse of AI Ethics' *Medium blog* , 8 December 2020, https://upfromthecracks.medium.com/on-the-moral-collapse-of-ai-ethics-791cbc7df872.

myself. It's more that incentives in the academic world are very much optimized around doing talks and publishing, etc. There are these worst cases, where there are people who are very public, but are well known in the whisper networks to be abusers, siphoning off all kinds of labour from junior people, while using language of liberation, or AI ethics or whatever—you pick your own vocabulary. And that isn't in service of, as you put it Khadijah, a duty to people. And what it means to have a duty to X, or a duty to people, is one analytic that I'm continually coming back to. I say duty to X because, depending on where you sit, that X is a variable. At Google for instance, it's a duty to the user (that's the way it's framed; people become users). In the non-profits, it's a duty to funders, or whoever. This is a long way of saying that a person's subject position is really important, and it takes so much to do the work of resisting those incentives, just because everyone else at your institution is just breathing down your neck.

I've started reading Sara Ahmed's *Complaint!*.[16] One of the things she talks about is how lodging complaints in the institution really illustrates what those incentives are, and what the inner workings of the institution are. There's really no academic analysis yet about how people get swept along in these tides of prestige and publication.

LI: I went into academia because I felt like there wasn't actually room in the tech sector for work that aligned with my values, and I didn't know that that was just a feature of capitalist alienation. So, another thing that you get swept along with in academia is this hope that, 'Oh, I want to do critical work. I want to be able to say things that I can't say at a company.' But to what end? That 'saying' doesn't necessarily lead to anything either. I suppose I'm suggesting that some people are chasing prestige, and some people are chasing an idealistic hope, but in both cases capital wins.

JG: Well, speaking of idealism in service of capital, you mentioned earlier writing letters to FAccT organizing committees. FAccT seems to occupy this important institutional position in the AI ethics / tech policy space because of its capacity to define what gets taken up as an agenda in the 'fairness' field, and to a degree, AI Ethics more broadly, as well as its capacity to generate networks, and facilitate industry–academy interaction. It seems to me that telling FAccT to take a stand could be a very meaningful action. Where did the impetus towards that action come from?

LI: I may delete all of what I'm about to say.

The impetus for the FAccT letter came from one attendee getting really angry at the town hall about Christo Wilson's paper that basically let a company, 'pymetrics,' define the terms of fairness auditing for its own hiring algorithm.[17] That paper was then trotted around by the company as an example of being independently audited so that local city councils and regulators would consider this algorithm ready to go. The process of working on that letter

16   Sara Ahmed, *Complaint!*, Durham: Duke University Press, 2021.
17   Christo Wilson et al., 'Building and Auditing Fair Algorithms: A Case Study in Candidate Screening', Proceedings of the FAccT Conference, Virtual Event, Canada, 1–10 March 2021.

then expanded into discussion of other issues. Khadijah was involved in the beginning. Alex was also involved in those conversations.

Asking FAccT to take a stand, or seeing that they won't take a stand publicly, is a meaningful action. I'm curious what the others think about this. As with a lot of organizing, it's learning by doing, and so there were a lot of conversations between me and Alex, me and Khadijah, and this network of people who signed the letter, and some of the people who didn't sign it but were glad it was happening. There were conversations asking, 'Yeah, is there a point in making a demand? Is there a point to making a demand about *this* particular thing?' It forced us to clarify, to some extent, our analysis of what the institution was in a way that could maybe be made public.

But to be honest, I also just wish that we could have a group meeting to talk these things out because it felt like it took so long, so many one-on-one, back-channel conversations. Issues of trust and time are so intense.

KA: The funny thing about FAccT is that I've never been to FAccT. I've been hate-attending on Twitter for so long.

For me, the letter very much encapsulated the 'who is our "community"' question. Because the chasm between the positionalities of people on there, between the 'Fuck the police, ACAB' people, and the 'I work for them' people, to me, felt unresolvable. But the thing that stood out to me is FAccT's organizing capacity. Institutionally, in person, it is impossible for us to replicate that with any kind of network of ourselves. Digitally, the hegemony that they maintained, for me represented the level of ambivalence, and why it's so hard to organize academics. Because fine, people are burnt out, and administratively I think it is somewhat difficult to organize a conference. But I just really struggled. I felt like there's a point at which you're not going to push those type of people forward, and they'll just refuse. Particularly, because one of the many reasons that I hated FAccT was that when I reached out it became clear that one of the people on the Executive Committee was one of the developers of the Alleghany County Family Screening Tool, and to me this was just beyond.

So I asked, 'Why don't we have our own conference?' The whole thing is based on free labour, but a conference specifically feels like something that we could actually pull off. Even if you did three workshops and you called it, I don't know, Alternate FAccT Conference, or the Ex-FAccT Drop-Outs Conference. But the motivation to do that…? I feel like if we mandated that people do it, they would do it. But the idea that there would be a groundswell just seems so outside of the collective imagination.

AH: One question I ask is why even organize around FAccT? And this is something that Lilly and I have had a lot of conversations about. These people are just going to just hunker down. But maybe it is worth forcing them to show their hand?

In the end, Lilly did a good job convincing me, but also I just feel like this is becoming a continual conversation around FAccT. I went to the first in-person FAccT in New York in

2018, and I remember someone standing up and they were just like, 'What the fuck is this? Why do we care?' They were talking about how all these conversations are basically immaterial, saying 'You're just thinking about fair ways to surveil people.'

LI: One thing about the FAccT letter is that the conversations around it helped clarify, through defining what's wrong with FAccT and having people sign on to saying publicly that this thing is wrong, that if we were going to start another conference like Khadijah's talking about, we would need to be clear on what some of its commitments would have to be.

The other thought that just keeps swirling around in my head is that it becomes really clear that FAccT's commitment is to maintaining a big tent or 'maintaining a table,' which is how they keep saying it. That's the term they used with PLSC too. But this reflects some fantasy that through the free exchange of ideas the right thing is going to happen.

JG: I appreciate the nuance that everyone has brought to this conversation. Dropping out is a difficult prospect, but you've really shown its relationship to the complexities of academic life. Researchers and scholars are constantly negotiating their relationships to coalitions and communities, the politics of money and prestige, institutional imperatives and academic freedom, and who we ultimately owe duties to. I can't thank all you enough for really reminding us all of what's at stake.

References

Abdurahman, J. Khadijah. 'On the Moral Collapse of AI Ethics'. *Medium* blog, 8 December 2020, https://upfromthecracks.medium.com/on-the-moral-collapse-of-ai-ethics-791cbc7df872.

———. 'Encoding Hindutva: Shalini Kantayya and Coded Bias', *Medium* blog, 2 June 2021, https://upfromthecracks.medium.com/encoding-hindutva-shalini-kantayya-and-coded-bias-721fe04f225f.

———. 'Holding to Account: Safiya Umoja Noble and Meredith Whittaker on Duties of Care and Resistance to Big Tech', *Logic: Beacons* 15 (2022), https://logicmag.io/beacons/holding-to-account-safiya-umoja-noble-and-meredith-whittaker/.

———. 'A Body of Work That Cannot be Ignored', *Logic: Beacons* 15 (2022), https://logicmag.io/beacons/a-body-of-work-that-cannot-be-ignored/.

Ahmed, Sara. *Complaint!*, Durham: Duke University Press, 2021.

Dickenson, Tim. 'Inside the Koch Brothers Toxic Empire', *Rolling Stone*, 24 September 2014,https://www.rollingstone.com/politics/politics-news/inside-the-koch-brothers-toxic-empire-164403/.

Harney, Stefano and Moten, Fred. *The Undercommons: Fugitive Planning & Black Study*, London: Minor Compositions, 2013.

Meyerhff, Eli, Johnson, Elizabeth, and Braun, Bruce. 'Time and the university', *ACME: An International E-journal for Critical Geographies* 10(3) (2011): 483–507.

Pasquale, Frank. *New Laws of Robotics: Defending Human Expertise in the Age of AI*, Cambdrige. Harvard University Press, 2020.

Phan, Thao, Goldenfein, Jake Mann, Monique, and Kuch, Declan. 'Economies of Virtue: The Circulation of "Ethics" in Big Tech', *Science as Culture* 31 (2022): 121–35.

Spade, Dean. 'Solidarity Not Charity: Mutual Aid for Mobilization and Survival', *Social Text* 142(38) (2020): 131–51.

——. *Mutual Aid: Building Solidarity During This Crisis (and the Next)*, London: Verso, 2020.

Wilson, Christo, Ghosh, Avjit, Jiang, Shan, Mislove, Alan, Baker, Lewis, Szary, Janelle, Trindel, Kelly, and Polli, Frida. 'Building and Auditing Fair Algorithms: A Case Study in Candidate Screening', Proceedings of the FAccT Conference, March 1–10, 2021, Virtual Event, Canada, 1–10 March. 2021.

ACKNOWLEDGEMENTS

There have been so many wonderful people who have helped us to bring this collection to life. The brilliant authors for not only contributing their time but for generously diving into the experimental "collective review" process. To Geert Lovink for his patience and support of our project, and for his commitment and vision to modes of publication that subvert the constraining norms of academic practice. To the editors and reviewers at *Science as Culture*, in particular Kean Birch and Kelly Bronson who edited the 'Forum on Big Tech' where we initially published on the 'economy of virtue.' To Elena Gomez for her swift and incisive editing. To the presenters who joined us at our first Economies of Virtue workshop in July 2021: Angela Daly, Sarah Pink, Brett Neilson, Mark Andrejevic, Julia Powles, Sy Taffel, Winifred Poster, Tsvetelina Hristova, Michael Richardson, Tanja Dreher, and Ed Santow. To Emma Kowal for her support and guidance in helping us to apply for the Academy of the Social Sciences in Australia workshop program grant. And finally, to the many interlocutors who have generously held conversations with us and more as we explored this thorny topic, especially Seth Lazar, Kate Devitt, Christine Parker, and Julia Powles.

CONTRIBUTOR BIOGRAPHIES

J. Khadijah Abdurahman (they/them/any) is an abolitionist whose research focus is predictive risk modeling in the New York City child welfare system and tech in the Horn of Africa. They are the incoming Editor in Chief of *Logic(s)* magazine, a UCLA C2I2 Fellow and the founder of We Be Imagining, a public interest technology project at Columbia University's INCITE Center. Khadijah co-founded the Otherwise School: Tools and Techniques of Counter-Fascism alongside Sucheta Ghoshal's Inquilab at the University of Washington, HCDE.

Laura Bedford is a Lecturer in Criminology at Deakin University. She is working to advance knowledge related to green criminology, environmental crime, resistance, and activism. She is particularly interested in problematizing the uneasy translation of hegemonic criminological theory and criminal justice practice outside of the Anglo-West.

Corinne Cath is a cultural anthropologist who studies internet infrastructure politics. They finished their PhD at the University of Oxford in 2021 and are a research affiliate at the Minderoo Centre for Technology & Democracy at the Centre for Research in the Arts, Social Sciences and Humanities (CRASSH) at the University of Cambridge.

Angela Daly is a socio-legal researcher of (digital) technologies. She is currently Professor of Law & Technology at the University of Dundee (Scotland) with a joint appointment between the Leverhulme Research Centre for Forensic Science and the Law School. She chairs the independent expert group on Unlocking the Value of Data for the Scottish Government and is a member of the Scottish Government independent advisory group on emerging technologies in policing, leading the workstream on law and ethics. She is also a fellow at the Information Society Law Center in the University of Milan (Italy) where she is working on facial recognition regulation research.

Jake Goldenfein is a law and technology scholar focusing on platform regulation, surveillance, and the governance of automated decision-making. He is a Senior Lecturer at Melbourne Law School, University of Melbourne, and an Associate Investigator in the Australia Research Council Centre of Excellence for Automated Decision-Making and Society.

Tsvetelina Hristova is a postdoctoral researcher at the Institute of Culture and Society, Western Sydney University. She works at the intersection of media studies, anthropology, and STS and her publications focus on the politics of sociomaterial practices of organisation and infrastructure and their relationship to labour management, migration, and political economy.

Alex Hanna is Director of Research at the Distributed AI Research Institute (DAIR). A sociologist by training, her work centers on the data used in new computational technologies, and the ways in which these data exacerbate racial, gender, and class inequality.

Lilly Irani is an Associate Professor of Communication & Science Studies at University of California, San Diego. She is author of *Chasing Innovation: Making Entrepreneurial Citizens in Modern India* (Princeton University Press, 2019) and *Redacted* (with Jesse Marx) (Taller California, 2021). She also organizes with Tech Workers Coalition and the Transparent and Responsible Use of Surveillance Technology (TRUST) Coalition San Diego, and sits on the board of United Taxi Workers San Diego.

Os Keyes is a PhD Candidate at the University of Washington, and an inaugural Ada Lovelace Fellow. They research gender and disability in AI, alongside the history of transgender medicine and science.

Declan Kuch is a Vice Chancellor's Research Fellow in Sustainability and Globalization at the Institute for Culture and Society at Western Sydney University. His research focuses on the interactions between democracy and emerging science and technology.

Monique Mann is a Senior Lecturer in Criminology and member of the Alfred Deakin Institute for Citizenship and Globalisation at Deakin University. Monique is researching the social justice implications of new technologies to improve the regulation of them.

Liam Magee is Associate Professor and Engagement Director at the Institute for Culture and Society, Western Sydney University. Liam's principal research interests focus on the application of social methods and information technology to the areas of urban development and sustainability.

Rodrigo Ochigame is an Assistant Professor in the Institute of Cultural Anthropology and Development Sociology at Leiden University, the Netherlands.

Sarah Pink is Professor and Director of the Emerging Technologies Research Lab at Monash University. Sarah is a futures and design anthropologist and filmmaker; her recent work includes the book *Emerging Technologies / Life at the Edge of the Future* (2022) and the documentary *Digital Energy Futures* (2022).

Thao Phan is a Research Fellow in the Australian Research Council's Center of Excellence for Automated Decision-Making & Society and the Emerging Technologies Research Lab at Monash University. She is a feminist STS researcher who studies the gendered and racialised aspects of algorithmic culture.

Michael Richardson is Associate Professor of Media at UNSW, where he co-directs the Media Futures Hub. His research investigates how emerging technologies shape and are shaped by culture and power. His next book, *Nonhuman Witnessing: War, Data, and Ecology After the End of the World*, is forthcoming with Duke University Press.

Jathan Sadowski is Senior Research Fellow in the Emerging Technologies Research Lab at Monash University. He is working on an ARC DECRA fellowship studying the political economy of insurance technology. He is the author of *Too Smart: How Digital Capitalism is Extracting Data, Controlling Our Lives, and Taking Over the World* (The MIT Press).

Sy Taffel is a Senior Lecturer in Media Studies and co-director of the Political Ecology Research Centre at Massey University, Aotearoa-New Zealand. He is the author of *Digital Media Ecologies* (Bloomsbury 2019). His research focuses on the intersections of political ecology and digital technologies.

Meredith Whittaker is the President of Signal. She is also co-founder and Chief Advisor at the AI Now Institute, and was Senior Advisor on AI at the US Federal Trade Commission.

www.ingramcontent.com/pod-product-compliance
Lightning Source LLC
Chambersburg PA
CBHW022039190326
41520CB00008B/647